THE WILD
WITHIN

THE WILD WITHIN

CLIMBING THE WORLD'S MOST REMOTE MOUNTAINS

VP

Vertebrate Publishing, Sheffield
www.v-publishing.co.uk

The Wild Within
Simon Yates

First published in 2012 by Vertebrate Publishing.
This paperback edition first published in 2019 by Vertebrate Publishing.
Reprinted in 2021.

VERTEBRATE PUBLISHING
Omega Court, 352 Cemetery Road, Sheffield S11 8FT, United Kingdom.
www.v-publishing.co.uk

Front cover: The South-West Ridge of Good Neighbor Peak, Mount Vancouver,
Wrangell-St Elias ranges, Alaska-Yukon border.
Photography by Simon Yates unless otherwise credited.

This book is a work of non-fiction based on the life of Simon Yates. The author
has stated to the publishers that, except in such minor respects not affecting
the substantial accuracy of the work, the contents of the book are true.

A CIP catalogue record for this book is available from the British Library.

ISBN: 978-1-912560-25-7 (Paperback)

ISBN: 978-1-906148-43-0 (Ebook)

10 9 8 7 6 5 4 3 2

Every effort has been made to obtain the necessary permissions with
reference to copyright material, both illustrative and quoted. We apologise
for any omissions in this respect and will be pleased to make the appropriate
acknowledgements in any future edition.

Design and production by Nathan Ryder, Vertebrate Publishing.
www.v-publishing.co.uk

Vertebrate Publishing is committed to printing on paper from sustainable sources.

Printed and bound in the UK by TJ Books Limited, Padstow, Cornwall.

FOR JANE, MAISY & LEWIS

Contents

Introduction 9

Cordillera Darwin – Tierra Del Fuego Map 14

ONE   That's Very Ambitious 15
TWO   Not Very Professional 37
THREE   The Way of the Gaucho 61
FOUR   All Your Front Teeth 81
FIVE   Life is Good 97
SIX   More Like Being Abroad 125
SEVEN   It Might Not Be the Hardest 143

Milne Land – Eastern Greenland Map 158

EIGHT   A Plane Crasher 159
NINE   It's Like Pantomime 179
TEN   I'll Never Do Anything Better 197

Wrangell-St Elias Ranges – Alaska/Yukon Map 212

ELEVEN   Not for the Faint-Hearted 213

Epilogue 229
Acknowledgements 238

'Thousands of tired, nerve-shaken, over-civilised people are beginning
to find out that going to the mountains is going home;
that wildness is a necessity; and that mountain parks
and reservations are useful not only as fountains of timber
and irrigating rivers, but as fountains of life.'

JOHN MUIR, *OUR NATIONAL PARKS*

Introduction

Stumbling from one snow-covered rock to another, I silently cursed as yet another football-sized lump slid from under my foot and I fell heavily on to the slope. The scree I had been scrambling up for more than an hour would have been challenging enough in the dry, but with its present coating of heavy, wet snow it was positively dangerous. Occasionally, I was reduced to pedalling motions with my hands and feet, as if fighting my way up an icy escalator – the 'down' one. A relentless westerly gusting across the slope made the job even harder, driving the snow with such ferocity it stung my face. Yet despite the discomfort I was enjoying the exercise after days of inactivity forced upon us by bad weather.

The day had started easily enough, picking berries as we wandered through sheltered forest below the mountains. Soon enough the obstacles began. Faint trails petered out and tangles of dense under-growth and fallen trees sent us on lengthy diversions. Huge moss-covered trunks toppled by mighty blasts off the southern oceans had to be scrambled over, timber-choked streambeds forded and steep banks climbed by clinging to tree roots and tussocks of grass. Time passed quickly in such terrain, but progress was slow. What had looked like a gentle stroll from below was clearly going to be a long and demand-ing day. This was not the manicured woodland of England, but a forest of *Nothofagus*, the native beech that blankets large swathes of southern Chile, Argentina and New Zealand.

Higher up we had to wade through peat bog and skirt around beaver dam lakes; close to the tree line the remaining forest became bush-sized and maddeningly dense. It had been a relief to reach the slope of snow-covered grass above the stunted trees, but then came the scree I was now struggling up.

Gradually the fan of slippery stones narrowed to a couloir that appeared to provide an approach to our chosen summit. We were simply following a line of weakness up the mountain, as we had tried to do in the forest below. The scree finished abruptly at a short, steep buttress that guarded the way to the top. I contoured leftwards along a rake towards a small col about 50 metres away. It was easier to be moving almost horizontally with the wind at my back, but the ground dropped steeply away at my feet and I moved cautiously.

The col brought relief from the tension of the rake and exertion on the slopes below. It was not, however, a sheltered spot. The wind gusted unpredictably through the shallow notch and I had to hold tight to the rock above before peering round the corner. An up draught smacked into my face. Beyond lay steep cliffs and ice-encrusted rock. I had hoped the col would reveal an easier way to the top. It did not. Crampons, ice-axes and a rope would be required to climb the ground above, and we had not brought them with us. This windy spot would mark the high point of our day's explorations.

Having stopped moving, my body soon chilled. I put on an extra jacket, swapped my thin inner gloves for fleece-lined over-mitts, and huddled against the rock to wait for the others.

Now I could fully appreciate the surrounding terrain. The view was striking in its desolation, an elemental landscape of storm cloud, snow-covered mountains, dark forest, lakes, rivers and sea. Shafts of sunlight cut through the cloud and picked out white horses in the Beagle Channel, which separated us on Isla Hoste from the mainland of Tierra del Fuego to the north. Yet for all the marvellous view my thoughts kept turning to the snowline. Here in the height of the southern summer it was down to 100 metres above sea level. Normally at this time of the year it would be at least a thousand metres higher.

A chance set of circumstances had led to my first visit to Tierra del Fuego back in 2001. Before then I thought of it as an almost mythical land, linked with the names of Charles Darwin, Robert FitzRoy, captain of HMS *Beagle*, and the missionary Thomas Bridges whose son Lucas fashioned their family history and closeness with the Fuegian Indians into a remarkable book, *Uttermost Part of the Earth*. And then there was the legendary Eric Shipton who spent the twilight of his long career as a mountaineer-explorer pioneering in the Cordillera Darwin, the largest range of peaks in this archipelago of mountainous islands. The reality of that initial visit exceeded my wildest expectations; these storm-racked islands captured my imagination and I would return again and again.

I had realised many years earlier that I climbed mountains because I relished the physical and mental challenge in that particular extreme environment. I felt I was re-connecting with the natural world – a world distanced from most of us in developed countries by our wealth, material comfort and the fact that we no longer need to engage with nature for a livelihood. Part of the lure was also one of escapism: life is simpler in the mountains.

After serving an apprenticeship on crags throughout England and North Wales, I graduated to winter mountaineering in Scotland, upping the ante on towering cliffs cloaked with snow and ice. This in turn led me to the European Alps, climbing routes of such difficulty and height they would sometimes take several days to complete. Next came exploratory alpinism on mountains or huge faces that had never been climbed before. Yet though, in retrospect, the path seems prede-termined, when I went to Peru in 1985 with Joe Simpson and made the first ascent of Siula Grande's West Face, I had no idea it would be the start of what looks like being a life-long calling. I moved on to the Karakoram, Himalaya, more visits to the Andes and to the mountains of Central Asia. But they would not be the end of my restless search.

Despite the remoteness of these mountainous regions, all have to some extent been shaped by people who have lived among them for centuries, sometimes millennia, marks of their presence extending far above the highest hamlets and summer camps. During nearly 30 years of exploration I have witnessed rapid change. Roads have been built to previously remote mountain villages, bringing commerce, electricity, schools and hospitals. Better infrastructure soon opened these areas to outsiders – people like myself. At first only a handful of adventurous climbers and trekkers penetrated deep into the mountains, but word spread and more general tourists quickly followed. Small towns grew to the size of cities and villages became towns.

I had been lucky to travel and climb in such places, and perhaps to experience them in quieter times. However passion and ambition was driving me on. I began to look at mountains beyond the margins of human habitation, increasingly appreciative of physical isolation and the commitment of climbing with just a single partner. Then the world changed again. As with road building, the communication revolution came late to the mountains but quickly gathered pace. Without really noticing how it had happened, I found myself entering these special places with computers and phones, and the lines between my mountain time, work and home became increasingly blurred.

The sound of sliding stones dislodged me from my thoughts. Andy Parkin, my friend and climbing partner, was nearing the col; Marcel de Letter, a likeable Belgian who we had met for the first time just a few days earlier, was not far below him.

'What's it look like?' Andy shouted as he started the traverse towards the col.

'We won't be going any further.' Nothing on this trip had been going to plan. Stopping short of the summit would simply add to our growing list of trials.

Andy and Marcel took cursory glances at the ground above before throwing down their packs and huddling beside me. They too donned extra clothing before digging out food and drink from their rucksacks. We sat in silence, heads bowed from the gusting wind, and ate our lunch.

It was not only the world that was changing. My own personal circumstances had altered fundamentally less than three years earlier when I had become a father. Far below us in a sheltered bay lay Marcel's yacht, *Iorana*, in which we had sailed to this isolated place. On board were my wife Jane and our two young children, Maisy and Lewis.

There are lots of familiar expressions to describe the emotions of becoming a parent. For me, the overriding feeling was one of love, mixed with responsibility. It is patently obvious when a newborn arrives that they are going to depend on you for everything for a considerable time. My immediate concern was material provision: I had to become much more focused on making money. But children also have pressing emotional needs. Logic would suggest I should have eased up on the risky activity of mountaineering; but I was late coming to fatherhood and my path was already firmly fixed. My pastime was also my job. Life became a complex juggling act between trips away and time at home, between work and family.

In fact, what happened was hardly a gentle compromise. As my work and personal life became busier, the decade also evolved into the most productive and rewarding of my mountain life.

Pacific
Ocean

Chile

Argentina

Paraguay

Uruguay

Brazil

Atlantic
Ocean

Falkland
Islands

ISLA GORDON

ISLA HOSTE

Beagle Channel

Mt Iorana

Monte Frances

Roncagli

Ada

Bove

CORDILLERA DARWIN

Admiralty Sound

Chile

Argentina

Ushuaia

ONE

That's Very Ambitious

Standing in line with a dozen other people on a narrow gravel shoreline, I looked out at the chilly expanse of Ullswater beyond the instructor as she completed our briefing.

'As you can see, the wind is strong and the lake's quite rough today,' Liz said. 'Whatever you do, please don't go out of the shelter of this bay.'

For me, it was a rare summer at home in England. Having committed to a sailing and climbing trip to Tierra del Fuego for the following southern summer on a friend's ocean-going yacht, it seemed wise to use some of the intervening time to get some practical sailing experience. My wife Jane and I had enrolled on a course at Howtown Outdoor Centre on the eastern side of Ullswater – one of the Lake District's largest and most beautiful stretches of water. By spending every Tuesday evening over a six-week period out on the lake we hoped to pick up the basic principles of sailing toppers – small one-man fibreglass dinghies fitted with a rudder and single sail.

On our first lesson the previous week it had been completely calm and impossible to put classroom theory into practice down on the water. We all simply drifted listlessly on the lake, paddling our boats back in with our hands at the end of the session. But today, as I waded into the water pushing the small dinghy in front of me, I felt nervous. Despite it being evening, the wind was showing no sign of abating and there were good-sized waves not far from the shoreline. The water beyond the small bay we had been instructed to sail around looked rougher still.

I climbed aboard and tried to make myself comfortable, but the wind quickly filled the sail and the boat rapidly accelerated. In no time I was struggling to hold on to the cord fixed to the end of the boom with one hand while trying to control the tiller with the other. I was soon skipping over waves as the yacht slewed across the water in an arc, feeling like it was about to capsize. Then the wind suddenly dropped, leaving the sail flapping noisily. My forward movement halted as abruptly as it had started. I sat and puzzled as to what had happened, trying to work out the direction of the wind and how I should set up the boat. It was not easy, there were so many different things to deal with. By moving the rudder I managed to get wind back into the sail, which produced another spurt of forward movement. However, it soon died like the first. This was baffling.

I looked around to see how the others were coping. One or two seemed to be doing quite well but most were also making faltering progress. The instructors moved between the dinghies in a small launch offering advice and encouragement. I persevered, cautiously trying to not go fully with the wind. Eventually I made some reasonable passages in a straight line, only to lose momentum when I tried to take a different tack.

I began to feel frustrated and reasoned that it would be best to simply throw caution to the wind – literally. I turned and let the sail fill completely, then held the dinghy on that course. I skimmed along, bouncing over the bigger waves, leaning out to maintain stability. This was more like it, I told myself as I rapidly headed out of the sheltered bay and into deeper water. The waves got larger, the wind gusting ever stronger. All of a sudden the cord attached to the end of the boom was plucked from my hand and the boat turned over, flinging me into the water. I surfaced almost immediately, gasping from the shock of the coldness. The lifejacket was doing its job well, keeping me at the surface with my head out of the water, so I floated for a while and took stock. The boat was upturned nearby and I was a long way out into the lake.

Having got my breath back, I swam a few strokes and regained the dinghy. We had been instructed how to right a capsized boat, however that had been in shallow water during the becalmed first lesson. I tried grabbing the keel and using my bodyweight to roll the boat upright; it would not move and after a couple of attempts I slumped back into the water. Then I dived down and tried pushing the mast up from below. The wind was stronger now and waves were breaking over the hull. It was obvious that I simply did not have the strength or technique necessary to get the dinghy back upright in such conditions. Embarrassingly, all I could do was wait to be rescued.

As it turned out I was not the only one having difficulties. Back in the bay others had overturned and the instructors were shuttling dinghies and clients back to the pier with two launches. My wetsuit had warmed and I felt quite comfortable. I relaxed, hanging limply from the side of the boat and waited my turn. Eventually, the launches made their way out to me.

'Having trouble are we?' Liz asked, as the rescue flotilla arrived.

'Couldn't get the damn boat back upright,' I explained rather feebly.

'So we can see.'

I passed her the line from the bow of my dinghy and climbed up the steps on the back of Liz's launch as ordered. The rest of the group stood waiting on the pier while my rescue was completed and boat retrieved. Some were shivering with cold by the time we returned. They did not look impressed with my excursion. We got the dinghies ashore and stripped them down. Then I walked silently back to the centre, feeling guilty for the trouble I had caused.

The lessons over the following weeks were less eventful and highly enjoyable. Good weather accompanied by breezes out on the lake allowed everyone to progress without too much difficulty, or me capsizing.

The final session promised something special – a chance to use our new skills in a race down the lake to a designated buoy and back to the pier at the outdoor centre. Everybody tried to take the best lines and tack at the right moment to optimise speed and distance covered. Racing was fun, it made you think about the classroom theory and how to apply it practically. All too quickly we were all back at the pier. I was sad that the course had come to an end – it had been a very pleasant way to spend a summer's evening each week – but now I could look forward to transferring my newly acquired skill to a much larger yacht later in the year.

Back in the centre everyone changed out of wetsuits and made their way into one of the classrooms for a final debriefing. After congratulating the group for their performance out on the lake, Liz began asking people what their aspirations for sailing were. A retired couple planned to buy a yacht to sail on Ullswater; a teenage boy said how much he had enjoyed the experience and wanted to come on a more advanced course the following summer.

'And what about you, Simon?'

'In six months time I'm going to fly to Ushuaia in Argentina, get on an ocean-going yacht and sail along the Beagle Channel to the head of a remote fjord. Then I'm going to go ashore and climb an un-climbed mountain.' It felt like a slightly ridiculous boast under the circumstances, but it was true.

'Well, that's very ambitious,' Liz said dryly, before adding, 'good luck with it all.'

❄ ❄ ❄ ❄

For more than three hours the plane had hugged Argentina's east coast on the long journey south. I was travelling to Tierra del Fuego in the company of Jane and two friends: my climbing partner Andy Parkin, and Elaine Bull whose sister Celia would be skippering the all-important yacht for our ambitious expedition. Gazing down on the desolate coastline, I recalled how nine years earlier on a trip to Cerro Torre I had travelled down this huge country by coach. The journey had taken the best part of two tiring, monotonous days. Flying was definitely worth the small extra cost and I wondered about my previous state of mind.

Eventually, the coastline gave way to open sea and I assumed that we must have left the mainland and were making the short crossing over the eastern end of the Magellan Straits to Tierra del Fuego. Land soon reappeared below and I felt that familiar surge of excitement; a sense of mounting anticipation that had swept over me at moments like this ever since my first trips to Asia years earlier. Cloud briefly obscured the view, then as the plane began to descend I started to see glimpses of mountains and glaciers, lakes and rivers. Now we were over sea again, but with land nearby on either side. This was wild country, unlike anything I had seen before. What really caught my attention was the dense, dark forest. All the low-lying land was blanketed in the stuff. The mainland of Tierra del Fuego in Argentina lay on the right and Isla Navarino in Chile to the left, directly below stretched the Beagle Channel. With the plane on its final approach, Ushuaia suddenly appeared. Its setting could hardly be more dramatic, the city crowded around a small harbour with buildings extending up surrounding hillsides towards mountains above. I caught a glimpse of a yacht making its way into the bay. It all flashed by and out of sight as we landed at the airport built on a spit of land projecting into the channel. All the tourist literature refers to this place as *Fin del Mundo* – the end of the world. It certainly felt like it.

We took a short taxi ride into town, found a room in a backpackers' hostel, then eagerly made our way down to the harbour. It was a fair walk round to the yacht club, which lies at the far end of a causeway splitting the western end of the bay. It's an exposed spot and we walked heads bowed as the wind accelerated across the bay, blowing plumes of dust from the unmetalled road. As we approached the yacht club we could see a boat heading for the pier.

'It's Celia!' Elaine exclaimed.

With perfect timing we reached the end of the pier just as *Ada II* arrived. Celia Bull was a picture of concentration at the helm, as she inched the vessel up to the mooring. Lines were thrown to us, accompanied by swift instructions as to where to tie them. Once the boat was secure Celia jumped on to the pier and ran up to Elaine, the sisters embracing and shrieking with joy. Then it was Jane's turn, Andy's and finally mine. Celia was buzzing.

'We've just come from Yendegaia,' she said excitedly. ' It's such a cool place. You're going to love it.'

I had seen little of Celia over the previous couple of years, during which she had taken up sailing and bought *Ada II*. Our friendship had been cemented 10 years earlier, when as part of a loosely knit group of climbers we had spent a magical week on the Scottish island of Eigg. For some time after we had lived near to each other in Sheffield and mixed in similar outdoor circles that formed part of the steel city's cultural life. A lively personality made her fun to be with and yet like many involved in adventure sports she could become focused and single-minded in pursuit of favoured projects. Celia had lost both her parents while still quite young, but they had left her well-provided for and she had used her inheritance to pursue her passions. That sense of purpose had enabled her to learn to sail and bring the boat down the Atlantic from Brittany to the Falkland Islands. When I heard she planned to bring the yacht into the vast archipelago of islands known to sailors as 'the channels' that runs down the coast of southern Chile all the way to Cape Horn we soon found ourselves talking about possible climbing opportunities. Her enthusiasm had been infectious.

We were shown around the boat and introduced to Francoise and Marianne – friends of Celia's from France who had just spent their vacation on board. I had few preconceptions of what the yacht would be like, yet was pleasantly surprised by both the size and luxury of the living areas. There was a communal area in the centre with a kitchen, dining table and seating; Celia's cabin and bathroom was in the stern while towards the bow a pair of cabins with twin bunk beds led through to a shared bathroom. A further space in the bow served as the storeroom. I could see it was not going to be a struggle living in this place for the duration of our trip.

That evening we all ate in a pizzeria on the harbour, before the lengthy flights from Europe caught up with us and we left early to crash out at the hostel. When we returned to the boat next morning Celia had her captain's head on. There was much to do and she wasted no time in delegating jobs. Andy and I needed to shop for food and supplies for the mountain and as we left the boat Jane and Elaine were already stripping out bedding that needed to be fumigated and washed following an infestation of fleas picked up at Yendegaia. We too planned to make landfall at this remote estancia.

Throughout the day we ferried shopping back to the boat, only to be sent on increasingly obscure errands. By late afternoon I found myself taking a taxi to an industrial estate at the far side of town to get a gas cylinder refilled. There, under an open-sided shed, I watched in horror as a man plugged a hose into the cylinder and to the accompaniment of a deafening hiss proceeded to vent what smelt like far more gas into the air than into the cylinder. The meagre bill explained his lack of concern for the wasted gas, but the casual disregard for safety was more baffling.

'I've got another job for you,' Celia said when I arrived back at the yacht. 'Do you mind taking a little dip?

'I suppose not,' I replied dumbly.

'Jolly good. I'll find a wetsuit for you for the morning.'

The yacht owners and their crews were a sociable bunch and though Celia had only been in the channels for a few weeks she had already got to know a good many people. As a woman skippering her own boat in this place she was something of a novelty and our

preparations were regularly interrupted by visitors of various nation-
alities. Although I knew little about sailing I sensed a great deal of
salty experience. The fact that these people had safely navigated their
vessels to Ushuaia indicated a certain level of competence. Some had
spent many seasons in southern waters and took charter groups to the
Antarctic. As *Ada* was French built and had been bought in Brittany,
where Celia had spent time learning to sail the new boat, French
crews were particularly friendly.

That evening we accepted a drinks invitation on *Darwin Sound*,
one of the larger yachts in the harbour. The crew sailed her around the
globe on charters and periodically met up with the owner, a Parisian
art dealer, who would take holidays on board. Laughter flowed along
with the wine and beer. I was warming to this scene. It had similari-
ties with the climbing world in terms of enthusiasm and the characters
it attracted. The glaring difference was one of money – to be a player in
this game required access to significant amounts of cash. The party
spilled over into dinner in town and later moved on to a bar where we
danced to a salsa band until the early hours.

I was still hungover when Celia presented me with a wetsuit the
following morning.

'The outlet from the toilet needs unblocking,' she said with a smile.

After I had squeezed into the suit, Celia handed me a piece of wire,
along with instructions of where to find the outlet. I waddled my way
along the pier and on to a lower jetty in front of the boat, as the girls
all screamed with laughter. When I took the plunge they laughed
even more. The water was bitterly cold. I swam quickly down the side
of the boat, took a breath and dropped below the water line. The girls
laughed louder as I dived again and located the small hole in the hull.
Several more dives were required to clear the blockage; I found it near-
impossible to keep myself below the water for any productive length
of time. As I wiggled the wire into the outlet effluent and strands of
toilet paper diffused into the water around me. Once the outlet seemed

clear I swam back to the jetty and hauled myself from the water. My head, feet and hands stung with the cold, but at least the job was done and I had provided some entertainment in the process.

Later, Francoise and Marianne said their goodbyes and left for France. The following morning we were able to vacate the hostel and move on to the boat. Now it was a waiting game. We were ready to leave, but Celia had discovered a problem with the engine. A mechanic had been called, but when he would turn up was uncertain.

In the busy run-up to our departure from home I had been put in touch with an Edinburgh-based company who were starting up an adventure website. Internet start-ups were in their infancy and people were still trying to figure out how to make money out of the dot-com business; Alicia and Keith Anderson who ran the company thought that a regularly updated news page about our expedition would help bring viewers to their fledgling site. On a bright sunny winter's day Jane and I met the couple in Edinburgh. We sat on top of Arthur's Seat learning how to upload text and pictures onto the page via a satellite phone connection. It turned out to be a long, slow and complicated process. We left the meeting with some very expensive electrical equipment including a laptop, phone, digital camera and a solar panel for recharging, all of which I had been carrying and guarding with more than a touch of paranoia since we arrived in Argentina. The thought of using the set-up had been filling me with dread but with time on our hands now was the moment to file our first report.

For several hours Jane and I sat on the grass outside the yacht club trying to make the equipment work. For some reason we could not connect with the server and eventually we took a taxi into town to send emails to Alicia and Keith asking for help and advice. When we returned the mechanic had arrived and was busy fixing *Ada*'s engine.

Early the following morning Jane and I were back at the clubhouse hoping to fix the computer problem. The moment seemed surreal and also had a touch of sadness about it. Some intangible part of what constitutes 'adventure' was being eroded. Here we were, stood by a payphone in a yacht club in Argentina in the most southerly city in the world, waiting for a call to come from a server in California, so that we could post entries on a website that would be looked at by people in Britain. I could hardly believe it when the call actually came. Jane patiently dealt with it. It took four hours and numerous further calls before a modest entry was finally uploaded on to the website. For those hours the world felt like it had shrunk; although our physical location had not altered, we no longer seemed quite so remote.

People from other yachts found the whole fuss intriguing and stopped to talk. A group of Latvian university lecturers, who had built a catamaran and were living their lifelong dream of sailing around the world, proudly showed us photographs of their journey – from the flotilla of boats that had seen them off in Riga to being de-masted off the coast of Brazil. They had very little money and were waiting for more to arrive from friends and family before they could continue. When the mast had been lost a Brazilian joiner had fashioned them a replacement from a tree trunk for $100. A Norwegian family who had bought a yacht in Auckland were doing some serious re-stocking before sailing non-stop to the Lofoten Islands at the other end of the Atlantic. In this place it seemed the abnormal was normal.

Our preparations almost complete, Celia took *Ada* across the harbour and filled the fuel tanks with diesel. It had been an interesting, but increasingly frustrating few days. On the fifth morning since our arrival in Ushuaia the officials from the Prefectura came on board and we went through the formalities for leaving Argentina. I felt relieved as they stamped our passports and a surge of nervous excitement as we cast off from the pier.

The day was fine with a steady breeze blowing puffs of cloud along the Beagle Channel from the west. Once we were out of the harbour Celia stopped the engine, shouted instructions and we helped unfurl the Genoa, which gave a powerful crack as it filled with wind and *Ada* began to move forwards under sail. Giant petrels and albatrosses skimmed low over the wave tops as the city slipped astern to be replaced by a rocky shoreline backed by dark forest and mountains. To the west I could see the outline of the Cordillera Darwin, the range we had travelled all this way to explore. Now I felt our adventure was finally underway.

It was late when we rounded the lighthouse at the end of a gravel spit guarding the inlet and town of Puerto Williams. The radio crackled to life as the authorities called the boat and Celia spoke to them in broken Spanish. We glided into the small port under engine passing a number of sinister looking, black Chilean Navy gunboats before mooring at the Mecalvi Yacht Club, an old ammunition ship that had been scuttled at the narrowing of the inlet to create an improvised pier. A group of jagged peaks – *Los Dientes de Navarino* – filled the skyline beyond. The Mecalvi's dilapidated appearance gave little indication that there were toilets, showers and a bar hidden within what remained of the superstructure. It was surprisingly cosy inside and the evening passed pleasantly with a new group of hardy sailors to chat with.

Williams was the last opportunity to obtain fresh food such as bread and so more shopping ensued the following morning. I soon excused myself and slipped off up the river inlet and into the forest. I had begun to teach myself fly-fishing in the previous months and was eager to try it out here. After a short while I found a clearing with enough space to fish. It was a beautiful spot and I eagerly assembled the rod, fitted the reel and pulled through the line. Then I chose a small brown fly and tied it on. As the first cast hit the water a mouth broke surface and took the fly. Within a short space of time I had caught a handful of fish and felt very pleased with myself. On my home river I had spent many fruitless hours watching fish rising around the fly without actually taking it. The Fuegian trout were much more obliging.

We had hoped to leave the next day, but the wind was blowing hard from the west, hurrying squally showers along the channel. Celia said that we would be wasting our time trying to go against such a strong headwind. Jane and I went fishing and passed a few hours working our way up the valley, catching sufficient to provide a small trout starter for dinner.

The next morning dawned clear and still. We motored back out into the channel and initially made good progress. Then cloud began to build in the west as the wind started to blow. Forward movement slowed and we augmented the motor with some mainsail, tacking back and forth across the channel. It was nice to be sailing, but it seemed to require a disproportionate amount of work. Whenever I returned from below deck I was disappointed by how little distance we had travelled. The wind increased as the day wore on, until our progress stalled completely and Celia sought refuge in a bay called Puerto Navarino. It was a little demoralising that the entire day's sailing had only brought us back to a point on the opposite side of the channel from Ushuaia.

We dropped anchor in the bay and waved to the Chilean sailors that monitored shipping from a white wooden hut on the grassy shore. A dirt road connected the place with Puerto Williams but it still looked like a lonely posting.

'The anchor is slipping,' Celia announced not long after we had stopped. 'We'll have to move.' We repositioned *Ada* several times until the anchor finally seemed to hold, but Celia was still anxious. 'We are going to have to take watches,' she said. At two in the morning Jane shook me awake and I got up to do my stint, periodically checking the GPS and going up on deck to look for signs of movement. The sky was clear now and filled with stars, but the wind was still blowing hard, whistling through the mast cables and slapping water against the hull as the yacht swung on her anchor chain. Time passed quickly as I sat in a trance-like state listening to the sounds of the boat and the sea.

I liked living on *Ada*. It had a similar rhythm and feel to an expedition base camp. The wheel of daily life turned around mealtimes and regular tea breaks, with chores and sailing seemingly fitted around them. However, it was altogether more luxurious than a tented camp. Here we had a proper kitchen, toilets, bunk beds and a nice central galley to gather, relax and eat in. Even when the weather was wild up on deck you could escape to this sanctuary below. Weight and volume were not the usual issue, either in terms of personal belongings, or food and drink. Yachts, I had discovered, have storage space everywhere, under tables and beds, in cabins on the walls, down in the hull, in the bow and stern.

The wind was howling furiously in the morning and although the water was relatively calm inside the bay, substantial waves and white horses were surging out in the channel. It was obvious we were going nowhere.

Jane and I went ashore intending to update the website and for the first time managed to connect easily to the server. The satellite phone cost a hefty US$7.50 a minute to use and pictures took a long time to upload. Mindful of this fact we posted a simple entry telling how we had taken shelter from the storm. As it turned out, it would be our last update to the expedition site. And unbeknown to us our postings were initiating a disturbing chain of events back home.

The daughter of one of our neighbours, Bethany, was feeding our cat while we were away. She was also following our progress on the website. She casually told her grandfather who ran a pub in the next village about us being caught in the storm. The story had then been passed on to a climber, Deano, who was one of the pub regulars. He mentioned the news to one of his friends, Mark Charlton, who is a locally based mountain guide. Mark immediately called Elaine Bull's husband and fellow guide Andy Cave. As the days passed with no further web postings Andy became increasingly concerned, fearing that the boat had sunk and began a fruitless search as to our whereabouts. The anxiety was only allayed when Elaine telephoned home from Puerto Williams at the end of her trip.

On the sixth day since leaving Ushuaia we woke to silence. The storm had finally blown itself out. We left immediately and motored across the Beagle Channel and into the Bahia Yendegaia. The water was flat calm and conditions bore no resemblance to the previous days. Andy and I sat up on deck in the sunshine, taking turns with the binoculars to view what lay ahead. Beyond the head of the fjord and above the forest the ice of the Stoppani Glacier was clearly visible with tantalising glimpses of the mountains behind. The landscape was on a grander scale now and somewhere in the cloud forming to the north and west were the peaks we had come to climb.

I had first met Andy in the mid-1980s on my annual visits to Chamonix in the French Alps. For a while he had been one of those rare individuals in the climbing world who had managed to excel in many different disciplines – rock climbing, ice climbing, big walling and alpinism. His achievements, both climbing with partners and alone, were formidable and growing. He was a rising star. From his home city of Sheffield, climbing had taken him around the world and he had settled in Chamonix where he could live among the mountains and hone his talents as an alpinist. Then disaster struck. While working as a guide he was lowering a client from the Riffelhorn – a small training peak above Zermatt in Switzerland – when the anchor to which he was secured ripped free. Andy fell 50 metres to the ground. Miraculously he survived the accident and the multiple injuries it caused, but years of operations and rehabilitation lay ahead. For someone so gifted and driven it was hard to adapt to the brutal change of circumstances and he suffered from depression. However, a rekindled childhood love of drawing and painting helped him through the dark times and eventually to make a living as an artist. Despite lasting disability he also returned to the mountains.

In 1988, Andy and I participated in an expedition organised by

Doug Scott to Makalu in Nepal. It was not a particularly successful trip in climbing terms but it marked Andy's return to big mountains after his accident and the cementing of our friendship. When we next went away together, in the Gangotri region of India in 1990, he was climbing well again and reached the top of Shivling (6,543m). After that our climbing paths diverged, but we kept in touch and occasionally met at the annual mountain film festival in Kendal where Andy exhibited his artwork. He had expressed an interest in coming to the Cordillera Darwin when Celia visited Chamonix and later she invited him along. For me it was strange to have a climbing partner chosen by someone else, but it was Celia's yacht and understandably she only wanted to share it with people she knew and was comfortable with. I knew we could get along, but how we would climb together was still to be tested.

As we turned the last headland in the fjord, the Estancia Yendegaia came into view. A cluster of brightly painted huts sat on a grassy terrace above a small bay. Beyond was woodland, backed by steep slopes leading up into the mountains. It was an idyllic place – but not today.

'Look, a cruise liner,' exclaimed Andy, sounding slightly disappointed.

'That will be the *Terra Australis*,' said Celia. 'It comes here every week.'

I was flabbergasted. We had come to one of the most remote and rarely visited mountain ranges outside of the polar regions to be confronted with a boat full of people. The shoreline was teeming with them and some were being led around on horseback. I could not help but think of how busy the world is becoming, even in the most unlikely of places.

An old sun-bleached wooden pier ran out into the bay with the skeleton of a ship's hull lying in the mud beside it. We anchored a little way back from the pier and Andy and I rowed over in the dinghy to tie a line to one of its rotten legs. Then we returned to the yacht to wait for the fuss to subside. We wanted to meet the estancia's resident gaucho Jose Alvarao, but for the moment he was busy.

The crew of the *Australis* were preparing to launch a dinghy. I thought they were going to pick up clients from the shore and was surprised when it headed in our direction.

'Celia. We've got visitors,' I shouted. Three men arrived and judging from the uniform one was the liner's captain. He stood up as they approached the stern.

'Can we come aboard?' he asked politely.

'Sure,' I replied.

'We have come to meet your captain. We have been hearing a lot about her.' Now I understood the purpose of the visit. They were intrigued by our infamous female skipper. As we drank tea in the galley Celia was subjected to a barrage of questions. The captain went on to explain how they were doing circuits in the channels from Punta Arenas to Puerto Williams, Ushuaia and then back again. As cruise liners went it was relatively small and could only hold about 80 guests, but it still looked massive to me in this isolated place.

'I wonder if we would be able to get a lift back to Williams with them?' Jane confided with me, as the trio were preparing to return to *Australis*. Jane and Elaine needed to leave two weeks earlier than the rest of us and if we all returned on *Ada* it would take up valuable time that we hoped to use exploring the channels.

'I guess it's worth asking,' I said, expecting the answer to be 'no'. Jane made a polite request to the captain.

'We will see what we can do,' came his helpful reply. 'I will have to get permission from Punta Arenas. I can give you an answer when we come back in a week's time.'

As the *Terra Australis* sailed away, we went ashore. Dogs walked the tideline and others were asleep on the verandas of the huts. A flock of upland geese were grazing behind the estancia as pairs of ibis circled overhead. As they came into land their haunting calls mingled with the sounds of the wind. Yendegaia once again felt like the wilderness I expected it to be.

We found Jose in the dilapidated shearing shed. He beamed a mischievous smile as we approached. A short, powerfully built man with black hair and a dark, weather-worn face, Jose was in his everyday outfit of cowboy boots complete with spurs, black pantaloons, an old woollen jumper and a black beret. Around his waist was a cloth sash with a large knife in a leather sheath tucked inside it behind his back. Jose looked every bit the gaucho he is. He embraced Celia and she handed him her gift – a carton of Marlboro cigarettes. I warmed to him immediately.

Jose invited us into the hut that serves as his home and made tea, heating the water on an imposing wood-burning stove that he continually fed with large logs. There were few personal belongings in the hut and just a basic array of cooking utensils. Yendegaia was no longer a working estancia. It had been bought by a group of environmentalists a few years earlier with plans to let the land revert to its natural state. The sheep and cattle had been cleared from the enclosed sections of the property and taken away by boat. Unfortunately, over the years cattle had escaped and multiplied into thriving feral herds living in the more peripheral valleys that radiated from the core of the property. There were also many wild horses. Jose's job was to eradicate these herds. He hunted, using his dogs to drive animals towards him so that he could shoot them. For this he was paid a small retainer, but mostly he lived off the land, almost outside the monetary economy. To boost his income he sold meat through the winter to crab fishermen and in the summer took visitors riding. His was a simple and hard life, lived in unforgiving country. Jose said he would be happy to help us get to the mountains. He was busy the next day riding with a group from the *Darwin Sound*, but we could leave the day after.

Andy and I used the spare day to bring gear ashore and pack. Later, Jane and I took a walk up the valley and spent a happy few hours fly-fishing. The fact that we caught nothing did not matter. Just being in that place was reward enough.

Back at the estancia an American couple had arrived overland, having traversed the wild country to the north from a roadhead near Lago Fagnano. It had been a demanding trek with several serious river crossings. We invited them to the yacht and over dinner Brendan and Nina told us of their incredible journey. While travelling in northern Chile they had impulsively decided to walk the entire length of the country following the Andean watershed. The two-year trek had been gruelling and logistically complicated; there had been many setbacks, but now it was nearly over and they were in a celebratory mood. They planned to complete their journey by walking to the southern point of Isla Navarino from Puerto Williams. They had little idea of what they would do after that.

At noon the next day we finished helping Jose load our kit bags on to the horses and all headed off up the valley. I had not ridden a horse since I was 12 years old and then I had simply been led along at walking pace. It was going to be an interesting place in which to re-acquaint myself with equestrianism. However my own troubles were nothing compared to those of Andy who struggled from the start. The lack of mobility in his left leg – a legacy of his pelvis being smashed in the Swiss climbing accident – meant that he had to be helped on to the horse. The damaged leg would not bend to fit in the stirrup and simply stuck out at an angle. It was obvious that simply sitting on the horse was painful for him.

The girls had no such problems. Elaine owned a horse and rode regularly at home, Celia had spent time riding here before we arrived, and Jane had ridden horses as a teenager. She had also been taking lessons before we left for South America in the hope of getting an opportunity to ride while we were away. Unlike Andy and me, they all knew what they were doing. Jose and the girls set off at a canter. We did not even attempt to keep up. Luckily, the horses knew the way and there was a well-worn trail running from the estancia into the broad, flat valley beyond. Andy groaned regularly and was continually shifting his weight on the saddle, attempting to get comfortable. Occasionally the others would wait at gates and allow us to catch up, only to race ahead again. We forded three rivers in quick succession before the valley widened further into a vast plain partially covered in trees. The whole property was in a state of decay with tumbled down bridges and broken fences. Nature was re-asserting itself over what had been cleared land.

The others made the most of the open terrain and spurred their horses into a gallop. Unfortunately ours followed. I pulled hard on the reins, but the animal just went faster. Andy was bouncing up and down on his saddle, barely in control and screaming with pain. Luckily after a few hundred metres everyone came to a halt.

'Sod that,' Andy growled as he rolled off the saddle and dropped to the ground. 'I'm going to walk for a while.'

Distances were smaller than they appeared and we made good progress up the valley even with Andy on foot. After following the course of the main river, we crossed a tributary and then turned towards a side valley that entered the plain. The land was boggy and Jose weaved a path following the driest route. Occasionally the horse's hooves broke through the surface and sank deep into the mud below. Sometimes they would panic and kick wildly trying to free their fetlocks.

When we reached the river flowing from the side valley I was surprised by its size. It was a good twenty metres across and although sluggish it was deep. We followed its edge briefly, until Jose turned his horse, dropped down the riverbank and into the water. Within a few strides the horse was swimming. I felt nervous, but little effort was required as the horses simply followed each other. After a few 'strokes' they regained their footing and climbed the opposite bank. We paused briefly in front of dense forest and immediately clouds of mosquitoes appeared and began biting. The horses were agitated and swished their tails trying to keep them away. Jose headed for the forest. Inside all was calm and free from the infernal insects.

Dead trees and branches littered the ground and it took time for the horses to thread their way around and over the obstacles.

'You would not even think of bringing a horse through this sort place at home,' Elaine said.

After we had cleared the dense section of forest we returned to the river. Here at least it was shallower and faster flowing. We crossed easily from one side to the other, following the line of least resistance up the valley until Jose was adamant that the horses could go no further. I felt we were still a long way from the mountains, but this would have to be the site of our base camp. We dismounted in a small clearing and helped Jose unload our kit bags from the packhorses. Andy was visibly relieved and walked around, occasionally stopping to stretch his stiffened legs.

We sat and chatted for a while, but there was little to keep the others at our campsite and the day was passing. It was soon time for them to leave.

I kissed Celia and Elaine and shook Jose's hand, thanking him for his help. It felt strange to be saying goodbye to Jane under such circumstances – mostly our goodbyes were done in airports. Because of the length of time we had taken leaving Ushuaia and reaching Yendegaia Jane and Elaine did not have much holiday remaining. Jane said they would come up to look for us the day before they hoped to leave. It was just 11 days later. We held each other not knowing whether we were parting for a few days or a month.

'Be careful,' Jane said as we kissed for the last time.

'Of course I will,' I replied with more certainty than I felt.

Jane climbed on to her horse and the girls shouted a final 'Good luck!' as they rode from the camp.

The sounds of horses' hooves and chatter receded beneath the constant roar of the river and wind blowing through the trees. Even though we were only a few hours' walk from the estancia and the yacht I felt incredibly isolated. We were surrounded by hundreds of square kilometres of mountain wilderness. It was a sobering thought. If we were lucky, somewhere up this valley lay the mountain we had travelled so far to climb.

Two

Not Very Professional

'Shall we take a walk up the valley?' I was keen to find out how close to the mountains we actually were.

'What about setting up the camp?' Andy replied cautiously.

'I wasn't thinking of going far. Besides we've got plenty of time to do that later.'

Andy looked thoughtfully at our gear strewn around the clearing. 'Yeah, sod it. Why not?'

I picked up my fleece jacket and headed upstream. The faint cattle trail we had followed intermittently to reach the camp clearing continued beyond. Occasionally there were obstacles to negotiate, limbs of old fallen trees, beaver dams and the muddy channels they make to get from one stretch of water to another. Everywhere were beech saplings gnawed off just above the ground. I was staggered at the amount of destruction caused by such small animals. Even some mature trees had been felled.

Beavers are not native to Tierra del Fuego. They were brought to Ushuaia in the late 1940s at a time when their pelts were fetching a good price and released into the wild in the hope of creating an industry. Unfortunately, the market for beaver fur collapsed and with no human or natural predators the animals flourished, rapidly spreading from their initial release point. The business idea had inadvertently caused untold ecological damage over a vast area, which was continuing to expand unchecked.

It was difficult to see how the cattle picked their way around all the debris but they obviously managed, as there was dung and hoof-prints everywhere. Not surprisingly, with Jose hunting them, the animals were very wary of people. We saw many signs of their passing, but never one of the beasts themselves.

As always it was good to be walking, particularly after the uncertainties that had beset this project. Somewhere above us were the mountains in which we had already invested so much time and effort. I felt a rush of anticipation as the reality of my dream finally began to play out.

Though it had been cloudy most of the day, now intermittent shafts of sunlight shone through the tree canopy, dappling the forest floor. It reminded me of childhood. Of how, as the spring days began to lengthen and warm, I'd walk with friends through the Leicestershire woodlands near our homes, exhilarated by feelings of freedom and space and enthralled by discoveries of new life emerging. Today I walked as I had always done in such places, occasionally pulling leaves from the trees and bushes and examining their delicate structures before crushing them between my fingers in front of my nose to release the aromas within. I paused regularly to study flowers or try and spot birds calling from the trees above.

I expected the valley to continue for a long way before reaching any junction and was surprised when after about an hour of gentle ascent the trees thinned out and we reached a fork in the river. The main valley continued straight on westwards but a smaller, steeper one entered from a more northerly direction.

'What do you think?'

'Let's try up here.' Andy pointed up the tributary.

It made sense to try this option first as it was obvious that there were no mountains for a considerable distance up the main valley. The steeper way offered the chance of getting among them more quickly. It also avoided having to cross the torrent. After a short rest we moved off up the side valley following a faint cattle or *gaunaco* trail up a grassy rib at the side of the stream. Guanaco are related to llamas and similar in size, but with a short uniform brown fleece. They are by far the largest animals native to Tierra del Fuego and in the past were hunted by the Fuegian Indians. Like the feral cattle they were shy and elusive.

The going was easy at first but the rib soon became steeper and rockier. I began to pull away from Andy, who always found such ground slower without full mobility of his left leg. His painful hours in the saddle earlier in the day can have done little to help either. Yet he never really complained, simply going at his own pace over terrain that many people without any disability would have struggled on.

The further I went up the valley the more excited I became. It was more of a narrow, steep gorge and I moved with increasing haste, almost desperate to see what lay around the next corner. Distances were much shorter here than we had originally estimated and I soon turned a bend to discover the valley floor filled by a wall of grey ice pitted in rocks. I wasn't really expecting this and for a moment stood dumbfounded, as if I had never seen such a feature before. Finally the coin dropped. It was the snout of a glacier. Now I was very excited.

I raced along the upper gorge hopping from stone to stone at the side of the stream, then scrambled through a jumble of boulders where the water emerged from under the ice. Once on to this I was able to zigzag up the front of the glacier snout. It was steeper than I assumed and required some care; water was running over the surface of the ice in the late afternoon sunshine, making it very slippery. I tried to follow lines of rocks and gravel embedded in the ice, but this tactic was not always possible and sometimes I was forced to make barely controlled dashes up glistening wet ice. Eventually the angle began to ease. Off the snout of the glacier there was more debris lying on top of the ice and I began to move more quickly as the valley broadened and flattened out. Suddenly I crested a rise and saw mountains. A ridge of minor peaks ran up either side of the glacier towards larger ones at its head. Cloud obscured the higher peaks, however, the rest of the sky had cleared and I expected to be granted a full view before long. I walked up to a high point on a prominent ridge of moraine in the centre of the glacier, threw down my rucksack and lay down among the boulders to wait for Andy.

The cloud was moving quickly, blown by the near-incessant westerly wind I had come to associate with this place. A huge pyramidal bulk on the south side of the glacier appeared first, which I felt sure was Monte Bove. It is the biggest peak in this part of the range, nevertheless I was still amazed at how much snow and ice Bove was holding, considering it is only 2,400 metres high and we were at a similar latitude to Manchester. As the clouds continued to lift and disperse a rockier summit became visible to the north. I immediately recognised this as the one in a photograph we had been given by the mountain explorer and doctor David Hillebrandt. It was the mountain we had come to climb. As I examined the whole scene more closely through binoculars I could hardly believe our luck. It was one of those rare moments when everything clicks: we had landed in the right valley, just a two-hour walk above the camp and the glacier approach to the base of our peak looked remarkably straightforward.

Andy appeared further down the glacier and I stood and waved to him. He waved back and walked up to join me.

'This must be the Bove Glacier. Some place, eh?'

'You're not kidding,' I replied enthusiastically.

We sat and took in our surroundings for a few minutes. I sensed we both knew we had found a special place and I wondered if anyone else had been on this glacier before. From our researches before the trip it seemed unlikely. It was strange to think that we were probably the first people into this entire valley and therefore to enjoy this view.

'I think we need to do a carry further up the glacier,' Andy said. 'We'll get the gear closer and a better look at the peak.'

'Good plan.' I nodded my agreement while staring above. Shadows were lengthening and it would not be long before night began to close in. I broke from my trance.

'Time to head back to the camp.' I picked up my pack, turned my back on the mountains and set off down the glacier.

I raced back in just 45 minutes and started cooking. Later, I opened my kit bag, pulled out my tent and pitched it on a suitable flat spot in the clearing. Then I blew up my inflatable mattress and laid it down inside the tent. Andy arrived and began his own unpacking. As I emptied the rest of my bag I felt increasingly anxious. Something seemed to be missing.

'Shit!' I shouted. 'I've left my sleeping bag on the boat.' I cursed some more. Andy simply smiled at this most basic of omissions.

'Sorry, I'll have to go back and get it.'

'Not tonight though,' Andy pointed out. It was nearly ten in the evening.

After we had eaten I changed into warmer climbing clothes and slid inside my bivvy bag. The night passed uncomfortably with just the thin fabric cover, but at least it was not cold.

'Good night?' Andy asked teasingly over breakfast.

'I've had better.' I was still embarrassed at my mistake.

'I'm going to stay put,' Andy said as I prepared to leave. 'I'm still sore from the horse riding yesterday and there's plenty to do here.'

We needed to build some sort of shelter to live and cook in and to sort out the food and supplies we had brought up, and I hardly needed help with carrying a sleeping bag.

I set off, sticking as close to the river as possible, though occasionally it was necessary to go deeper into the forest to get above rock buttresses that dropped straight into the torrent. On the way in on horseback we had avoided these obstacles by fording the river. At some point however, I was going to have to reach the other side on foot in order to get back to the estancia. It was not a prospect I relished. Here the water was too deep and fast flowing to cross. I kept a look out for a likely spot, hoping to find a fallen tree or branch that at least partially cleared the river, but there was nothing.

By the time I emerged from the forest I was worried. The river was now a little more sluggish, but still maybe ten metres wide and too deep to wade. The only way across at this point was to swim. Then in the distance I noticed a narrowing with some tree debris stretching out to mid-stream. I hurried towards it and as I got closer noticed some old fencing wire spanning to the far side about a metre above the water. It was far from ideal but I had found a place to cross. I stripped to my underpants and put my clothes and wellies inside my rucksack. Walking over the branches with the wire as a handrail was easy enough but the watery bit was obviously going to be trickier. I dropped my weight on to the wire and took the plunge. The glacial water made me gasp as I sank up to my chest, but luckily the rucksack acted as a float and stopped me going deeper. With a series of rapid tugs on the wire I pulled myself across and up on to the bank. Amazingly, only a small amount of water had leaked inside my rucksack. Shivering, I hurriedly re-dressed, happy to be over the river and still have dry clothes.

Soon I was out in the main Yendegaia valley. Here the terrain was flat and much more open with just small patches of trees. However, a lot of the ground was boggy and the walk back to the estancia took longer than I expected. It was mid-afternoon before I arrived and the place was deserted.

Fortunately a dinghy was lying on the beach near the old pier. It did not have oars but we had laid a line to the pier from the boat to prevent *Ada*'s anchor from dragging. I pulled the dinghy into the water and jumped inside. By pushing against the pier legs I soon reached the rope and was able to hand-over-hand along it back to the yacht. I tied the dinghy to the railings, climbed on to the deck, slid open the hatch and peered down into the galley. The girls and Jose were sat around the table playing scrabble. They looked up in surprise.

'Hello,' I said feebly.

'Simon,' Jane replied, looking puzzled. 'What are you doing back here?'

'I left my sleeping bag.'

They all dissolved into fits of laughter and I felt the same flush of embarrassment as when I had told Andy.

'Do you want a cup of tea?' Jane asked a little more sympathetically.

'That would be nice.'

I hurried through the galley and into our cabin. The sleeping bag was lying in its stuff-sack in the middle of my bunk. How had I possibly overlooked it? I tried to reassure myself that it was the unfamiliar surroundings and complicated approach to the mountains that had led to the mistake; but I had left things behind before. On expeditions so much time is taken up packing that the climbing can almost seem like a secondary activity. Occasionally you get things wrong. I had got away lightly with an uncomfortable night followed by an unwanted hike and icy river crossing. If I had forgotten to pack something as vital as my sleeping bag when actually on the mountain the repercussions could have been much more serious.

I had planned to go back to the camp the same day, but I knew it would be difficult to get back before darkness fell. The girls had arranged to go riding with Jose the following morning and suggested that we all return to the camp together. If I spent the night on *Ada* I would save both the walk and a repeat dip in the river. It was not a difficult decision. I opted to stay.

Later that evening we all went ashore. The sky was clearing again and the wind tailing off. I could already see a general pattern to the weather, which was at its best early and late in the day. Celia went out into the bay with Jose to check his lobster pots and we watched while picking our way along the shoreline. They busied from one spot to another, Jose laboriously hauling up the lines and then wrestling the large baskets into the dinghy before dropping them over the side again.

The ground between the huts on the beach was littered with pieces of old farm machinery and hidden away among trees was a large, derelict, wooden shearing shed. The estancia had obviously once been a major operation, but those days were long past. Now it felt more like a run down museum, a relic of a pioneering era when people thought a worthwhile living could be farmed from this place at the end of the world. Nature was reclaiming the land: wooden fences were falling apart, trees were growing on previously cleared land and the huts on the beach were on the verge of falling apart. It was saddening to witness the failure of an enterprise after so much hard work, but at the same time uplifting to see the wilderness re-asserting itself. If ever land was too wild to tame, this place certainly felt like it.

By the time we returned to the huts Jose and Celia had finished checking the pots in the bay. Jose walked along the beach clutching handfuls of king crabs by their legs.

'*Centolla*,' he said dismissively.

'Jose's fed up of eating them,' Celia explained.

Centolla are considered a delicacy in Chile and Argentina and much further afield. The ones held by Jose were a beautiful shade of pinky-red, with nearly round bodies, a pair of small short claws and long thin legs, all covered in sharp spines. In season, fresh *centolla* caught by fishermen in their small boats out in the Beagle Channel are flown daily to the fish markets of Paris and Tokyo.

Jose retrieved a large pan from his cabin and set about dealing with the crabs. One at a time he placed them on the ground on their backs, placed his boot on their stomachs and simply ripped their legs off. The legs went into the pan and the bodies were discarded. Jose, we were learning, was not squeamish when it came to killing things.

In the evening we brought some salad over from the boat and ate the *centolla* with Jose in his cabin. It tasted delicious, whatever the manner of the crabs' death. Jose meantime stuck to his staple of roast beef and a few potatoes.

Afterwards we made a driftwood fire on the beach and stood drinking beer and chatting before returning to the yacht. Sitting on deck as the light started to fade we noticed the still water around the boat begin to come to life. Initially, there were small splashes on the surface that sounded like raindrops hitting the water. The splashes came and went, moving from one location to another. Soon large tracts of water were boiling with fish; an enormous shoal of sardines had come into the bay. Celia rushed to get a net from the bow of the boat and with one scoop caught about 20 fish, which we put in bucket of seawater for breakfast. Later, once it was dark, we started to pick out larger silhouettes in the water with the beams of our headtorches. The splashing got louder as the bigger fish fed on the sardines. We launched the dinghy and managed to catch one in the net. It was an ugly brute with a small body that tapered away from a large head, its enormous mouth filled with wickedly sharp, backward pointing teeth. Nobody dare pick it out of the net and we dropped it back into the water. We called them 'Jurassic fish', learning later they were a type of hake. The feeding frenzy continued into the night. Lying in my sleeping bag I could hear the hake thudding on the hull. I realised we had witnessed something very special and dreamt of times past when the world's oceans would have been teeming with fish, the land covered in forest inhabited by a multitude of wild animals and the sky alive with birds. It was comforting to know that pockets of such places still remained, but shocking to think of the damage that humans have wreaked over a relatively short space of time.

By morning the sea was calm and the fish had gone. The only sign of their visit was a high tide line of dead sardines, beached in their panic to escape the predators. There were even some hake among them. A few seagulls were pecking lazily at the fish, almost as if they did not quite know what to do with so much food.

After a sardine breakfast we went ashore, helped Jose saddle the horses and headed up the valley. At the camp Andy appeared from his tent and came over to greet us as we tied up the horses.

'I hope you don't mind, but I decided to spend a night on the boat,' I explained.

'I've been keeping busy.' Andy pointed to a newly constructed hut in the centre of the camp. We had brought a sheet of plastic and some nails in Ushuaia. Andy had put them to good use in my absence, making a timber frame and covering it with the plastic to produce a weatherproof shelter where we could cook and relax while at base camp.

'Fantastic,' I enthused, walking round the structure and admiring his handy work.

'I'll put a brew on shall I?'

The goodbyes were briefer and less heartfelt this time around and once the others had left Andy and I worked together putting finishing touches to the shelter. It was nice to finally be on our own and to focus our thoughts on the mountain we had come so far to climb. After dinner we shared a carton of wine and chatted enthusiastically about the days ahead.

I slept soundly in the comfort of my sleeping bag, but when I woke there was the unmistakable sound of water dripping on the tent. It was raining again and a quick check of the barometer showed that the air pressure had plunged overnight. I could hear wind howling above the tree canopy. It was already apparent that we were going to need a lucky break with the weather to be in with a chance of getting up something. However, there was little indication of that happening; the few spells of better weather we had seen were just hours long and confined to early mornings and evenings with the air pressure remaining stubbornly low.

There was little rush to start the day, so I lay in the tent and read until hunger finally forced me outside. It was a grey and dank morning and the river was noisier than before, swollen by all the rain that had fallen, however, I was pleased to see that our hut had remained dry. I filled a pan with water, fired up the stove and made some tea.

'It doesn't look like we're going anywhere today,' I said as I delivered a brew to Andy's tent. He gave a knowing nod but did not look particularly concerned. Andy was hardly new to the expedition waiting game in this part of the world; he'd done several lengthy trips to the FitzRoy region of Patagonia, often on his own.

By mid-afternoon the rain had stopped and bursts of sunshine appeared through breaking cloud, making a mockery of my weather forecast.

'I think we should make a carry to the glacier,' Andy suggested.

'Yeah, we've still got plenty of daylight left.'

We hurriedly agreed on a rack of climbing equipment, sorted out a few days' worth of food and added a stove, pans, gas, ropes and a lightweight mountain tent to the mix. Then we split the load and packed, adding our own personal climbing equipment for good measure. As always the rucksack felt uncomfortably heavy. I consoled myself with the thought that not all of what we were taking would be carried on our backs once we began to climb.

Despite the weight it was satisfying to be moving again and we made rapid progress back to our high point of two days earlier. As before, the cloud was clearing, ushering in another fine evening. A shallow valley up the central part of the glacier provided gently angled walking over increasingly bare ice and I followed this to a large boulder that lay stranded on the surface.

'This will do for the stash,' I said as Andy arrived.

'We're not going to struggle to find it,' he observed. The boulder towered above us and was by far the most significant piece of debris visible on the glacier.

'Exactly, and we'll need to rope up a little higher up.'

Further on the ice was covered in snow and rose more steeply. The slope was riven by crevasses, some were open gashes while others lurked just beneath the surface. The way did not look difficult but it would require care.

We emptied our rucksacks on to the ice and gathered everything under the boulder, taking care to cover the bin liners of food to keep off foraging birds or animals. The gear and food amounted to quite a pile. I topped it off with my ice-axes, then we shouldered our nearly empty rucksacks and set off down.

'Now I guess we wait for some settled weather,' I said with an optimism I did not feel.

The following morning cloud and wind had returned and light rain was falling in the forest. A glimpse at my barometer confirmed what I already knew – the air pressure had dropped again. Conditions in the higher mountains a few kilometres to our west would be much worse. Climbing, like sailing in this place, was obviously going to be a test of patience.

After breakfast Andy got out his paper, paints and charcoal and began to work. He always kept himself busy and I admired his industrious approach, even though I sometimes relished the chance to live the slower, simple life that being in such places allows. At other times he made me feel lazy.

Spurred into action I took the laptop and satellite phone into a small clearing, determined to try again to update the expedition website. My resolve did not last long. For some reason I was unable to log-on. The battery in the computer seemed to be getting very low and so I set up the solar panel in the hope of doing a recharge. The kit was still all new and baffling, and to me looked incongruous in such wilderness: a piece of cutting-edge technology in a forest that must have changed little since it colonised this land at the end of the last ice-age. Andy showed a brief interest in the equipment, but as the low battery meant I could demonstrate none of its capabilities he soon drifted back to his painting. I vowed to try again later.

Voices broke the silence and moments later Jose and the girls rode into camp, all smiles and moving confidently on their horses. It looked like they were having more fun than we were.

'We've just come up to take a walk to the glacier,' Elaine enthused. 'We thought you might have gone up.'

'We carried up yesterday. Now we're waiting on the weather and pressure.' My reasoning did not sound very convincing, as again the weather appeared to be clearing.

While the girls took a walk up to the glacier Jose sat on a log in the centre of the camp and smoked regular cigarettes between cups of strong black coffee. He was not one for walking and anyway his cowboy boots and spurs would have prevented him going far. When the girls returned we chatted a little before they began to make ready to ride back to the estancia.

Jane seemed uneasy, putting me in mind of a time a number of years earlier when she had accompanied me to beneath a mountain in Pakistan. The peak was large and formidable to look at, and would give my climbing partner and I some difficult days. Jane had become upset when it came time to leave and we later confided that neither of us had found the experience particularly helpful. The mountains above the Bove Glacier looked nowhere near as intimidating, but this was still a committing climb. There was no search or rescue provision should anything go wrong. Once more Jane had shared our preparations and approach to the mountains, and also the consequent mounting tension. However, we were now in very different headspaces: Jane, Elaine and Celia were on holiday while Andy and I were psyching ourselves for a piece of serious exploratory mountaineering.

There were no tears this time. We embraced, kissed and said our goodbyes, knowing we were unlikely to see each other again until we had at least attempted the peak.

'We'll come back up to see how you are getting on in a week's time,' Jane said as she turned her horse to leave. All too quickly they had gone and once more we were left with nothing but the sounds of the forest for company.

Later, it rained and the weather was no better the following morning.

Once again I set up the solar panel and plugged it into the laptop, but after what should have been a full day of charging, the computer still would not operate. I packed all the equipment away in disgust and did not touch it again. It had been a lot of effort and anxiety to post one brief message on our expedition website and I would not repeat the experiment again. My first brush with 21st-century global communications had been less than successful, more a salutary experience.

As we shared a meal in the hut that night our restlessness was palpable. The barometer remained stubbornly low. Conditions were no better in the morning. Desperate to escape the camp, I walked up the hillside away from the river. As I got higher I felt a childlike urge to see beyond the leafy canopy. I picked a suitable looking tree and climbed to the top. By precariously balancing on the highest branches and gently standing upright I got my head above the leaves. There was sunshine down the main Yendegaia valley over the estancia and the sea beyond, but dark, brooding clouds over the mountains at the head of our valley.

'I think we should go tomorrow whatever the weather,' Andy said when I returned to the camp. 'At least we'll get a feel for the place even if we have to come back down.' I understood his reasoning, but did not want to get caught high on one of these mountains in a storm. We had already seen how the wind could blow in this place.

'I guess you are right,' I replied cautiously, but also aware of a level of apathy creeping into camp life. 'It'll certainly be good to get out of here for a while.'

By mid-afternoon the following day we were back at our gear stash on the Bove Glacier. The morning weather had started badly again and we had waited until after lunch before leaving. It had been a wise decision, the clouds were parting and waves of warm sunlight were moving down the glacier. We loaded our rucksacks, put on our harnesses and carried on. Soon we reached the point where the slope steepened and was split by crevasses. It was time to rope up. Progress became slower as the snow deepened and we were forced to weave our way around the slots. Occasionally our feet would break through the slushy snow into a hidden chasm below. It was laborious work, but eventually we cleared the zone of crevasses and reached a plateau that led to the head of the glacier. At eight in the evening we called it a day, put up our lightweight tent and began melting snow. Then we turned our attention to the mountains.

'What do you think?' I pointed to our peak at the back of the cirque.

'I can see a line up that couloir to the right of the ridge,' Andy replied thoughtfully.

'Yeah, and it looks like there's a gully splitting the upper headwall.' This welcome line of weakness had not been visible on the Hillebrandt photograph, which must have been taken from further to the north.

At four o'clock next morning Andy's alarm signalled the start of our climb. He lit the small stove hanging from the centre of the tent and made drinks. Outside it was clear and still. Then we packed in silence. As we left the tent it began to get light. It seemed strange simply to abandon the tent in such a place, but we knew we would not be able to use it on the mountain – the terrain was too steep.

A short walk across the glacier took us to the foot of the face. Our planned line followed a vague set of features up the centre. By following slopes up the right of a buttress we hoped to gain access to a faint couloir running into steep snow slopes below a final tower. A prominent gully line then breached the tower.

Once over the bergschrund below the face we packed away the rope and climbed simultaneously up easy-angled slopes just to the right of the buttress crest. Already a large bank of ominously dark cloud had drifted into the cirque from the west and the wind was getting up. I sighed to myself as it started to snow – it was going to be a hard day.

The ground steepened and I was forced to move further rightwards into a broad couloir where I found a small section of rock protruding from the snow. It would provide an anchor, we would need to climb roped from here on. By the time Andy arrived I had chopped a platform, made a belay and uncoiled my rope. He unpacked his rope and handed me the remaining climbing gear. I crossed the gully in deepening snow and headed for a steep, rocky corner on the far side. Here my progress slowed. It was snowing hard and I could barely see what I was doing as I swept snow from the rock, only to find it almost bare of ice. Bridging my feet wide and making a series of insecure pulls on my axes I moved upwards, but it was taking a lot of time. Occasionally I glimpsed Andy through the whiteness, being deluged by snow from above and blasted by wind from below. Already our worlds had been reduced to the small zones of snow and ice immediately around us – two separate struggles at either end of the ropes. Bushed, I reached the top of the corner, anchored myself to the rock and pulled up the remaining rope. Andy inched his way towards me through the maelstrom.

'That took hours,' he complained when he joined me, looking chilled to the bone.

'I had to clear away the snow,' I replied defensively, 'and the rucksack was heavy.'

'You should have left it.' It was fair criticism. I had not done much mountaineering over the previous year. These days when I did climb in the mountains it tended to be on expeditions abroad. In truth I felt a little rusty; unlike Andy I did not live in an alpine playground where I could take short trips into the mountains whenever I wanted. Now it was my turn to wait. The climbing above looked desperately hard.

Andy abandoned his rucksack before moving above me. He stopped at a small overhang and painstakingly cleared several cracks of ice and placed gear in them. Somehow he was going to have to move leftwards. I could not see how he was going to do it.

'Watch me here,' he said after clipping one of the ropes into the gear.

'I've got you,' I replied nervously.

Andy jabbed his left axe into what looked like soft, granulated snow lying on the slab above the roof and gently pulled down. It ripped straight through. Undeterred he tried again. This time the axe held and he transferred more weight on to it, removing his other axe from lower down and bringing it up to place alongside the first. Now he was out of balance, his feet scrambling for purchase below the overhang with virtually his entire weight on his arms. In a series of quick and insecure moves he moved left. At the far side of the overhang Andy needed to establish himself in a groove. The axe placements petered out and I watched with increasing concern as he tried to swing his weaker left leg across, before tiring and scuttling back. He nearly fell moving back off the overhang, but at least then he was able to rest.

After a few shake-outs of each arm Andy went straight back to it. I could tell from his body language that this attempt was do-or-fly and watched the ropes carefully. By quickly hooking his axes into their previous placements he moved back to the hanging groove and then stalled, his left foot pedalling for purchase. Then it stuck and he managed to rock on his axes and stand up, balancing on the very tips of his crampons. I watched helplessly; if he fell he was going to take a nasty swing into the corner below me. Somehow, precariously balanced and breathing hard, he managed to take a peg from his harness and at full stretch insert it into a crack above his head. I stayed braced, ready for the fall I was sure would come any moment. Andy started tapping the piton into the crack. The first few taps were tentative, so that he did not knock it out, but he was soon hitting the piton with force and after a few heavy blows a high-pitched ringing came from the metal. It was secure. With a precise movement he reached up with a tie-off and clipped the karabiner through the eye of the piton. Then, agonisingly slowly, he pulled up a loop of rope, as I hurriedly fed it out to him, and carefully clipped it into the other end of the tie-off. Andy let out a huge sigh. The tension lifted. A moment of danger had passed.

Now he was able to shift his feet and alternately rest weary calves while inspecting the moves above. He probed tentatively with his axes and found placements, but they were very insecure; the tips hooked on tiny edges. Suddenly came a series of powerful moves, Andy pulling from one improbable axe placement to another, crampons scratching on the rock for purchase. He disappeared from view and soon the rope stopped moving. Wet snow was falling very heavily and small avalanches were sliding down the gully line to our left with increasing regularity. I waited patiently.

A muffled cry of 'Safe' finally drifted down. I had become cold and was happy to busy myself again. I tied Andy's rucksack on to one rope and removed most of the belay. When the ropes came tight I let the rucksack go and it spun across to my left; Andy hauled it up until it wedged below the peg.

'Climb,' Andy shouted. I removed the remaining gear and set off. Almost immediately I was in difficulty. The axe placements above the small roof were terrible and there was little for the feet either. I lunged sideways; the axes seemed to hold better but I was getting tired.

'Tight!' I yelled, approaching the groove. I swung left into it and dangled on the rope. I couldn't see what to do next. I tried the tiny placements for my axes, only for them to pull whenever I tried to weight them. My rucksack was not helping, even so I was amazed at what Andy had climbed.

'Keep me very tight here,' I urged. By making small movements as Andy took in the rope I inched upwards, embarrassment growing at my inability. As I reached the wedged rucksack I gave it a shove from below and Andy pulled it up. Retrieving the piton was a prolonged struggle. I simply hung on the rope and hammered away at it until eventually it dropped from the crack. Andy could see me now and was smiling at my discomfort. Finally, I put together a decent series of moves and arrived at Andy's belay a little more composed.

'Doesn't look so bad above,' said Andy. I was relieved to hear it.

After a brief rest we swapped the remaining gear and I led off into the snow and mist. It had developed into a foul day. The climbing was easier – ice under damp, heavy snow – but very insecure. Steep snow, poor ice, wind and regular avalanches that threatened to push you off meant complete concentration was required. At times the visibility was so bad that it was difficult to pick a way, nevertheless even as the weather deteriorated we continued to gain ground through the whiteness. Time slipped by. We had taken so long with the start of the climb that evening came quickly. It was difficult to tell how far we had come up the face.

'What about a bivouac?' Andy said, joining me at a stance at about eight o'clock. It was more of a statement than a question.

'Where?' The same thought had been crossing my mind but I had seen nowhere that looked suitable.

'That cone of snow up to your right,' he replied, undaunted by my negative response. 'We can make a platform.' I did not see it myself, but Andy moved across to his cone and started digging. By the time I joined him he had already hit ice below the snow. We soon made a body-length shelf, though annoyingly it was only wide enough for one to lie down and offered little shelter from the wind and incessant avalanches.

'We're going to have to dig up as well,' I suggested. The light was beginning to fade and with no alternative sites nearby we would have to make the best of where we were. By digging carefully we managed to make an L-shaped chamber that bulged out on the inside. It was big enough for both of us to sit up and get out of the snow but our feet remained outside. It was dark by the time we both squeezed in.

Somehow Andy managed to get the stove going in a tiny space to his side, while I struggled to stop myself sliding towards the entrance. As I tried to wedge myself upright I punched a hole in the wall of the shelter. Spindrift poured through and into my sleeping bag until I managed to stem the tide with a few snowballs.

'I don't think I've ever been anywhere as cold and wet,' Andy said, handing me a drink.

'Scotland,' I replied, from memory born of grim experience.

'Well I haven't climbed there for years.'

'It's about as cold and wet, but if this was Scotland we'd be in a nice warm pub by now.'

Andy kicked away the snow that had piled up over the bottom of his bivouac bag and for a brief moment my headtorch beam illuminated the storm raging outside. Then an avalanche poured down, covering the bag and obscuring the view. Despite the circumstances we slept, waking periodically to kick accumulated snow from our feet. My sleeping bag got wetter and wetter and by daylight a puddle of water had collected under us. The weather had not improved. As we ate a leisurely breakfast I wondered how long we could hold out. Our position was beginning to get serious, spending another night out in similar circumstances did not bear thinking about. And yet I felt strangely comfortable with no pressing need to go down; in all likelihood we would encounter similar conditions on another attempt.

By mid-morning it was evident the storm was easing and we prepared to leave. I was pleasantly surprised on getting outside. It was misty and still snowing slightly, but the outline of the sun was visible through the cloud. Its warmth slowly permeated my wet clothing. We had left the ropes dumped in the snow the night before and they had become tangled and took some time to free. At one end was our gear secured to an ice screw. I carefully excavated it and immediately recognised something was missing. I quickly checked my harness and then probed feebly in the snow.

'Shit! I've lost my figure-of-eight.'

'That's not very professional,' Andy commented, barely looking up from his own preparations.

'I can't have clipped it in properly last night,' I said apologetically. It was a double blow as I used the device for belaying as well as abseiling.

'Here take this.' Andy handed me his belay plate. Then he tied into the ropes, grabbed the gear and began climbing. He followed ribs of snow and runnels of poor ice until he disappeared from view. I climbed quickly when it was time to follow. It was good to be moving, to get warm and to drive some of the moisture from my clothing, but as I took the lead I realised the bivouac had taken more out of me than I would have thought. I slowed. Then the sun burst through the clouds, draining me further. At the belay I took off my rucksack and daubed sun cream over my face.

'Lets leave the sacks and go for the summit,' Andy suggested as he joined me.

'Are you sure? I think there's still a fair way to the top and what if the weather changes? The bivvy gear will be here.'

'I think we can do this faster without it,' he said forcefully.

'Okay.' Andy had been making the right calls up to this point, but I still felt uneasy about coming down the face. Our original plan had been to descend an easier-angled ridge from the summit further to the north. Now we would be abseiling the route and I had lost my descender.

We left the bivouac gear and sleeping bags in my rucksack and put some spare clothing, a little food and water in the other. Then Andy led off. He moved fluidly without the extra weight on his back and I followed quickly. A further rope length brought us to below the summit headwall. It was my turn to lead. Above, the thin gully we had looked at from the glacier cut through the black, overhanging, rime-covered rock above.

Snow and ice conditions had been gradually improving with height and here I was delighted to move up steep névé into the bottom of a corner. I placed a piece of gear in the left rock wall, clipped the rope through it and set off. There was a thin ribbon of ice in the corner and to my delight it took axe placements first time. I simply stacked one placement above the other, my left foot on the ice, the other out on the rime of the right wall. This was like climbing in Scotland at its best, I simply knew the axe placements would not fail. All too quickly the steep climbing was over and I found myself in a broader, more gently angled gully. I raced up this until the rope came tight, placed a belay into the rocky left wall and brought Andy up. For some reason I could not fathom, he followed the pitch very slowly.

'It looks like the top up there,' I said, pointing aloft as he joined me at the stance. I was barely able to contain my excitement as Andy disappeared above. The rope came tight. I dismantled the belay, followed up the broadening gully, cleared a small cornice and then walked up an easy-angled ridge in the mist. Andy was sitting in the snow on the top.

'The cloud lifted earlier,' he said simply.

We sat in silence as the mist drifted eerily around us. Suddenly a window opened to the east and we could see our approach route up the Bove Glacier and across to the Yendegaia valley beyond. More mist parted revealing Monte Bove, its weather-beaten, rime-covered west face a contrast to the rockier eastern side. We walked around the summit taking photographs as each new vista presented itself, from the foothills to the east and the ice cap in the north to the Beagle Channel glittering in the evening sun to the west. There were streaks of cirrus high in the pale blue sky and clumps of cumulus over the Pacific that looked like mushrooms. It was the most remarkable panorama I have ever had from the summit of a mountain.

At one point Andy was stood on the top smiling, waving at his shadow projected on to a misty cloud several kilometres away to the east. It was the first time I had seen a Brocken spectre and we laughed together, shadow dancing like children before making our way down the ridge.

On the top of the cornice Andy got to work and dug a T-shaped trench into the rime. Then he placed a snow stake in the trench bottom and ran a sling out along the base of the T – towards the edge – before threading the end of a rope through and tying it to one end of the other. This would be our first abseil point. It was 7.30 in the evening.

'Can you use a karabiner brake?' he asked

'Not very well.' I knew that it involved threading the rope through two pairs of karabiners, but not exactly how it was done. However, I did know that if it was done wrong it could fail.

'Here take this.' Andy generously handed me his descender.

'Thanks,' I replied, feeling very grateful.

Then he threw the ropes down and started to abseil. When Andy's weight came off the ropes I took one final longing look at the sun setting out to the west then slid down.

On the second abseil I went first and entered the steep corner I had led on the way up. The rime on the wall to the right of the corner was covered in scratch marks of crampons and the tiny notches of axe placements. I realised why Andy had taken so long to follow the pitch: he had been unable to climb the ice in the corner. The lack of mobility in his left arm meant he was unable to place that axe higher than his right in the thin ribbon of ice. Instead he had climbed the wall; it looked ridiculously hard and yet he had said nothing. At moments like this I had nothing but admiration for the man.

Our descent began to pass in a blur. We quickly reached the stashed gear, re-packed and carried on down. A little later darkness fell but it was a clear, still night. We continued by headtorch, clearing the bergschrund with a final scary abseil to the glacier. Then we walked below the face until we hit our upward tracks in the snow and followed them down. It was 2.30 in the morning when we reached the tent and we did little more than throw down our mats and sleeping bags, take off our boots and dive inside. The down filling of my sleeping bag had morphed into clumps with the consistency of wet papier-mâché. I decided to remain in my waterproof shell. It was wet and cold, yet within moments I was asleep.

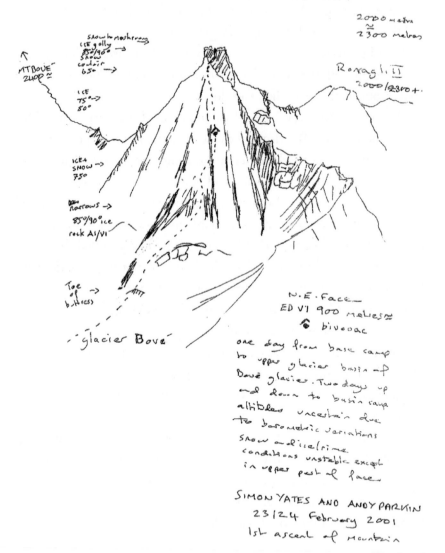

UN-NAMED SUMMIT

2000 metres
≃
2300 metres

Rovaglii II
2000/2300+.

MTBOVE
2400 ≃

Snow mushrooms
ICE gully
850/900 →
Snow
couloir
65° →

ICE
75° →
80°

ICE+
SNOW →
750

narrows →
85°/90° ice
rock A1/VI

Toe
of
buttress

Glacier Bové

N.E. Face
ED VI 900 metres ≃
bivouac

one day from base camp
to upper glacier basin of
Bové glacier. Two days up
and down to basin camp
altitudes uncertain due
to barometric variations
snow and ice/rime
conditions unstable except
in upper part of face

SIMON YATES AND ANDY PARKIN
23/24 February 2001
1st ascent of mountain

Andy's drawing of the route up the peak we had climbed. We later discovered it was not on our rudimentary map and had no name. We called it Monte Ada.

THREE

The Way of the Gaucho

It was eleven in the morning when I woke, feeling warm but steamily damp. Andy was still asleep. I unzipped the tent and peered outside. Our mountain lay in front of me and, as always, it was hard to believe we had actually climbed to the top. It was as if the previous days had been a dream. Reality was less appealing: a leaden sky heralded more bad weather. I scooped snow into the pan and fired up the stove. Andy began to stir beside me.

'You all right?' I asked.

'Yeah, not bad; I'm still feeling pretty wasted though.'

'You made the best choice of pit.'

I pointed at our sleeping bags. Andy had decided on a synthetic filling; although heavier before the drenching his bag had not absorbed water and there was still form and shape to it. In soggy contrast, my down-filled bag looked like a lumpy bin-liner pulled across my body. We laughed at my misfortune. Luckily it did not matter. Before the end of the day we would be back in the comfort of base camp.

Breakfast was a slow business. We were both desperately tired and although we said nothing I sensed little enthusiasm for what was likely to be a tiring walk out. It was two in the afternoon before we broke camp in wet, driven snow and trudged forlornly down with bowed heads. The snow on the upper part of the glacier had thawed since our approach and we broke through the crust to our knees with every step. It was a relief when we came off the snow and could take off our harnesses and the rope, but now it was raining hard. Progress became more of a stagger as we slipped on bare ice running with water. Andy was finding it difficult and took several bruising falls before we reached our stash at the boulder. There was now more kit and spare food to add to our loads.

'I'll take all this and both ropes.'

'Are you sure?' Andy replied, wanting to do his bit as ever.

'Of course, it's my day job, carrying large rucksacks.' It was a bit of an over-simplification, but when I work leading commercial expeditions there are many days when portering seems a big part of the deal.

'Oh, all right then.'

Thankfully Andy was not going to let his admirable independence get in the way of pragmatism. He was hardly going to be travelling light anyway. Once the repacking was complete we both had huge loads to carry down.

'If it's okay, I'm going to press on.' I said, shouldering the sack. 'I'll put the kettle on.'

'Sure.'

I had got cold during our break and needed to regain some body heat. Despite the days of exertion and the weight of my sack I felt strong and moved quickly down the glacier. The rain intensified in wind-driven pulses as the cloud base dropped, obscuring the mountaintops. We had been lucky to be in the right place at the right time. The brief window we had been granted to climb in had now closed. There was little to see or savour. I simply put one foot in front of the other and tried to maintain a swift pace without falling on the patches of ice.

I paused at the snout of the glacier. Here the ice dropped away steeply into the river valley and it was essential to pick a good line. I eyed the terrain and tried to link together the longest sections where the ice was pitted with rock debris, knowing that this would offer the best traction. Even so there were plenty of bare stretches. Having visualised my route, I descended cautiously, placing and weighting the tips of my ski poles before each step. Or I simply ran down the bare ice aiming to slow up on the next embedded rocks, stumbling to regain balance whenever I slipped.

Finally, it was done and I reached the muddy gravel by the river beneath the glacier. Hurrying on, I contoured above the water and out of the steep ravine. Rock gave way to vegetation and the ground became slippery again, but I made short work of it and was soon back in the main river valley stomping through dripping forest. It had turned into the sort of day all too common in the early winter months at home in Cumbria – cold, wet and windy.

I reached base camp at seven in the evening. It was dank and uninviting but at least it was well-stocked with food. I dumped my rucksack against a tree, dived into the hut and hurriedly ate some salami on crackers. Then I went to the river, filled a pan with water and made tea. After emptying my rucksack I made tomato sauce to accompany the pasta I planned for dinner and started a fire. There was still no sign of Andy. The light was fading.

It was almost dark when I heard the crackle of sticks breaking underfoot. Moments later Andy entered the hut.

'I thought that was going to never end,' he said, shaking his head. He looked completely ragged. 'The end of the glacier was fucking awful. I was lucky not to break something. I was on my arse most of the time.'

'I wondered how you'd find it. I'll make a brew.'

We chatted a little while we drank and ate, but what we needed above all else was sleep. We could bask in the glow of our success later. As soon as the meal was finished we headed for our tents.

Sunlight was casting the shadow of branches across my tent when I woke. In the pleasant warmth, the down in my sleeping bag was almost dry and returning to its former lofted glory. There was little to remind me of the previous days of struggle until I stepped outside. Andy was up and busy. Nearly everything he had taken on the mountain was already hanging from bushes to dry. It was just the day for it, though after an initial burst of activity the morning passed lazily. It was nice to relax yet at the same time I was hoping for a visit from the girls. Elaine and Jane were due to leave Yendegaia the following morning and had promised a last ride up to see us.

'I'm going down to the estancia,' I told Andy at three in the afternoon, my patience exhausted. 'I want to see Jane before she leaves.'

'Sure. I'm going to hang out here.'

'I'll be back up to clear the camp as soon as possible,' I said, stuffing my sleeping bag into my rucksack. The way down was familiar now and the forest felt more benign, less threatening and remote than it had done before the climb.

I met the girls 20 minutes below the camp, threading their way between huge limbs of dead timber in the densest section of forest.

'It's Simon,' shouted Celia.

'We did it,' I told them. 'Got down last night.'

'Fantastic,' Jane said, looking visibly relieved. At least on this trip she would leave knowing we were safe. 'Was it hard?'

'Hard enough. We had some pretty shitty weather, but got lucky on our summit day.'

'We've been having a great time,' Jane enthused. 'Learning to be gauchos.'

Celia and Elaine said they would go and get Andy. It was a nice gesture. They left with Jane's horse and we walked back through the forest towards the river, swapping stories. Jose had been keeping them busy gathering firewood, riding and castrating horses.

'Something horrible happened though,' Jane added in a hushed tone, which seemed mildly ridiculous as no one could hear. 'Jose was teaching us how to lasso and he pulled a down a foal; it fell badly and broke one of its front legs.'

'What did he do?'

'He killed it. Slit its throat.'

'Well, I don't suppose he could take it to the vet.'

'We all felt really guilty,' Jane continued. 'It wouldn't have happened if he wasn't showing us. We've been eating foal since it happened.'

It was a stark reminder of where we were. The remoteness and isolation of this place meant that the remaining domestic animals on the estancia were there to work or as food, and under certain circumstances both. There was little room for sentiment.

We did not have long to wait by the river before Celia and Elaine returned with Andy. With only three horses between five of us it was necessary to shuttle across the river. Once over, I rode pillion behind Jane as we headed back to the estancia, Andy doing his best to keep up on foot.

That evening we dined on the finest rack of foal and roast potatoes in Jose's cabin. Two sisters from Buenos Aires – Rose-Marie and Florencia – had arrived. They had some association with the trust that oversaw the management of the estancia and planned to walk out to the north. Their manner seemed out of place in a tumbledown hut at the end of the world and I suspected their more natural habitat to be glittery metropolitan soirées. During dinner they monopolised conversation and took it upon themselves to translate for Jose, even though Celia and Andy had been managing to converse with him in Spanish.

'This is the way of the gaucho,' they would say at the end each translation.

Thankfully the sisters went to bed early and left us to our party. The wine and beer flowed as we celebrated our success and a last evening all together. Elaine and Jane said their farewells to Jose before we drunkenly made our back to the yacht.

❄ ❄ ❄ ❄

In the morning Celia ferried Elaine and Jane over to the *Terra Australis*. By the time we reached the liner the girls had been served cocktails in an airy lounge. They had entered a different world from the one we had shared over the previous weeks; we laughed at this sudden change of circumstances but even so it was a sad moment. Their time in this place had been special and now it was coming to and end. Laughter mingled with tears as we said our goodbyes. Tears were still running down Celia's face on the dinghy back to *Ada*. A few minutes later *Terra Australis* weighed anchor and motored from the bay.

We had arranged with Jose to go and clear our camp from the forest. In bright afternoon sunshine we rode up the valley but could get no further than the river. The storms while we had been on the mountain and the warm sunny weather that had followed meant the Rio Neimeyer was swollen with meltwater. Jose was not prepared to cross and we returned to the estancia empty-handed.

Plans had already been made for the coming days. Rose-Marie and Florencia were ready to start their trek and Jose had offered to escort them as far as a pass from the Lapataia valley. Celia was keen on doing more riding and I was happy to take the opportunity to see more wonderful country. Jose also assured me that there was good fishing to be had.

'I'm going to stay and paint,' was Andy's verdict on the excursion. 'I don't think I can stand two days on a horse.'

Next morning we headed off at a canter, the dogs weaving across the path of the horses and occasionally snapping at their hooves. Jose looked comfortable and relaxed; even when his horse appeared to be walking it moved faster than everyone else's. When we reached the broad flats a little inland he broke into a gallop. The other horses followed. My inadequate riding technique was painfully exposed as I bounced in the saddle. At times I thought I was going to fall, but somehow managed to hold on. The day was certainly passing at a faster tempo than our previous ones on horseback. I was beginning to realise what an efficient means of transport horses could be.

Jose stopped at the wide river that drains the Stoppani Glacier and I caught up. It was a good 50 metres across, deep and flowing quite quickly. White glacial flour billowed to the surface and swirled around, making the water look even more menacing. Jose advanced without hesitation, urging his horse into a stumble down the bank where it took a couple of strides on the riverbed and started swimming. The dogs dived in and were immediately swept downstream. Our horses needed no prompting either. I lifted my wellies to stop them filling with water. It was a serious crossing and I knew from many encounters with glacial streams and rivers that if anyone parted company with their swimming horse survival would be touch and go.

By the time Jose hit the far bank the dogs had already drifted out of sight round a bend. He raced off to retrieve them as one-by-one the rest of us gained the riverbank. I felt a surge of relief as my horse's hooves touched the bottom and it was able heave itself out of the water.

'That was interesting,' I called to Celia, with a frivolity I did not feel. We joined Jose down river where he was fishing out the dogs. Some had made it across under their own efforts, but the smaller ones were having difficulty – paddling frantically but going downstream rather than across. Jose made several forays into the water, plucking the dogs out by the scruffs of their necks and dropping them on the bank. Thankfully he did not ask for help.

The crossing behind us, we continued up river for a short way before heading into a side valley. In a small clearing below a forest of imposing, mature trees lay the ruins of a sawmill. Once it had turned out planks that were loaded on to the boat now gently rotting alongside the pier back at the estancia. In its heyday 60 people had worked on the estate. Entering the forest, it was easy to see why the mill had been located here. The trees were by far the biggest *Nothofagus* (Antarctic beech) I had ever seen, with trunks up to an arm-span in width. There was also a good trail – a leftover from the logging days – weaving uphill between huge stumps and the remaining trees. Jose kept up a good pace and soon the trees became smaller and began to thin. We emerged on to boggy grassland that led gently up to a watershed and then more steeply down the other side. A huge, broad valley fringed with peaks opened up in front of us. It was incredible to think that all this land was still part of the same property.

Following a shallow river course, we rode quickly down to the tree line where a tin-roofed shack came into view. Jose called this place '*la casa*' (the house). Its simple beauty was complemented by its remoteness and isolation. It was unimportant that the building was little more than a shell with wooden beds inside. There was a hearth, a plentiful supply of pre-cut firewood and an axe. All we needed now was dinner. I unpacked my fishing rod and made for a beaver dam lake. The fish started to bite almost immediately and I quickly hooked one – a pretty trout, greenish back dappled with bright orange spots shading to a lighter orange belly. It was too small to eat and after admiring its delicate markings I returned it to the water.

The sisters appeared armed with a length of fishing line wrapped around a tin can, a simple spinner and weight on the end of the line. They soon bagged two good-sized fish before losing interest and drifting back to the *casa*. Their visit stiffened my resolve to catch something worthy of the pot. I tried several different changes of flies but the fish had stopped biting. The backwoodsman seemed to have been upstaged by the city socialites; not that it really mattered, it was a lovely afternoon and the setting beautiful.

A strange sight greeted me back at the *casa*. There was a pile of steaming, half-digested grass lying on the ground and the dogs were all asleep.

'What's been going on here?' I asked Celia as she appeared in the doorway.

'We went out hunting with the dogs; Jose managed to lasso a large calf and brought it back here, tied it up and killed it.' The tone of her voice dropped to a whisper. 'It was all a bit gruesome; he fed the offal to the dogs. Rose-Marie and Florencia found it quite upsetting.' I looked again at the steaming grass and realised it had been in the animal's stomach. My disappointment at not catching a fish big enough to eat seemed even less important.

That night the sisters ate the trout they had caught but passed on the offer of beef. For now, they were less keen on the way of the gaucho.

Jose and I left early next morning while the others slumbered on in their sleeping bags. Apparently there were bigger fish in Lago Lapataia, a large lake further down the valley. Jose was going to drop me at the lake, go back to the *casa*, take the sisters to the start of their trek and then return to escort me back. Though we tried to move quickly, the trail was faint and there were treacherous stretches of peat bog. The horses panicked when their hooves sank deeply and at times we had to dismount and lead them on lengths of rope. It was two hours before we reached Lago Lapataia and halted at a hut by its northern shore. Jose took the saddle and bridle off my horse, then rode away.

I immediately felt very isolated. This place added new meaning to the phrase 'the middle of nowhere'. The vast lake was cloudy with glacier run off; dry fly fishing was not going to work, as the fish would not see the fly on the surface. I tied on a wet fly and began to fish. Soon I was absorbed in the simple activity of casting and gently pulling in the line. Periodically I moved a few yards. There were no bites or other signs of fish. After a while I took a break and my attention turned to the weather. It had been sunny when we arrived, now the sky was filling with grey cloud and a cool breeze was blowing from the north-west. I fished a bit longer then gave up and sat in the hut to wait for Jose. As the wind steadily rose I became increasingly anxious. The weather was changing quickly. I thought through my options and concluded I needed to leave. However, I had never ridden on my own and nor did I feel confident about finding the trail back to the *casa*; furthermore, the horse would need saddling before I could go anywhere. It all seemed rather daunting. Then it began to rain and I knew

I would have to get on with it.

The horse was tied to a tree and grazing peaceably. It was promisingly co-operative as I led it to a railing outside the hut. I managed to get the bridle over the animal's head and the bit into its mouth. Buoyed by success I put on the saddle and pulled the girth tight. Finally, I mounted the horse, flicked the reins and, to my surprise, set off.

The first obstacle was a river crossing. The horse barely broke its stride as we went down the bank and into the water. It was not as serious as the crossing the day before, but I still felt a surge of relief when it was over. Two more crossings of the same meandering river followed in quick succession and with each I felt my confidence growing. Finding the trail was not proving as difficult as I expected, as the horse seemed to know the way.

For a while the rain held off, but the wind was gathering strength and I had seen enough of the weather in this part of the world to know that a storm was building. Hopefully I would get back to the *casa* before it hit. Where the trail was clear I urged the horse to trot and we soon reached the peat bog. I dismounted and to hurry along simply led the horse by the reins, ignoring the longer length of rope that was coiled around its neck. The horse struggled a little as its hooves broke through the surface of the bog, but I kept pulling, marching on. In the centre of the bog the horse stumbled and its back legs sank deeply into the mud. It panicked and in a rapid series of lunges, reared up and surged towards me. A hefty kick from a front foot caught my left thigh and knocked me on my back. I screamed and let go the reins as the horse thrashed past me, only stopping once it had found firm footing. My thigh ached and I knew I was going to have a big bruise later. But I had been lucky, a kick like that could easily have broken my leg. I hobbled to the horse, uncoiled the rope, as I should have done in the first place, and then led the reluctant animal through the rest of the bog from a safe distance. Now I moved with greater caution, only too aware I could not afford a serious accident in this place. By the time I reached the *casa* the wind was near storm force, driving waves of sleet down the valley. There was no sign of the others. I took the tackle off the horse, tethered it to a bush and made a fire.

Night was approaching when I heard dogs barking, quickly followed by the thud of hooves. I hurried out to see Celia and Jose gallop up to the hut. There was snow in the air and Jose was visibly relieved to see I had made my own way back; he would not have had time to collect me from the lake in the remaining daylight. I'd made the right decision.

'It was a very long way,' was all Celia said as they brought the saddles into the *casa*. She and Jose were wet and exhausted and I wondered how the sisters would be faring on their first night under canvas. Not very well in all probability.

We ate some more of the calf before settling down for the night. Not that the night itself was very settled. Driving rain replaced the sleet and snow as ferocious gusts of wind tore at the building. The *casa* had obviously suffered from similar batterings in the past. Sheets of the corrugated iron roof flapped so noisily in the blasts that I thought they would be ripped off. Amazingly, they held.

Conditions were little better in the morning and I expected Jose to sit tight until the weather improved. To my dismay he did not. We saddled the horses in driving sleet and Jose loaded the remaining quarters of the calf on to the two spare horses. The way back to the pass was directly into the wind and most of my warm clothing was still at our base camp. Without socks, gloves or my fleece hat I was soon uncomfortably cold. I shivered my way to the high point and only began to feel warm once we were down in the forest above the saw-mill. The colder temperatures thankfully meant the river was less swollen with meltwater and we crossed it with relative ease. As we galloped the final stretch the clouds began to part and shafts of bright sunlight illuminated the valley. I was relieved to get back to the estancia.

Andy was painting on the porch of Jose's hut when we arrived. He looked tired and drawn.

'Some storm, eh?'

'I thought the hut we stayed in was going to blow away,' I replied. 'What's it been like here?'

'I was up all night, worried the yacht was being torn from its moorings.'

Later we learnt that the storm had caught a large cruise ship in the Drake Passage – the stretch of water between Cape Horn and the Antarctic Peninsula. A huge wave had broken over the vessel and smashed the bridge. There had been a number of injuries and lifejackets were issued to the passengers and crew in case they were forced to abandon ship. The thought of going into life rafts, in that water, in such stormy conditions, is scary indeed.

Our time in Yendegaia was coming to an end. Celia was keen to move on and Andy and I were looking forward to seeing the mountains we knew lay further to the west. The next day was calm and sunny. Only the fresh snow on the peaks gave any indication of the storm that had passed. We took a final ride up the valley and cleared our base camp, leaving just the shelter, which Jose said could be useful for his hunting trips.

That evening Jose roasted a sizeable chunk of the beef brought back from Lapataia and we shared it in a farewell meal. Andy spoke of his winter solo trips to the FitzRoy region of Argentina – of the weeks he'd spent waiting in remote huts and of his epics on the mountains. There were parallels with Jose's life in this wild place. The gaucho often went months without meeting another person, seemingly quite happy with just his dogs and horses for company. I guess the big difference was that Andy spent time in such places for recreation, Jose for his job.

Two days later we finally got *Ada* out of the Bahia Yendegaia and into the Beagle Channel. There had been a false start when strong headwinds forced us back to the sanctuary of the estancia. We felt a little uncomfortable about imposing on Jose again, having already said our goodbyes, and so left him to his solitude. When the winds were still unfavourable on the second morning we did not even pay him a visit. Conditions finally improved and allowed us to sail in the afternoon. After more than two weeks spent in and around Yendegaia it was refreshing to be back in the Beagle Channel. I was ready for a change of scenery.

The slopes and valleys running down to the shores grew ever steeper as we motored west and the channel gradually narrowed. Occasionally, tantalising glimpses of glaciers and snow-capped peaks appeared through the cloud. Squally showers tracked along the channel to meet us and progress slowed in the increasing swell. As *Ada* crawled past the Chilean navy post at Yamana – a white hut on the shoreline with the national flag painted on its tin roof – someone waved to us from the balcony. A little further on the channel forked and we crept into a narrow passage between the mainland and the chillingly named Devil's Island, stunted trees somehow clinging to its windswept outline. The island slid astern and a bay appeared on the mainland; at its head a huge icefall spilled down from the Hollandia Glacier and seemingly into the trees behind the beach. It was one of the most dramatic views I had ever seen.

'Caleta Olla,' Celia shouted, as she turned *Ada* into the bay and began issuing instructions for mooring. Andy and I uncoiled bundles of rope for laying lines to the shore and prepared to drop anchor. However, there was a surprise to come. As we sailed deeper into the bay, a cove came into view hidden by a small hill on its seaward side and cliffs on the other. Radiant turquoise water lapped on a crescent beach fringed by trees. It was so beautiful I almost expected it to be surrounded by hotels and packed with tourists. A single French yacht – *Le Broulard* – lay at anchor.

We spent a full day exploring around Olla before sailing further west to the fjord of Seno Pía. At its mouth we slipped through a gap in a submerged moraine ridge, gazing in silent awe at the surrounding granite cliffs and waterfalls that dropped straight into the sea. Further in, the fjord became choked with ice calving from two enormous glaciers. Frustratingly, the weather remained uncooperative. Each day started clear but soon cloud would build in the west and be driven by steadily increasing winds, bringing rain and gales. Then after dark the rain would stop and stars appear through breaks in the cloud. Yet despite the weather I knew it was a privilege to be in such a place and felt a touch of melancholy knowing our journey was coming to an end.

Four days after leaving Yendegaia, rough conditions forced Celia to turn *Ada* around and seek refuge in the nearest anchorage – Bahia Tres Brazos, a large fjord that cuts deep into Isla Gordon on the south side of the Beagle Channel. As Celia manoeuvred *Ada* into a small inlet within the fjord, Andy and I readied lines and lowered the dinghy. The entrance to the inlet was narrow and the wind gusting wildly. Celia was still new to the art of turning the boat in these tight spaces and her face was tense with concentration. Once in the inlet she shouted to drop anchor. It held, but the yacht was still being blown from side to side and there was a very real danger of hitting the surrounding rocks. We needed lines to the shore to keep *Ada* in central position.

'You go,' I heard Celia shout to me from the stern of the boat. I immediately went over the side and into the dinghy, untied it and paddled for the shore. I was quickly blown backwards faster than I could paddle forward and soon passed Celia, a look of horror on her face. I was trailing a line to secure *Ada* so there was no danger of my actually being blown away, but I needed to reach the land. With huge, frantic strokes I succeeded in running the dinghy aground, pulled it on to the rocks so it could not be swept away, then started scrabbling along the shoreline. We needed to get the rope quickly back beyond the bow of the boat but it was no easy task. The shore was covered in dense scrub and rose to a small headland. I had to thread the rope around bushes and at one point swing around a tree, metres above the sea, while still keeping hold of the rope. I was rushing and soon the inevitable happened: I slipped and plunged up to my chest in the icy water. I was out within seconds, clambering up the rocks still holding the line. The cold was bitter and by the time I had tied the rope to a suitable tree I was shivering uncontrollably. Then I had to repeat the exercise, this time dragging the dinghy below me in order to use the line to haul myself back to the yacht.

'Why didn't you go with Andy?' Celia asked as I climbed on board.

'You shouted for me to go,' I said defensively.

'I shouted 'two go',' she explained, laughing at our simple communication error before turning serious again.

'We need another line out. Put the engine on the dinghy and go with Andy this time.'

After lowering the motor to Andy in the dinghy I climbed in, started the engine and moved towards *Ada's* bow where Celia had readied another line. She passed it down to us and Andy tied it to the side of the dinghy. I revved the motor and we sped off across the inlet as Celia fed out line. She could barely keep up and out of the corner of my eye I saw a loop of rope snag round her ankle and pluck her off her feet. I knew the line would go tight and so spun the dinghy around. Within moments we were skimming back over the rope, which was now likely to snag in the propeller. I snatched and pulled the hinged engine out of the water just in time. Celia got back on her feet and I manoeuvred the dinghy much more slowly to the shore.

Later, over a bottle of wine at the dinner table, we joked about our joint incompetence. It had hardly been a textbook demonstration of how to moor a yacht.

The weather was no better in the morning, but we managed to remove the lines and slip anchor without mishap. After days of struggling westwards into relentless headwinds under motor now it was time to go eastwards back to Puerto Williams. Out in the main channel, Celia cut the engine and we set to work. It was time to sail. The Genoa cracked as it filled and the yacht surged forward. Although it was hard graft and we got soaking wet and bitterly cold, it was a joy to take turns on the wheel. As *Ada* surged down the waves of an increasing swell we screamed to the thrill of it all.

We were tired when we reached Caleta Olla that evening and an even bigger day lay ahead, sailing all the way to Williams with a great tailwind that only dropped as we reached the port. We were ready to celebrate. After showers in the yacht club and dinner on the boat, we headed to the Mecalvi Bar. The slope of the bar floor became more difficult to handle as the evening progressed, but it was Saturday night and we were going to make the most of it. We walked into town and in a residential side street found a nightclub called Euphoria. I pitied the neighbours. Euphoria appeared to be an ordinary house with most of its internal walls ripped out, and it was rammed with people – mostly with men, Peurto Williams being primarily a naval base.

As one of the few women in the establishment, and the only one with long blonde hair, Celia got a lot of attention. Over the course of several hours of dancing Andy and I did our best to shield her from the advances of the Chilean sailors. Tempers got a little frayed.

'Shall we sort them out,' Andy shouted to me at one point.

'I don't think that would be wise.' The odds were hardly in our favour.

Eventually, we stumbled back to the yacht, happy but exhausted.

We all felt terrible in the morning, and in a day made more gloomy by our hangovers helped Celia strip the yacht of its sails and rigging. Then we took off the cockpit and stowed everything neatly in the bow. Finally, we moved the boat to the shelter of the pier where it would spend the winter. It was time to go home.

Andy and I secured a lift to Ushuaia on a yacht belonging to an Argentinian called Mono, who had taken Jane and Elaine back earlier. He looked like a giant, broad-shouldered Father Christmas. Celia, meanwhile, had received a better offer.

'The guys have asked me if I want to crew *Darwin Sound* back to Rio del Plata,' she announced after visiting the French friends who had arrived in the port. She could barely contain her excitement at the prospect of sailing such a boat all the way up the Argentine coast virtually to Buenos Aires.

'You should go for it,' Andy said.

'I think I will.'

❄ ❄ ❄ ❄

We left Puerto Williams late. Mono operated to his own schedule and did not return from town with the necessary paperwork until lunchtime. Then he needed lunch. The final farewell was painful and as we chugged from the harbour I wondered when we would all meet again.

We did not get very far. Mono simply motored across the channel and we spent the night in Argentina tied up alongside the pier of the Estancia Remilino.

'We should not stay on this side of the channel,' he confided. We were technically 'illegals' since we could not complete Argentinian immigration until Ushuaia. 'But no one will know.' Mono, I would come to learn, lived to his own rules.

I woke to the throbbing sound of the yacht's engine. It was barely light. Andy and I rushed to get up but by the time we got on deck Mono was already casting off.

'I think there's a storm coming,' he said. 'I want to get back to Ushuaia before it arrives.' The wind was blowing strongly from the west and the sky filling with wispy cirrus, often a precursor of bad weather. A faint glow of orange marked the sunrise over the eastern end of the channel. As we motored noisily along, Mono prepared a simple breakfast below deck while Andy and I became transfixed by the sky. I took one photograph and then another as an explosion of oranges, mauves and reds rippled across the underside of huge lenticular clouds hovering above the eastern horizon. The show seemed to go on for hours and only when daylight was nearly full did I think of looking to the west. There the white outlines of the Cordillera Darwin peaks stood clearly in all their remote beauty between the sea and a dark violet sky and I knew I would have to return to these empty mountains as soon as possible.

As we approached Ushuaia a yacht came into view coming from Puerto Williams, gaining rapidly on Mono's boat.

'It's *Darwin Sound*,' he said, examining the vessel through a pair of binoculars. It was bewildering, we had been told they would sail directly to Rio del Plata, but soon its distinctive white hull and twin masts were clearly visible. Mono called them on the radio.

'They are going to Ushuaia to get fuel.'

Darwin Sound caught up quickly and as it came alongside Celia appeared on deck and started waving to us. She made her way to the bow of the yacht and hung over the railings with her arms stretched up and out like Kate Winslet in *Titanic*.

❄ ❄ ❄ ❄

On our last day in Ushuaia Andy and I met up with a couple called Luis and Carolina, who ran the only mountain guide company in town. They were helpful, friendly people and invited us to their house for dinner. They had made three trips to Yendegaia and after the meal showed us some slides. There were views we were familiar with and others that were new. A set of pictures from a winter trip was particularly interesting. One showed a tent glowing in the darkness with a chimney poking out of the entrance, followed by a photo taken inside showing the wood burning stove the couple had fashioned out of a dried milk tin and the chimney made from cans.

'Outside minus twenty,' Carolina said. 'Inside, only underwear.'

They had not been particularly lucky on their attempts to climb at Yendegaia but had obviously had a lot of fun.

'Hey, look at that,' Andy said as Luis switched to an image that clearly showed Monte Bove along with the peak we had climbed and a chain of three mountains to the north.

'These are the Roncagli Peaks?' Andy asked, pointing at the trio of peaks.

'Yes,' Carolina and Luis agreed.

'Then the peak we climbed is separate.' Andy was tapping at his map as he spoke. 'It doesn't even have a name.' I took the map off him and studied it intently. It was not the best of maps, little more than a sketch really, but it was all that was available. There was simply a ridgeline from Monte Bove to the Roncagli peaks.

'It's not even on the map,' I added.

'Exactly,' said Andy, sounding like a lawyer who had just unearthed a damning piece of evidence.

'I guess we can name it then. What do you want to call it?'

'Monte Ada,' Andy said without hesitation.

❄ ❄ ❄ ❄

I called Jane, before starting the long series of flights back home.

'Haven't you heard?' she asked.

'Heard what?'

'There's Foot and Mouth in the country, our area has been worst hit.'

My shoulders slumped as she listed the farms that had already been affected and people we knew who had lost livestock. Pyres of burning carcasses darkened the countryside around our village, the movement of livestock had been banned and many farmers were virtual prisoners in their own homes. Sweeping restrictions had been introduced to prevent anyone walking across farmland or the open hills. People's movement was effectively confined to the man-made world of buildings, towns and roads. It was a brutal return to reality. The weeks of freedom in the pristine wilderness and limitless space of Tierra del Fuego had come to an end.

There was other news. Apparently I was going to be a film star.

FOUR

All Your Front Teeth

'This is an iconic rock,' Kevin said melodramatically, pointing at the site of our 1985 base camp.

'No it's not, Kevin,' Joe replied bluntly. 'It's just a boulder.'

Seventeen years after our misadventure on Siula Grande, Joe Simpson and I were back together in the same remote valley of Peru's Cordillera Huayhuash range. Accompanied by director Kevin Macdonald, assorted production staff, mountain guides and porters we had returned to make a film based on Joe's bestselling book – *Touching the Void*. Our first testy interview at base camp rather set the tone for the two weeks of shooting on location.

Filmmaking had already been going on for some time before the trip to Peru. Early in the spring of 2002, as he was getting a feel for the project, Kevin had travelled up to Cumbria to talk to me, then towards the end of May I went down to London and told my story to camera over a long day of interviewing in a studio near London Bridge.

During the lunch break I sat on a terrace overlooking the river with co-producer Sue Summers.

'The tide's coming in,' I said in passing.

'How do you know that?'

'The water is running upstream.'

'Oh Simon. You are so practical,' she replied, in a tone that made me think she was either completely clueless or being snidely cynical.

After that nothing much happened for a while; I was beginning to discover the stop-start nature of filmmaking.

There was plenty to keep me busy. My second book had gone into paperback at the start of the year and there was a steady series of bookshop events and lectures arranged to promote it. After years of working for and with others taking groups on commercial mountain-eering expeditions, I had bitten the bullet and decided to set up on my own. It was quite time-consuming: forming a limited company called Mountain Dream, getting to grips with the legal and account-ing issues and producing a brochure and other promotional material. A break was also essential and Jane and I spent a short vacation on Colonsay, a small island in the Inner Hebrides.

Eventually, the film producers resurfaced and there was a flurry of activity: a meeting in London, a medical for insurance purposes and some vaccinations before the long flight to Peru.

As we approached Lima there was a remarkable moment when the plane dropped below the cloud base and in full view was the entire Cordillera Huayhuash, the scene of our epic on Siula Grande's West Face clearly visible in the centre of the compact group of peaks. Sadly there were to be few such moments during the rest of our time in Peru.

We followed our old trail into the Huayhuash, filming as we went, and set up a base camp a little further down the valley from our 1985 site. All went well to begin with, but over time the interviewing became increasingly aggressive and intrusive. Unpleasant patterns began to emerge. Joe was asked to reconstruct his life-saving crawl down the moraine for hours at a time, day after day. It soon became apparent that the director was after more than just ridiculous amounts of footage. It struck me as abusive.

Filming took place low on the mountain to begin with, then as people became acclimatised we moved to a high camp on moraine at the side of the glacier opposite the 1,300-metre West Face. Initially we had only planned to have three days at the top camp before splitting into smaller groups to film in different locations. However, filming at altitude proved more tiring and time-consuming than had been envisaged. It was also logistically difficult to move the heavy 35mm cine camera gear around and to charge the batteries from the generator back at base camp. On the second day it was agreed to spend an extra couple of days at the moraine camp and get all the mountain photography completed at the one spot.

On the penultimate day at the high camp John Whittle, one of the guides responsible for safety while filming, and I climbed up and along a nearby ridge, arduously breaking trail to a point below a crest at 5,300 metres. We deliberately left the short rise to the top free of steps so as to have virgin snow for the 'summit shoot' the following day. Back at camp we slumped wearily into the tent and later other guides began drifting back from their day's work on the glacier. They were complaining about the schedule suddenly being altered. Kevin had decreed that we would all return to the base camp the following day. Some of us, myself included, would have to come back up again to complete the summit shoot that John and I had just prepared.

One of the guides had told Kevin that it would be totally demoralising to have to go down and come back up. I was incensed. The guides had been doing physically demanding and dangerous work at altitude for four days, John Whittle and myself for five. The food had been inadequate, at times just stale cheese rolls making it up to the high camp. In my opinion Kevin didn't appreciate how difficult it was working at that altitude. My hours of trail-breaking would be for nothing; by the time we returned our steps would have blown over.

I intercepted Kevin on his way back from the glacier.

'You've obviously not worked on a building site,' I told him, … 'because you've still got all your front teeth.'

I made as if to head-butt him, but stopped short. Then in slightly more measured terms I pointed out that he had struck a deal with the guides and that they were working on a promise. Kevin looked dumbfounded.

The movie world is autocratic and I doubt that anyone had spoken to the great director in such terms before.

'You shouldn't have done that,' one of the guides, Paul Moores, told me a little later. In view of what was to follow months later they were knowing words.

My intervention did have results though. At a hastily convened meeting with the guides Kevin reinstated the original schedule. We would complete the filming the following day and return to base camp.

A little while later I went over and apologised to Kevin.

'I should think so,' he replied.

I found his reply arrogant and our relationship never really recovered. Kevin took to openly calling me 'mad' while I silently thought he was just plain sad. This mutual antagonism worsened after a particularly nasty interview he conducted with me at base camp just before we left the mountains. Apparently, the reason for my 'building site' confrontation was due to repressed emotions from 17 years earlier. It was rubbish of course and I told him as much in front of the camera.

Moreover Kevin's ignorant questions came only hours after Jane had emailed saying she had been taken to hospital with a suspected miscarriage. It was all a bit much. Jane and I were dealing with some serious and complex ongoing medical issues and I had reached a point where I did not care for Kevin and his silly psychological mind games – he was only making a film after all. He was visibly shaken when I told him the facts and was briefly apologetic. But contrition did not last long and he quickly reverted to type, defending his interview before scurrying away to consult with his line producer. She was sent back to ask me if I kept a diary. After that Kevin stayed away from me, perhaps scared that I really would give him a thumping.

The walk out was a chance for me to try and burn off some anger but trouble flared again at the overnight stop and back in the town of Cajatambo. For someone whose business was communication, I found Kevin strangely unable to deal with me in a simple and direct way.

He later confided to one of the guides that I was worse to work with than Mick Jagger; I guess the old rocker must have mellowed in his old age, but I took it as a compliment anyway. It was a relief to finally get on the bus, return to Lima and fly home.

Jane lost the baby just days after my return from Peru and I had little more to do with the filmmakers.

None of these happenings made it into the finished film, which begs the question: what was it all about? From my own point of view, not a lot. The process was difficult enough for all involved anyway without generating a lot of additional stress. The guides – many of whom I like to think of as mates and deeply respect as mountaineers – were put in a very unpleasant position. For me, the time with the filmmakers and indeed the finished product, were nothing to feel proud of; the whole process ended up being far too divisive and exclusive for that.

In the wake of the 1985 epic, and particularly after the *Void* was released, I was asked many times if Joe and I were still friends. As with other media events, rather than answering questions the film merely threw up a raft of new ones. I got the impression people thought that having been through such an experience together Joe and I should either be the closest of friends or bitter enemies. Reality is always more complex.

Over the years I have climbed with many different partners. For the days, weeks and sometimes months spent together, they are intense and intimate relationships, almost like a marriage in some respects. But by their very nature they are also deeply pragmatic and circumstantial partnerships, as with a colleague at work. And as in everyday life, climbing relationships do not always last. For a variety of reasons, they can be very fleeting, last for a certain time and then fade away, or be lifelong. Two of my most longstanding male friends are past climbing partners, but equally there are others I have had little or no contact with since our climbs together. I cannot recall having a serious falling out with a climbing partner on a trip, but there have been a few who I would not want to share a rope with again, and some probably feel the same way about me. I was more promiscuous with who I climbed with when I was younger. Now I am picky and no doubt my contemporaries are too.

Joe and I never climbed in the mountains together again after Siula Grande. Initially his injury precluded it – I was, after all, on the North Face of the Eiger just a few weeks later – and I moved on to climbing with other partners. While never close, we remained mates, mixing in similar circles in Sheffield until I left the city in 1993. I had become disillusioned with living in a community of almost exclusively 'outdoor' folk; it seemed like every hour spent not climbing was spent talking about it. I needed a clean break and left to start a different life in the backwaters of Cumbria with Jane. Joe stayed in the city and I had little contact with him, or indeed with many of the other people I knew from that time. The filmmaking process did make me realise how different we had become. I was climbing mountains, married, living in a small rural village hoping to become a father – Joe wanted none of these things. Apart from the traumatic incident on a mountain in Peru back in 1985 we no longer had much in common.

I remember clearly how on my first meeting with Kevin, conducted over a pint in a pub in Kendal, he had listened to my matter-of-fact description of the events on Siula Grande. When I told him of my previous return to the area in 1998 to try and climb Siula Chico next to Siula Grande with Mick Fowler he looked disappointed and commented, 'best if we keep that quiet'.

'We might have to ask you to ham it up a bit,' he confided, towards the end of our chat.

I guess I did not provide the filmmakers with the drama they were after, but they were resourceful and simply took on the job themselves.

Was it difficult going back to the mountains after making the film? That's another question I've been asked too many times. Not in the slightest. On one level I had to – that was where I made my living –

also they still remained special places to me. What I had absolutely no wish to do was to return with people who saw the mountains as no more than a backdrop to a story, and who would violate my intimacy with such places.

Over the autumn of 2002 I managed to get together a small group of clients to go to Monte Francés. The prospect of going back to Tierra del Fuego was exciting, as was the challenge of guiding people in a place where few even climbed for themselves. What was most reassuring was that I was going to the mountains with people who were enthusiasts and who, like me, loved being there.

Late the following January I arrived in Ushuaia with my friend Micky Fox and Dutchman Marcel Bessemer. We took a taxi into town to the Nido de Condores – the Condor's Nest – a small guest-house recently opened by Luis and Carolina. It was a nice place with a relaxed atmosphere, up the hill a little from the centre of town.

That night we ate out with Luis and Carolina and caught up on two whole years. Argentina had been through turbulent times, with a financial crisis a year earlier and an almost overnight 300 per cent devaluation of the peso. It had caused terrible hardship and social unrest, though as a tourist destination Argentina had become a bargain. Ushuaia was already seeing an upturn, with visitors pouring into the town. As ever, Luis and Carolina were positive and full of plans for the future.

'I have a small problem,' Mono said when I met him in the morning. 'My boat is in Williams and I cannot bring it to Ushuaia.'

'Sounds like a big problem to me.'

I had kept in touch with Mono and followed the progress of the construction of his new yacht – *Mago del Sur* (Magician of the South). Our group was to be the boat's inaugural charter. Mono had registered the boat in Panama and as a result had fallen foul of the bureaucrats in Ushuaia, who were insisting that as an Argentinian he should register the boat in his home country. Mono's immediate response had been to take *Mago del Sur* to Puerto Williams in Chile while he considered his next move.

'We can take my old boat to Williams,' he said. 'I just have to re-float it first.'

He had four days in which to do it if we were to keep to our schedule. Meanwhile we got on with preparing for the mountains and hit the supermarket, wheeling up a line of stacked trolleys at the checkout. It is amazing how much food and supplies four people need for a two-week trip. Fellow customers and staff evidently took a different view and looked at us like we were greedy.

Gus Morton flew in the day before we were due to leave Ushuaia; unfortunately his bag did not. Gus was an enthusiastic character, who spent his work time commuting around Europe from his home in Luxembourg inspecting nuclear power stations. Luckily, he also has a good sense of humour. A lot was hanging on the following day.

Next morning we made out way down to the yacht club to help Mono. His old boat was on the wharf in a huge homemade metal cradle that ran on rails into the water. We helped lower the boat into the sea, then sat back to wait for the incoming tide to float it free from the cradle. The water flowed and ebbed and nothing happened. Mono vowed to try again the following day. We had better luck with Gus's bag, which had arrived by the time we returned to the hostel.

When the boat failed to float again, Mono cracked and telephoned a friend. All our gear was then loaded on to a little yacht called the *Unicorn*. Finally, we were free of Ushuaia and on our way. *Unicorn's* skipper was another Mono, a hospitable man who plied us with tea and biscuits as we made the crossing to Williams.

Mago del Sur proved worthy of our patience and Mono proudly showed us round his new boat. Built to Mono's own specifications, the large yacht featured a retractable keel, allowing it to get into shallow anchorages. It was still unfinished and a little industrial inside, but was more than fit for our purpose. That night we had a barbeque on the pier outside the Mecalvi and forgot about the hitches of the previous days.

It was dark when we arrived in Caleta Olla the following evening, having motored along the Beagle Channel on a calm, sunny day. I woke early the next morning and eagerly went up on deck. The place was just as I remembered: the sheltered bay, a strip of shingle beach fringed with trees, the still, turquoise water. It felt invigorating to be back.

We worked hard through the day carrying loads up from the boat to a campsite in a small clearing below the glacial lake under Monte Francés's impressive South Face. Towards evening we built a plastic shelter from a roll of polythene and then spent our first night in the tents. After more load carrying next morning I wanted to see what lay further up the valley.

'I'm going to check out higher up,' I told the others. Gus was keen to come along.

Above the camp the forest was quite dense, but a faint guanaco trail led up to some rock slabs beside a waterfall. At the top of the slabs we climbed up over a moraine ridge and looked down on a small lake. It was a dramatic place. An icefall dropped from the Francés Glacier into the back left corner of the lake and a band of granite cliffs stretched across the cirque to a waterfall cascading down from the right-hand side of the glacier. It was obvious we needed to gain the glacier somewhere near the waterfall, but where? A broken gully line to the right looked like it might just provide the solution. Our next problem was getting around the lake.

Here the beech trees were low and compact, and it was a matter of trying to push a way through. Again, there were guanaco trails to follow but they were easy to lose. We worked our way over a rock bluff and struck lucky – a moraine ridge, hidden by the trees, contoured around the lake. We followed it easily to a grassy hillside by a stream that flowed from the waterfall in the cirque. I was moving well and raced ahead, keen to see if the gully would provide a feasible way up to the glacier.

'I'm going to go back down,' Gus announced.

'If you are okay, I'll press on a bit and see you later.'

'Sure.'

I carried on up towards the waterfalls, then veered rightwards up steep grassy slopes. The gully soon narrowed to a wet chimney capped by a huge chockstone. I climbed it a short way before swinging on to the left wall to enter a mossy corner. By carefully kicking steps in the moss I precariously gained height until able to make a lunge for some stunted beech. The trees were remarkably solid and I monkeyed up them and a rocky corner to a shelf that led horizontally back into the gully, blocked by another chockstone. This time the right wall offered the most promising way. I launched out of the gully bed, hauling on beech saplings and blobs of hard, dull-green moss that looked like lumps of coral. This was unusual climbing and although I was solo-ing, with a potentially fatal fall below, I was really enjoying myself. A precarious traverse along a ledge with loose flaky handholds led back into the recess, which I followed to more open hillside.

For a while it was easy going up grassy slopes, until I entered a continuation of the gully, rubble-floored with another large chock-stone above. To the left was a wall split by a mossy chimney that spouted water and led up to a cave capped by a small roof. There looked to be a way around the roof on the right.

Water poured down my sleeves as I tackled the chimney, which was easier than it looked. Inside the cave I delicately traversed right and into a corner below the lip of the roof. There were positive holds in the corner at the roof, but it would be a committing move without knowing what lay above. I felt confident and lucky. I stepped up into the corner, pulled up around the roof and wedged myself in a notch, hands searching above. Suddenly the way was not so obvious. I had a brief wave of panic, then slowed my breathing and made a quick sequence of layback moves to better holds that led into a grassy gully. After walking a little way up the gully to a snow patch, I could see rocky shelves leading diagonally leftwards to the glacier. It looked as though I'd found a pretty neat way of gaining the glacier; feeling well satisfied I turned back down.

Reversing the layback moves was a little nerve-racking, but once the roof was turned, the descent was mostly easier than climbing up had been. I quickly reached the base of the gully and as it started to rain caught up with Gus before the waterfall.

'It's a good way up,' I was able to report.

Back at the camp the weather played games with us. The barometer went on a roller-coaster ride as days of rain alternated with drier days that in all certainty would be too windy higher up. One morning we left for the mountain only to be turned back by more rain a short way from the camp. It was a frustrating time that tested everyone's patience, but luckily I was with old hands who understood the need to wait.

On the seventh morning the cloud started to clear after a night of heavy rain. The wind had dropped to a whisper. We went up. Having done the legwork to find the way, we moved swiftly through the forest and around the lake before roping up to climb the gully. The glacier slopes were straightforward but it was a long way to the ridge and we were fully exposed to wind now blowing across Francés's South Face. Heads down, we continued until we reached a hollow behind a rock pinnacle on the ridge. It was windy but flat.

'We'll camp here,' I said.

The wind pulled at the tents as we put them up and it was quite late by the time we were finished.

'Shall we have a crack at the summit?' Gus asked.

I was thrown for a moment, but there was a certain sense to it. We would kick ourselves if the weather was bad in the morning.

'It doesn't look far,' I said, thinking aloud. 'Yeah, let's do it. Pack a headtorch.'

'I'm going to stay here kid,' Micky said, as we hurriedly prepared to leave.

'Are you sure?'

'I'll go in the morning.' I knew Micky well enough not to question his decision – he was his own man.

It was a race against darkness and we all knew it. I kept up a relentless pace at the front of the rope, only pausing to catch breath. We climbed over rolling crests along the ridge as sunlit spindrift danced around the steeper summit cone above. The snow deepened, forcing us to make a lengthy detour around a huge crevasse before heading towards a final pyramid. Then the scale of everything around us suddenly shrank. I knew this moment: we were near the top. A small, steep gully split the slope above and gave a short section of climbing on excellent ice. Then it was a simple matter of weaving a way through rime-covered gendarmes to the summit.

The Roncagli peaks, the very top of Monte Ada and Monte Bove sat to the east of us just above the boiling cloud, their summits catching the last rays of sun. We shook hands and quickly took some photographs. It was too cold to linger. As we made our way back down the clouds cleared and an orange moon rose above Bove.

The weather was even better in the morning and Micky got his summit day too. We left the camp early and climbed back to the top, following our steps from the night before. As we looked at the mountain wilderness all around I was calm and happy, my enchantment with this place now deeply rooted.

Monte Francés was first climbed by the British mountaineer Eric Shipton in 1962 and did not receive a second ascent until 1992. We had just made the third ascent. As far as I knew this made Monte Francés the most climbed mountain in the entire range. I laughed at the thought – three parties in a little over 40 years. Unlike many other ranges, you could hardly say the Cordillera Darwin was getting busy.

There was a price to pay for upsetting the filmmakers, I discovered when *Touching the Void* was released in late 2003, as they rounded on me and gave me a good old hand-bagging in the national press. The director stuck to his amateur psychologist story about repressed emotions and I also learned that I had had to be restrained after our altercation at the high camp. Co-producer Sue Summers described me as 'opaque and unfathomable'. As the villain in the story I was a soft target and they were selling their product. A fair bit of vitriol was also directed at Joe, but as a successful author with a bestseller on his hands he was much less assailable, and over the years he had become a skilful manipulator of the media.

Still, I'm hardly the first mountaineer to fall foul of pundits who delight in questioning the morality of those undertaking activities that involve self-imposed risk. The fact that our misadventures and epics play out in remote and inhospitable locations with few witnesses and, unlike many sports, no live TV footage, simply plays into their hand. I'm quite sure I won't be the last such victim either.

'It's a very important story,' yet another American TV producer said earnestly down the phone around the time of the film's release in the US. 'We want to tell your side of it in an honest unbiased way.' I recognised the spiel by now and thought about people being killed in Iraq, the AIDS epidemic in Africa and the hundreds of millions around the world who would pass the day without enough food. As I saw it, nearly 19 years after the events on Siula Grande the only thing that remained important about the story was its ability to generate cash. The events had little to do with me any more, or even what actually happened, they now belonged to the second-hand storytellers.

The Oprah Winfrey Show contacted me, but I declined the request to appear on America's top talk show. Judging by the tone of the emails with which they continued to bombard me, rejection did not happen very often. The final message was a desperate plea for a quote that they could somehow use on the show. It gave me quite a laugh.

When I later told the Oprah story to the American mountaineer Carlos Buhler he was aghast. 'You could have set yourself up for life on the back of that,' he said. The thought had never even occurred to me. I simply saw no reason to fly halfway round the world to be bayed at by a hysterical audience.

'Tell me about this secret life you have been living?' my Dad said on the phone one day. He had just read in his daily national newspaper that I was married with three children and had given up climbing in the early 1990s to pursue a business career. Other newspapers – including ones you might have imagined had higher standards of journalism – carried similarly ridiculous stories. Yet some of the same titles would later ask me to write for them. How does that work? I had entered a different world played to rules that are incomprehensible to the rest of us.

I cannot deny that for a while the lies and half-truths made me bitter and angry. It was shocking to be thrown back into the name-calling of the school playground, but like most media storms, it raged only in a teacup. Eventually a story loses its selling power and the circus moves to another town. Needless to say I did not get mobbed on the streets of my own unassuming town – Penrith, in Cumbria. The only lasting legacy is occasional recognition by fellow tourists on the streets of Kathmandu.

'Are you Joe Simpson?' they walk up and ask.

I would soon find my way again, happy and comfortable in my own world and with the good people around me. There were also more pressing and real things to deal with.

A few months earlier Jane had discovered she was pregnant. Because of the possibility of having a baby with a genetic abnormality she booked to have a nuchal scan 13 weeks into the pregnancy and we travelled to Newcastle for the appointment. We had been told a consultant and genetic counsellor would be present for the scan, but there was just a junior doctor. He looked visibly sick when we explained

Jane's case history and suggested rescheduling the appointment to a day when the other staff were present.

'We've come over from Cumbria,' I explained. 'We know the issues involved and don't really want to make the journey again.'

'Well I am perfectly happy to do the scan, but I need to make some calls first.'

Having spoken to the consultant, the young man conducted the scan. It took some time for him to move a cursor around the screen clicking on various points to make the crucial measurements. His face was a study in concentration.

'To me that looks like a perfectly normal baby,' he said finally.

We could hardly believe it. After all the years of trying, the grief of miscarriages and the all-consuming visits to specialist fertility and genetic units around the country, Jane was finally pregnant with a healthy baby. She was going to have a child and we were going to be parents. Our eyes watered and tears of relief and joy ran down our faces.

In late February, just a couple of months before our baby was due, I travelled to Canada to speak at the Vancouver International Mountain Film Festival. Under the directorship of Alan Formanek, a Slovak climber who also stages a similar event in Bratislava, the festival is very much pitched at grass-roots enthusiasts. Alan arranged digs for me with two student volunteers, Jeremy Frimer and Jay Piggott. Both were dedicated and talented climbers and it was a pleasure to share their youthful passion for the sport for a few days. Jeremy and I also shared a fascination for the Cordillera Huayhuash, in fact, Jeremy was writing a climbing guidebook to the area. It was my first visit to Vancouver and I could not have had better hosts and guides. We spent many hours of intense discussion over cups of tea at the lads' house and over pints of beer in various pubs and bars. So much so that when Jeremy came to introduce me to the festival audience he told them that I lived on a diet of tea and beer.

The trip to Vancouver also enabled me to catch up with Celia who was renting an apartment just up the road at the ski resort town of Whistler. Life had changed radically for Celia since our time together in Tierra del Fuego: she was now a parent. Given the free and adventurous life she had been living on *Ada* for so long, it had come as a surprise when I first learnt that Celia was going to be a mother. Baby Dylan was the fruit of a short-lived relationship with an American called Woody who she met in Puerto Montt at the end of a voyage through the Chilean archipelago. She had decided to have the birth in Canada.

Celia looked tired but well and it was nice to spend a little time with her again and to meet Dylan, who was just a few weeks old. I was also able to test my inept skiing skills at what is supposedly one of the best resorts in North America. Whistler certainly compared well to my limited experience of skiing in Europe. The pistes were much less crowded and there was a huge base of snow, but the biggest difference was how politely people queued for the lifts. There was no disguising the bitterly cold temperature however, and after managing just half a day on the piste I was exhausted and in need of a warm bar.

'I must be the only person who has spent a winter season in Whistler and not done any skiing,' Celia joked one evening. She also had a lesson for me.

'Here you go,' she said, handing me a crying bundle of Dylan. 'You can get some practice.'

I put him over my shoulder and walked round the room, gently patting him on the back. All too soon I would be walking the same soothing circles with our own baby.

Early on the second day of climbing Monte Ada in 2001 after an awful bivouac on the face below.

1   The intrepid Celia Bull at the helm of her yacht *Ada II* leaving the harbour in Ushuaia.
2   Andy Parkin on *Ada* in the Beagle Channel. Celia chose Andy as my climbing partner for the first of our Fuegian expeditions. It subsequently developed into a lasting and fruitful climbing partnership.
3   The head of the bay at Yendegaia with *Ada* at anchor near the estancia buildings.

4 Setting off from the estancia on horseback up the Yendegaia Valley.

5 Our first view of the mountains up the Bove Glacier. Monte Bove is on the left with the peak we had come to climb capped by cloud to the right.

6 Moving towards the steep gully that dissected the headwall, which provided the only feasible way to the summit of Monte Ada.

1   Looking west along the Beagle Channel to the Cordillera Darwin just before arriving back in Ushuaia.
    I knew at this powerful moment that I would return.

2   Joe Simpson and me re-enacting our former selves for the cameras in Peru, 2002.

3   Filming Siula Grande's West Face that we had climbed 17 years earlier. I did not share the same world-view
    as the director – Kevin Macdonald – sitting with the white cap.

4   On Monte Francés's South West Ridge with the Beagle Channel below and Isla Gordon behind, 2003.

5 On the summit of Monte Francés with the Roncagli peaks, Monte Ada (centre) and Monte Bove, all catching the last rays of the setting sun.

6 Andy Parkin climbing on the second day of our ascent of Hispar Sar, Pakistani Karakoram, 2004. Route finding was not difficult – we followed the massive 1,500-metre couloir up the South-West Face. The feature had compelled me to return following an attempt 15 years earlier.

7 On our fourth day of climbing on Hispar Sar we reached a shoulder on a ridge above the couloir with stunning views of peaks to the south.

8 The vista to the east from the same spot was equally dramatic showing the top section of the Hispar Glacier, the Hispar La pass, with The Ogre – the largest peak – in the background.

1 Paul Schweizer – my partner on the Alverstone climb in 2005. We would return to the same region to climb Mount Vancouver four years later.
2 Our drop-off by ski-plane on a lobe of the Alverstone Glacier with the mountain's West Face behind.
3 Paul Schweizer on Alverstone's lonely summit. Mount Hubbard in the background.

High on Alverstone's West Face on our first day of climbing, with a backdrop of the vast glaciated wilderness that characterises the Wrangell-St Elias ranges. Mount Vancouver is in the distance.

There is a surprising amount of space in the British Isles if you go looking for it. For over a decade I have travelled regularly with my wife Jane to the Scottish Islands and we have nearly fulfilled our ambition of visiting all the inhabited ones. It has been a fascinating and entertaining journey. In Shetland we camped on the stunning beach at Burrafirth (1) and watched an otter skipping through the swell while attempting to make a meal from some eider chicks. The Shetland ponies dragged all our food from the porch of the tent and ate it overnight, which meant a lean Sunday as the shops were closed. On Unst – the most northerly – we were amused by the elaborately decorated Bob's Bus Shelter (2), which even has its own website.

3   On the back of a commercial expedition to Monte Francés I got the chance to sail around Cape Horn in 2006. Here at an anchorage on Isla Hermite the barren archipelago of islands looked and felt very similar to those off Scotland at the other end of the Atlantic.

4   A micro-storm blew up, adding atmosphere to our passage around the Horn.

FIVE

Life is Good

Jane's labour had been going well but the midwives and doctor began to get concerned about the baby's racing and, sometimes, erratic heartbeat. They decided the baby needed to come out. Nothing had prepared me for the brutality of the final stages of the birth, but the fact that the doctor who had been wearing smart trousers and a delicate floral blouse suddenly appeared in what looked like a trawlerman's outfit complete with wellies should have given me a clue. The bed was adjusted to a more upright position, as footrests were pulled out and a bucket slotted neatly in between them. Something with a fancy French name, which in reality was little more than sink-plunger, was attached to the top of our baby's head and then pulled, as Jane was summoned to push. An alarm was sounded and more midwives rushed into the room. Two of them jumped on to Jane's bulge as the doctor continued to pull. Our baby was propelled into the world and placed gasping on Jane's stomach. It was a girl.

'Hello,' Jane had time to say before a midwife ran out of the room with the baby.

It was 1 a.m. on 27 April 2004 and our daughter Maisy had been born. It felt like the massively significant moment it most certainly was, however, I was unaware how much the magic, commitment and responsibility of becoming a parent would grow and change over time. In many ways, as this childhood was beginning my own very extended one was coming to an end. For nearly 20 years I had roamed the world's mountains free of many of life's responsibilities. It had been an incredible journey, from childhood explorations in the fields around my Leicestershire family home to some of the remotest mountains on the planet. Now another slightly more planned and controlled adventure was beginning. So much would be different, not least our shopping bill. Having for most of my years forgone a substantial degree of comfort in the quest for experience I was surprised by the amount of things a child needs and the consumption they generate. It soon became apparent that once you have children you inevitably become a mega-consumer like everybody else in the developed world, whether consciously or not.

Maisy's arrival coincided with a relatively quiet period in terms of work and climbing commitments. I had a few lectures booked locally and an invitation to a climbing festival in Italy pencilled in for the summer, followed by a trip to Pakistan with Andy in the autumn. It was a time for visitors and visiting as we introduced our new daughter to family and friends.

Between the socialising I made plans. A web of contacts built up over many years in the outdoor community enabled me to begin piecing together a series of lectures for the winter. After my recent experiences with the media it was refreshing to be dealing once again with people who were straightforward and had no hidden agendas. Even so, it was time-consuming work and occasionally frustrating when promising lines led to dead-ends; at its best, arrangements fell almost effortlessly into place. I relied almost exclusively on the internet and email for information and communication, constantly marvelling at what these new tools could do. The logistics of a tour are complicated: dates, venues and travel between them all have to fit. The final piece of the jigsaw was to arrange the shipment of my books to various locations, so that I had copies to sell after each show. I was acutely aware I could have not have pulled together the whole venture by myself without the aid of communications that had only come into common use over the previous decade. I'd started with modest ambitions for the tour but boosted by success I widened its scope. In the end I filled the first three months of 2005 with engagements, taking in the United States, New Zealand, Australia and Iceland. I felt quite pleased with my efforts.

I stood waiting in the departure hall at Manchester Airport with Jane and Maisy next to a trolley piled high with two huge kitbags – the rather cumbersome travel accessories of a mountaineer – hoping the heap would serve as a suitably conspicuous meeting point. Andy was late and I was becoming anxious about missing our flight to Islamabad.

The delay at least gave me time to reflect. Fifteen years earlier in the company of my regular climbing partner at the time – Sean Smith – I had made an attempt on a mountain called Hispar Sar on the north side of the Hispar Glacier in the heart of the Pakistan Karakoram. A huge couloir splits the mountain's South West Face. The line looked so compelling that from base camp we had hiked for three days to reach it, suffered two nights of storm while attempting to climb it and then marched down for a further two days to regain our base camp. The memory of that perfect line and the quality of the climbing had stayed with me, coupled with a desire to return to Hispar Sar. A photograph sent to Andy convinced him to come along. Sometimes you find life going in circles; this particular episode had just taken a long time to come around.

I was beginning to resign myself to catching a later flight, with all the hassle and expense that was likely to entail, when Andy arrived. He was struggling to control a trolley stacked high with his own kit and looked stressed. One of his bags fell on to the floor and, red-faced, he wrestled it back on to the trolley.

'Train from Sheffield was delayed,' he gasped. Andy never seemed to have much luck with travel arrangements, but took great pleasure in relating this latest fiasco as we hurriedly completed check-in.

Once free of our bags, with boarding cards in hand, we all retired to a coffee shop to take stock and compose ourselves before the flight. I was used to these farewells by now – most of my adult life has been a series of them – but this was the first since Maisy had been born. It felt strange, even a little uncomfortable, holding our baby in my arms while trying to retain the focus I knew was required for the next month. We were, after all, going to travel halfway round the world to a troubled country and attempt an unclimbed peak in a remote location. Fatherhood certainly put the mountains and our efforts to climb them in a different perspective. Being a middle-aged survivor of a pastime that had been responsible for the deaths of many friends and acquaintances, my attitude had already shifted markedly with age and experience. Even so, as I hugged Jane and Maisy at the departure gate saying my goodbyes I was deeply conscious of the changed reality. I sneaked one final look at our beautiful daughter as I walked through the door into security and framed the vision in my mind for the weeks to come.

As it turned out it was also the end of an era on another level. It would be the last expedition on which I would be unable to contact others by telephone while in the mountains.

After a four-year absence it was wonderful to return to northern Pakistan. The events of 11 September 2001 and the Western world's response to them had made the country a no-go area. It was not that Pakistan had suddenly become more dangerous to travel in, more a question of governments acting against perceived risk. Many Western nations had advised their citizens not to travel to Pakistan, thus invalidating normal travel insurance. The prospect of personally picking up the bill for a very expensive helicopter rescue in the event of an accident had meant that many trekkers and climbers stayed away. The mountainous area in the north of the country remained calm and peaceful and the people as welcoming as ever to visitors, but there had been virtually none. It was heartbreaking to see the tourism infrastructure I had watched slowly build up since the 1980s – when the opening of the Karakoram Highway boosted access and interest – lying empty and unused. Literally overnight the tourists had stopped coming and were only now, nearly three years later, beginning to trickle back in. The loss of jobs and income for what is an impoverished area anyway had caused much hardship, but with their typical stoic resilience the mountain people of Pakistan's Northern Areas were getting on with life, hoping the visitors would return.

Six days after leaving Britain we arrived at our base camp. Jutmal, a small, grassy ablation valley high above the Hispar Glacier, is a magical spot. It looks out over a river of ice and rubble far below with a line of peaks either side running up to a snowy pass – the Hispar La – at the head of the valley. Our camp was a tiny oasis in a landscape so vast, stark and barren it looked every bit the geological building site it literally is. And yet here was perfection. A tiny stream ran through the grass, radiant butterflies fluttered between colourful flowers and the place hummed to the sound of grasshoppers. It had the surreal atmosphere of an exhibit in a garden show.

We paid off the 12 Hispar porters as we would not need them for the next two weeks. Only Nazir Ali, our cook, would remain, having secured the job because unlike others he was willing to be left on his own in such a place. When not working, Ali occupied himself by listening to cricket matches on his short-wave radio and fastidiously washing and drying his clothes. We were lucky he was so self-contained, as we were away for much of the time and the camp received not a single visitor.

Over the following week we made excursions to scope out our mountain from different angles and to move food and equipment to an advanced base camp. These outings also helped acclimatisation, though with a storm confining us to the base camp for two days, we were not as well-prepared for climbing as we would have wished. It would have to do; we were running on a tight schedule. On 25 September we took a well-earned rest. The previous two days had been arduous, climbing the steep, unstable moraine that formed the final approach to our route. Andy had found it particularly difficult, the limited mobility in his left leg preventing him from boulder-hopping, which was the simplest way of moving over such terrain.

Despite our small setbacks I felt happy, by a stroke of luck the rest day had fallen on Andy's fiftieth birthday. Over the years, I had never really given much thought about Andy's age. In many ways he seemed a timeless figure. His physical appearance had altered little during the time I had known him and his frugal lifestyle had remained similarly unchanged. I had only found out his birth date by chance, when I forwarded copies of our passport pages to the airline. Andy had made no mention of the milestone but I felt it was appropriate to mark the occasion. To this end I'd bought a bottle of duty-free whisky at Manchester Airport and decanted the precious liquid into a plastic water bottle to ensure it survived the journey. I waited until mid-morning when Andy was sprawled out on the grass in the sunshine painting, then presented him with the gift.

'Happy birthday,' I said with little ceremony. Andy examined the opaque white bottle with its yellow-brown contents cautiously. I understood his concern. 'It's not piss you know.'

Andy smiled, opened the bottle and sniffed at the contents approvingly.

'Cheers,' he said, taking a swig. ' I wasn't expecting that.' A bottle of liquor in Muslim Pakistan had obviously thrown him, but over the next few hours he warmed to the idea.

By the following evening we were back at our advanced base camp and ready to go. At dawn we crossed the remaining short section of glacier and reached a snow cone at the base of the couloir. Above, steep icy runnels over rock slabs gave some superb climbing before the angle eased. Route finding was not a problem; we followed the great gully until late in the day then moved right into a small snow basin, hoping to excavate a bivouac ledge below a rock wall. We managed to dig only a narrow shelf but reasoned we could sleep end-to-end; with no alternative it would have to suffice. In the twilight we hurriedly prepared for the night.

'Merde!' I heard Andy shout. A clump of three stuff sacks clipped to a karabiner accelerated away down the route.

'That's the food and the brewing kit gone,' he said despondently, after prolonged swearing in his naturalised French.

'We could always go down and get some more,' I offered. Dropping the bags was an annoying mistake made in haste, but Andy was being hard on himself. Our position was hardly serious – a few hours of abseiling would take us back to the glacier and our camp. However, the look on Andy's face told me thoughts of retreat had not even entered his head. A quick inventory revealed we still had most of the gas and instant noodles; a few chocolate bars also remained. As we bedded down for the night, Andy prepared what was to become our set evening meal – a bowl of instant noodles washed down by several cups of lukewarm water.

The night passed slowly, sporadic deluges of spindrift adding to our discomfort. It was a relief to start moving again at daybreak and we continued uneventfully up the more gently angled central part of the couloir in fine weather. A two-tiered bivouac in soft snow provided a more amiable place to pass the next night and a much simpler location from which to resume climbing the following day.

Our early start was fortuitous. As I led the first pitch it started snow-ing, bombarding Andy with regular avalanches. Steeper climbing, poorer weather and lack of food slowed our progress. Late in the after-noon an icefall gave access to the uppermost basin of the couloir; this blanked out above and Andy led a difficult mixed pitch to gain a knife-edge ridge. It was dark by the time I joined him.

The bivouac was sensational; all we could do was hack out a small shelf along the crest of the ridge. I sat uncomfortably wedged against a small rock buttress while Andy lay out precariously below me. The night brought wind, snow and biting cold; as it got light I could scarcely believe that we had managed to sleep in such a place. If Andy had made any sudden movement or rolled over in his sleep he would have fallen from his perch.

Now he had work to do, methodically clearing rotten snow to climb a runnel of honeycombed ice up the side of the ridge crest. It was the hardest pitch of the climb. Our lack of sustenance was really taking its toll. I felt weak and slow as I moved up waves of exposed corniced ridge to a flat shoulder. It took until mid-afternoon before we reached the easy-angled slopes that led to the summit.

'I'm tired,' I said to Andy as he joined me at a stance. 'Can we make it to the top and back before it gets dark?'

'Weather looks settled. We could always go early tomorrow.'

I nodded my approval. What a bivvy site! The upper part of the Hispar Glacier lay below us to the east, rising up to the Hispar La; beyond was Snow Lake, while to the south the jagged outline of The Ogre dominated the skyline. I pulled my damp sleeping bag from my rucksack and spread it on a foam mattress. It was a neat place to do some drying. That evening we finished the last of the noodles and went to sleep happy, the alarm set for midnight. We did not sleep for long. The wind got up, cloud moved in and by ten in the evening we were enveloped in storm. Midnight passed with no improvement and we stayed put. By dawn conditions were no better. With only vapour left in the remaining gas cylinder it was folly to continue. We packed our rucksacks and started to abseil.

It was a long day. The storm intensified and the couloir we were descending excelled in its function as a natural drainage line. Lower down we were regularly swept by increasingly large powder snow avalanches and eventually conditions became so bad that we could only move at carefully timed moments between deluges. It was a relief to finally escape the fall line and to be able to wade down the snow cone to the glacier. At the foot of the slope I found our three bags of food lying mockingly in the snow.

It continued to snow heavily in the night, but we ate well and it felt luxurious inside the shelter of the tent. After a lengthy breakfast we loaded our rucksacks and staggered off down the glacier. The snow-covered moraine lower down proved tiresome but by midday we had only to cross the Yutmaru Glacier to reach the base camp. As we started across the storm blew in again and visibility dropped. Soon we were lost.

'This is the first time I've not had my compass with me,' Andy observed at one of our many stops to ponder where to go next.

We weaved around on the glacier, trying and failing to recognise features in the driving snow. The hours slipped by. To be benighted was the last thing we needed. Finally, with dusk approaching, the cloud lifted momentarily. We had wandered off the side glacier and were now on the Hispar itself, below the point where we needed to climb the moraine in order to get to Jutmal. We had to retrace some steps, but at least we knew where we were. Exhausted and relieved, we reached base camp and the comfort of the kitchen tent just after dark. Nazir Ali kept the stove roaring well into the night.

Walking out of the mountains, I had time to reflect. It was disappointing not to have reached the summit of Hispar Sar, to bag the first ascent of the peak and to get a view of the great mountains to the north. But we had climbed the couloir, completing what was a perfect line, and in that respect the circle was now closed. The vision of Hispar Sar's South West Face would no longer occupy my thoughts, bidding me to return. My perception of the mountains of Pakistan and passion for climbing them was changing. This was the place I had spent my formative years of exploratory mountaineering, returning again and again. Here I had learnt to climb day after day while coping with extremes of heat and cold, hunger and thirst. It had been a formidable training ground and had served me well, but I sensed it was time to move on. The trip to Tierra del Fuego had altered me and shifted my perspectives. Perhaps the enforced absence from Pakistan had helped clarify my thoughts, focusing them increasingly on mountains free of human influence. People had lived in the Karakoram valleys for thousands of years and although the mountains themselves remained raw and elemental, even high on the glaciers there were clear indications of man's presence.

Back in Gilgit I suffered a more telling reminder of the presence of people. The rudimentary sanitation that characterises much of the developing world threw me a dose of Giardia. It was my first re-acquaintance with the disease for many years and I had forgotten how unpleasant it was. Our last night in town passed with a churning stomach, cramps and the signal sulphurous belches. Early next morning, on the flight to Islamabad, I suddenly felt very nauseous, made a dash for the toilet, but only managed a few steps before heaving a wave of vomit down the aisle of the plane.

'What can we help you with today, sir?' asked the assistant at the car rental desk. It was mid-January and I had spent late autumn and the festive season at home after the Pakistan trip. Now I was in Albany, the capital of New York State, to begin the lectures series I had organised the previous year. It felt exciting. For the next three months I would be travelling continually, climbing occasionally, meeting many new people and some old friends.

'I'd like a car please,' I replied with a dose of English sarcasm that produced no reaction. It rarely did in this country.

'And what kind of car are you after?' the man continued undeterred.

'The smallest, cheapest one you've got.'

The man handed me a brochure and proceeded to run through the various models and insurance options. The vehicles all looked large to me.

'Haven't you got anything smaller?'

'No, sir.'

None of the other rental companies had either. I hired the smallest large car available and spent a lengthy time locating it in a vast parking lot. At home it would have been called a family saloon. The trunk (boot in English) swallowed my kit bag and could have accommodated several more. On opening the driver's door a metal arm came out and presented me with the seat belt buckle. Eventually I worked out that I could not put the automatic gearbox into drive without pressing down the brake pedal. It was like driving a sofa. The only pleasant surprise was when I came to fill the vehicle with fuel: to someone accustomed to European prices it seemed I would be motoring virtually for free.

I had no preconceived ideas about what to expect from this part of my tour, dealing with the logistics had taken time enough. I was aware that New England had some good ice climbing venues and that was about the sum of my knowledge. I motored north into the Adirondacks where I had scheduled my first gigs. It was hilly, heavily forested country. Considering that the great cities of Montreal, Boston and New York are all relatively nearby, it was virtually empty, with only the occasional small settlement. I had been invited by an outdoor shop called The Mountaineer to attend their annual 'Mountainfest' in Keene Valley, a pretty little town in the heart of the hills. The shop was easy to find: it was one of the few businesses in the place and right on the main road. Vinny, the owner, was a helpful sort who made me feel incredibly welcome, his easy manner typical of the folk around this very grass roots festival. Over the following days I instructed ice climbing, drank and ate with the local mountain guides and on the Saturday evening gave my presentation to a packed school hall. It was all great fun, but the highlight was still to come.

I teamed up with a local guide and went to climb at Poke-O-Moonshine – a steep, clean, granite crag around a hundred metres in height that thanks to some seepage from the hillside above is one of the areas premier ice venues. Like many of the cliffs I visited, it was just a short walk from the road. The plum line was called *Positive Thinking* – a cascade in its upper section, reached by a striking streak of ice all the way from the ground up a steep rock slab. The climbing was sensational.

Then it was back on the road, a slow journey east out of the Adirondacks and into Vermont. On one of the rare sections of straight road I put my foot down. It was a mostly empty highway but not a well-timed move. A short time later I caught sight of red flashing lights in the rear-view mirror. The police officer was very polite and told me I was speeding. I tried pleading the ignorant foreigner, but he was having none of it and retired to his car with my passport and driving licence. He was gone for a very long time. I thought about going to ask what was the delay was but had been given clear instructions to remain in my car. Eventually he returned.

'So you've been to Peru?'

'Yes.'

'What was that like?'

'Very nice.' He seemed more interested in the countries I had visited than my traffic offence. At least it explained the delay: I think he had simply been looking at the stamps in my passport. Finally, he gave me a ticket.

'What should I do with this?' I asked.

'Fill it in and return it with payment for the fine.'

'What if I don't pay?'

'If you commit an offence in New York State in the future you'll be in big trouble.'

I took the officer's advice and up to now have committed no further offences in New York State.

After talking in colleges in Middlebury and Colgate I returned to Albany and flew to Utah. Salt Lake City was brash and modern compared to the quaint towns and rolling landscape of New England. The people were similarly different. The city was also sitting in an unpleasant haze of photochemical smog. It was hard to believe I was still in the same country.

My host, climber and writer Mikel Vause, met me at the airport. Mikel is an English lecturer at Weber State University in nearby Ogden where, at his instigation, I spoke to a class of students on the theme of how to write mountaineering literature – not a subject on which I would claim great expertise, but I muddled my way through. We climbed ice, took a hike into the mountains above the cloud and in between excursions wallowed in the hot tub at Mike's house. On the final evening I spoke at a charity dinner, before the smog delayed my flight home.

There was little time to settle into any domestic routine. In fact, I barely had time to recover from the jet-lag before I was getting into the car for a road trip lecturing across England. Then all too soon it was time to fly abroad again. Boarding the flight with Jane and Maisy I became aware of looks of dismay from passengers in the seats around us. It was a 12-hour flight from London to Los Angeles and, not surprisingly, they felt they had drawn a short straw sharing it at such close quarters with a nine-month-old baby. The looks were similar when after less than three hours on the ground at LA we got on a further flight to Auckland. It was a brutal introduction to long-haul flying but amazingly Maisy was taking it in her stride. At the end of both journeys people commented on how marvellous she had been. I felt distinctly disorientated as we took a final flight to Christchurch on South Island.

Christchurch is home to the New Zealand Alpine Club who had arranged talks for me right across the country, starting in their headquarters city. Friends who had emigrated to the islands had already been in touch offering places to stay, so the club's advanced publicity was obviously working. Gary Kinsey, who I had met on my first alpine summers in Chamonix many years earlier, and his partner Christine kindly offered the use of their house in Christchurch. It would serve as a base for our time in New Zealand.

Though we were exhausted by the flights there was much to do. We hired a car, met with Geoff Gabites, president of the NZAC to discuss further publicity, and dealt with newspaper interviews. I also became a first time user of a mobile phone. Up to now I had managed to avoid owning a mobile, however, I had been instructed to get one by the publicist who was handling the Australian leg of the tour. I did warn her that it might be of limited use in a place like New Zealand but she seemed undeterred. Much of one day was spent with a photographer on a crag above the city, as he tried to get just the photograph he was happy with. Then we left, driving south into the night.

It was a joy to wake upon the side of Lake Tekapo on a beautiful sunny day. Like most visitors, we were keen to experience New Zealand's mountains and coastline and we stayed for several days with a friend in Glenorchy near Queenstown, walking in the hills by day and spending evenings around the barbeque. Later in Queenstown my phone picked up a signal and immediately started buzzing. I patiently listened to the messages. A few were from old friends wanting to say 'hello' and offer hospitality, but most were from Stephanie the publicist in Sydney. The first were simple instructions to telephone journalists, Stephanie's voice slowly becoming sterner in tone. The later calls were of a more pleading and finally hysterical nature. She was audibly relieved when I spoke to her. Despite my warning, she was evidently struggling with the concept of a place without a mobile phone signal. In the end the journalists got their stories and I had a laugh. My new communication device had already caused a surprising amount of misunderstanding.

Back in Christchurch I embarked on the lecture series, yo-yoing between venues up and down both the north and south islands. Mid tour, we spent three days walking the Queen Charlotte Track at the top of South Island in the Marlborough Sounds. Maisy slept much of the time in the papoose on my back and our bags were taken by ferry between overnight stops. Compared to the treks we had done in the Himalaya it was easy and very civilised – the perfect introduction for our young daughter.

After the trek we headed down the west coast and spent two nights with Alan Wilkie and his family. I first met Alan in the Alps back in 1984 and he had come to England for a while before returning to New Zealand. I had heard nothing from him since. We had quite a lot to catch up on.

Bizarrely, my last two engagements were in Dunedin down at the bottom of the South Island and Auckland up at the top of the North Island the following day. Flights were required for the final leg and Jane was left with a bit of a drive to return the car to Christchurch. The scheduling may have been a little odd but it did mean that we had seen a lot of the country and it had been very sociable. I look forward to seeing all those people again in another 20 years' time.

❄ ❄ ❄ ❄

My cousin Melanie lives in Sydney and she and her husband were waiting at the airport.

'G'day,' Bruce greeted us.

That evening, sat around their swimming pool, was calm and relaxed. The following days were not. Now I was in a large capital city and an up-market adventure travel company – World Expeditions – were calling the shots. They wanted to get as much promotion from my visit as possible. Stephanie had been very busy. A blur of travel, meetings, publicity and talks began with nearly a full day at the headquarters of the Australian Broadcasting Corporation giving countless interviews. After two nights in Sydney I said 'good-bye' to Jane and Maisy and moved on to Canberra, Brisbane and Hobart where I paused for an extra day to catch up with a former climbing partner.

Paul Pritchard had been visiting Tasmania back in 1998 on a climbing road-trip with Celia Bull when he suffered a horrific accident on the Totem Pole – a world-famous slender sea stack on a remote stretch of coastline to the east of Hobart. While abseiling to the foot of the climb he dislodged a rock with the rope; it fell some distance before hitting him on the head, bashing a hole in his skull. He was left hanging in the surf unconscious and bleeding profusely. Celia had somehow summoned the strength to single-handedly winch Paul 20 metres back up the stack, secure him to a ledge and then go and alert the rescue services. Her amazing effort saved his life, however their relationship did not last through his long and painful rehabilitation. Later, Paul returned to make a film about the events and became reacquainted with one of his intensive care nurses in Hobart – Jane Boucher. After a spell of living together in North Wales they married, returned to Tasmania, and started a family. The lecture tour had given me a great opportunity to catch up with an old friend and to see something of Tasmania – I doubt I would have been able to make the journey otherwise. Paul looked happy and relaxed in his new home and was able to show me a few of the special places he had discovered. Then it was time to move on again.

The tour concluded with consecutive nights in Melbourne, Adelaide and Perth. It was a good place to finish. My brother Matthew was a long-time resident of the city, having emigrated there in the late 1980s. Jane and Maisy had arrived direct from Sydney a few days earlier. Now there was time to relax and spend some precious time as families together before travelling home.

Towards the end of our adventure in Pakistan, Andy and I had inevitably got round to talking about future projects. He was keen to go back to Alaska and had in mind a route he had previously attempted solo. I had made a couple of visits myself, guiding the standard West Buttress route on Denali, the highest mountain in North America. I had thoroughly enjoyed the place and the mountains, and the other big draw was its accessibility. There was none of the tiresome and expensive bureaucracy involved with visiting many of the peaks of the Indian sub-continent, nor lengthy and time-consuming approaches. Despite being a wilderness, this was very much the developed world and motorised transport could be utilised all the way to base camp. It would be a simple and quick trip to organise.

We had done little in the way of preparation except apply for a Mount Everest Foundation grant to help out with our costs. With departure looming it was time to make some more detailed arrangements. I telephoned Andy at his Chamonix home.

'Ah, Simon,' he said. 'I've been meaning to call.'

'We need to start sorting out a few things.'

'Sorry kid, I can't come.' Andy sounded devastated. 'My knee's blown out. I'm going to have to have an operation.'

It was a bitterly disappointing turn of events for Andy, but not completely unexpected. The lack of mobility in his left ankle and hip consequently put more pressure on the knee. There was some good news though: the doctors expected him to make a speedy and full recovery. I wished him well with the surgery.

I still wanted to go away and climb but doubted if I could find a climbing partner at such short notice. There was another small problem: our proposed climb was Andy's project and therefore I would need to find a new objective as well.

A few days later I received a timely email. Paul Schweizer, an American philosophy lecturer living in Edinburgh, wondered if I might be free to climb in North America in May. Though we had not climbed together before, we had met many times over the years and spent quite a bit of time in each other's company at British Mountaineering Council winter meets, introducing visitors from around the world to the delights of Scottish winter climbing. At our last meeting, after a lecture I had given in Edinburgh, we had casually talked about climbing together, but I had thought little more about it until now. I knew Paul was a very competent mountaineer: he had quietly amassed a series of notable ascents around the world over a lengthy period, and as someone who had been around, I reasoned he was likely to stay around. More importantly I knew that we would get along. It makes the whole expedition experience so much more enjoyable if it is harmonious. Although you can never be sure how people are going to react in serious, potentially life-threatening situations in the mountains it certainly helps to not start yelling at each other. I gave him a call.

'I got your email.'

'And?'

'I'm keen to go. Where were you thinking of exactly?'

'Well, I went to the Wrangell-St Elias many years ago. I'd love to go back there.'

'Sounds good to me.' I knew little about the ranges except that they were a vast area of heavily glaciated wilderness spanning the Alaska-Yukon border, and they contained Mount Logan – Canada's highest mountain and the second highest in the North America. For me it was new territory and that made it particularly attractive. 'Do you have something in mind?'

'Not really,' Paul replied thoughtfully. 'But I can do some research. There's plenty to go at.'

We quickly concluded that we needed to fly into the range with a pilot called Andy Williams based at Kluane Lake and booked flights to Whitehorse, state capital of the Yukon, for late April. However, we had still not found a climbing objective by the time I needed to travel again. My next speaking engagement was taking me to Iceland.

❄ ❄ ❄ ❄

It was cloudy for most of the flight to Reykjavik and I only started to get an idea of the land below as the aircraft was making its final approach. The patterns were unfamiliar. What looked like streams or rivers were surrounded by crumpled rock split by cracks and fissures. Finally, I realised what I was looking at. It was lava covered in luminous green moss. I had seen nothing like this before.

My first point of contact was a man called Gummi who ran an adventure travel company. He picked me up at the airport in a huge four-wheel-drive complete with ridiculously outsized tyres. These were not for show, but essential for driving over icecaps and crossing rivers. Soon they were being put to good use. We quickly left the main road and headed into the hills – except these were not hills as most of us know them but small volcanic ash cones and craters. Occasionally there were pools of steaming water or bubbling mud. Then as we made our way back towards Reykjavik came more lava flows: some were bare, some covered in moss and others sprouting willows from within their fissures. As we neared the capital the landscape became more industrial with small power stations dotted across the horizon, networks of pipes crossing the land and linking greenhouses. It was hard to know what to make of it all.

The geothermal energy plants situated around Reykjavik – I would soon learn – tap into subterranean lagoons of super-heated water and produce two very useful products: electricity and hot water. Once the steam is put through turbines to produce electricity the wastewater is then piped around the city to heat homes and businesses. This meant that buildings were super hot, with windows left open despite the frigid temperatures outside. All hot tap water smelt strongly of sulphur and taking a shower had the odd effect of leaving you smelling worse than before.

Gummi's family were perfect hosts and I spent a pleasant couple of days exploring Reykjavik before being passed from one group of interesting people to another. Although I had little idea who, if anyone, was overseeing these arrangements for me, they all seemed to work seamlessly. I met with a journalist who was writing an article to promote my lecture and was taken to the hot springs at Geysir and the fantastic *Gullfoss*, or 'Golden Falls'. The setting of the *Alping* – Iceland's original parliament – at Thingvellir in a rift valley formed by the parting of the North American and European plates, was particularly atmospheric. The weather throughout was variable in the extreme, temperatures fluctuating wildly from several degrees above freezing to many degrees below. There was snow, sunshine and rain – sometimes within a few hours of each other. I spent a long day winter climbing on the Trollwoman's Horn, north of Reykjavik, visited the nearest icefield to the capital and spent an evening talking with a retired scientist who had worked on Iceland's whaling fleet. My lecture – the reason, of course, that I had come to Iceland in the first place – ended up feeling like a sideshow, somehow slotted between a myriad of other activities.

On my final day I was picked up by a man called Haldor and driven through a blizzard into the lava fields outside Reykjavik. We stopped at what to my eyes looked like a random spot and set off walking across the snow-covered rubble. After a few hundred metres Haldor found the ravine he was looking for and we climbed down and entered a huge cave. It was the mouth of a lava tube and over the next few hours we explored deep inside. The tube gradually narrowed until it broke into a series of small tunnels that ended with the final dollops of lava lying on the floor. They looked like petrified cow turds. It was one of the most unusual days out I could remember.

I left with a set of unique impressions and a sperm whale tooth that now rests on our mantelpiece. Although I had no idea at the time, it would be the first of several visits to this geologically busy island on the northern fringe of Europe. I would come to relish its surreal, empty landscapes and make lasting friendships with some of its charming, quirky inhabitants.

Shortly after arriving home the Nottingham-based taxman and world-renowned climber Mick Fowler sent me a couple of inspiring aerial photographs of the huge West Face of Mount Alverstone. Paul soon discovered that only two routes had been climbed there and both avoided the largest section of the face. With just two weeks remaining before our departure we decided Alverstone was the mountain for us.

Whitehorse is a functional town on the banks of the mighty Yukon River. 'One horse would be more appropriate,' I commented to Paul, after we had completed what was an unavoidably short stroll around its centre. It looked like it could do with another gold rush. Still, at least we were able to orientate ourselves quickly. We also learnt there had been a month of unseasonably warm and settled weather.

We ate a late breakfast, shopped for food, packed, and booked a taxi to take us to Kluane Lake the following day. After hiring a satellite phone and buying some gas cylinders we were ready to head north. Once out of town the properties lining the road tailed away until there was just stunted pine forest. Some of the trunks had been shattered by the winter frost.

We stopped at Haines Junction to register as required at the Kluane National Park headquarters. A ranger ran through some paperwork, before sitting us down in front of a television.

'You'll need to watch this video,' he said almost apologetically. I soon understood why he perhaps felt it unnecessary viewing. The video was obviously pitched more at backpackers and skiers who could suddenly find themselves in unfamiliar environments and situations. Where Paul and I were going required a complete understanding of wilderness survival; if we didn't know the stuff in the video already, we would be out of our depth from the moment the plane dropped us on the glacier. The formalities over, we got back in the taxi and continued to Kluane Lake. There was little at the airstrip other than a hangar and Andy's house on the far side.

'Come and see me in the morning,' he advised. 'If you need somewhere to stay there's a bunkhouse.' He pointed into the trees beyond the runway. I marvelled at how simply everything fell into place in this part of the world. It was a far cry from the mountains of Asia with its teeming cities, creaking infrastructure and dysfunctional bureaucracy. Here there was enough space and money for things to happen without treading on any toes. Nearby, in the mountains, there was simply beauty and space.

It was sunny in the morning and Andy's plane was out of the hangar. We wandered over and found him inside.

'The forecast is not so bad,' he said. 'But I've seen this weather before. We won't be flying today.' There was high cloud to the west and a few puffs hanging lower over the mountains. We spent a bit of time chatting and I warmed to Andy immediately. He looked to be in his fifties and spoke in the slow, deliberate, understated manner that I recognised from the mountaineering world in people who knew what they were doing. Us being demanding was not going to change his call. We would wait until Andy said he was ready to fly.

The low cloud had lifted by morning and Andy deemed the day fit to fly. We were delighted, having already exhausted the limited visitor attractions at Kluane Lake. After loading up the plane we showed Andy our map, pointing out where we hoped he could land us.

'I'll see what I can do,' was all he said.

The plane lifted gently from the gravel airstrip and flew low into a broad river valley to the west. Andy started to gain height up slopes to the south of the river. This was skilful flying. The plane gained lift each time we crossed one of the rock ridges that ran down the hillside. Soon we were flying high over vast plains of gravel and braided rivers that emerged from great glaciers. The mountains lay straight ahead.

The scale of the landscape was awesome and Paul and I sat silently trying to take it all in. Then Andy began pointing to the horizon.

'Shit,' I heard Paul say. 'There's cloud to the west.' Where we had hoped to land lay hidden beneath it.

'I can land you this side.' Andy offered.

'No, thanks,' we replied in unison.

'Okay. We'll have to try again later.' Andy turned the aircraft as he spoke.

Back at the airstrip a Canadian group had arrived. They were going to Mount Logan and, like us, would have to wait.

Next day Andy decided to take the Canadians in first. Logan was his bread-and-butter charter and he reasoned that he could take a look around before committing to our more unusual flight.

This time conditions were perfect and the plane was spiralling down below Mount Alverstone almost as soon as we had recognised it. We flew once over the upper section of the Alverstone Glacier and then Andy gently landed the Helio Courier on a high side glacier. We came to a halt, but Andy kept the engine running.

'Get out!' he shouted.

We jumped down, unloaded our kit and gave the thumbs up. Moments later the plane accelerated away in a plume of snow, bobbed down the glacier and drifted into the sky. The remoteness hit as soon as the engine noise faded away. The mountain landscape around us was vast and silent, its glaring whiteness amplified by the sun high above.

We set up camp in the lee of a rognon, then wandered in something of a daze up our little side glacier to a col. Below lay the huge Hubbard Glacier, running northwards towards the squat bulk of Mount Logan in the distance. The scale was so enormous that it was difficult to accurately judge distance. It was going to take some time to get the feel and measure of this place.

Looking back to our mountain, Alverstone's West Face was golden in the afternoon sun. The prominent West Buttress on the left side of the face had been climbed in 1995 and the broad gully to its right a little later. The rest was an open book. This is what had brought us to this place.

'What do you think?' I asked.

'Well, the couloir looks kinda compelling,' Paul replied. On the right hand boundary of the main face was a good-looking line that led almost to the top of the mountain. Further right the face became more broken and was studded with threatening séracs.

'I guess we can go and take a closer look tomorrow.'

Two evenings later we left our base camp. Andy had done a good job and the foot of Alverstone's West Face turned out to be a mere hour and a half walk away. The skis we had lugged all the way from home were left behind to serve as tent pegs. We camped beneath the face with four day's food and gas and a minimal rack of climbing gear.

Early the following morning we began solo climbing on reasonably angled hard névé. We made rapid progress up the gradually steepening slope, but soon the sun came round and warmed the shattered granite that formed the upper part of the face. Rocks started to fall – small at first, then gradually increasing in size and frequency. We were in the fall line. About 800 metres up the couloir narrowed. As we hurried to get through the dangerous bottleneck I heard the high-pitched humming of falling rock but did not have time to react. A pair of rocks hit me almost simultaneously on the left forearm and shoulder.

'Fuck!' I shouted, grabbing the arm, which immediately swelled and stiffened.

'Are you okay?' Paul asked with a worried tone.

'Yeah,' I replied feebly. 'I don't think it's broken, but it might be time to dig the ropes out.'

It was a wise move. Soon the sun crept down the face, turning the névé to bare ice. To fall here would be fatal. The climbing was now on 50-degree ice with short steeper sections and the intense sun meant sporadic rockfall continued throughout the day. We moved diagonally to the right out of the central runnel to lessen the danger; even so occasional rogue rocks bounced our way. Progress faltered as the withering heat took its toll. But there was nowhere to stop. Finally, at nine in the evening, Paul reached a snow bank above a small icefall. We excavated a platform, 1,200 metres up the face, put up the tent and slumped inside. I felt quite drained. We managed to make a brew and eat a little before the need to sleep overwhelmed us.

It was late when we woke. My arm felt sore and had developed some colourful bruising. We were still tired and needed to rehydrate. The morning passed to the accompaniment of a constant roar from the stove. It was early afternoon before we were ready to leave and the sun was glaring directly on to the face.

Easy-angled slopes led right from our campsite and then up more steeply to the edge of the upper rock buttress, bordered by a gully on its right hand side. Regular salvos of rocks peppered the gully, but we had to cross it. I watched nervously as Paul waited for a lull before making a lung-bursting dash to the far side. It was one of those mountain moments that are unavoidable sometimes – you simply have to chance your luck. I rolled my dice and our lucky streak held.

Seven more rope lengths of good 60-degree ice led to a flat col on the summit ridge. The top looked to be close. We dumped our rucksacks, untied the ropes and wandered silently up to the summit. For the first time we could see Mount Kennedy to the east, its huge north buttress illuminated by the evening sun; Mount Hubbard appeared to the south.

'Hey, well done,' Paul said simply as I joined him on the summit. We shook hands and slapped each other's backs. It was time to savour the views and take a few photographs.

Back at our rucksacks we put up the tent. The sky became hazy as the evening drew on and a strong smell of wood smoke hung in the air. Somewhere beyond all this snow and ice a huge forest fire was blazing. The night was still and bitterly cold. In the morning we wandered easily down Alverstone's north flank to the Great Shelf and peered down into the upper section of the Alverstone Glacier.

'There's no easy way down there,' I said disappointed, 'and it faces west, so it's going to get some rockfall.'

'We could try dropping down into the Dusty Glacier and getting back to the Alverstone from there,' Paul replied thoughtfully. 'We should be able to get down over there.' He pointed to a col on the other side of the shelf.

'Got to be worth a try.'

It was short walk to the col and although we could not see the complete route to the glacier the snowy face below did not look too steep. We decided to go for it. An abseil took us over the cornice and on to the face and for a while we walked comfortably down snow slopes, but the angle gradually steepened. Now the slope was broken with bands of threatening séracs. Avalanche debris lay far out into the glacier below. With no prior knowledge of the face, route finding between the séracs was a little nerve-racking. Lower down, we reached a sérac that stretched right across the slope. It was impossible to skirt around.

'We're going to have to abseil,' I told Paul.

I chopped a bollard in the snow and set up the ropes for the descent. The thought of using snow as an anchor and trusting all your weight with it is never pleasant. I descended slowly, trying not to put any unexpected load on the rope, but the ground got steeper. Then my heart sank. There was a huge crevasse at the base of the sérac. I abseiled gently towards it, knowing what I'd have to do but not looking forward to it one bit.

With a deep breath I kicked off the icy wall and let myself free-fall to a clumsy landing on the lip of the chasm.

'Safe,' I shouted, knowing we were not.

As Paul came slowly down I viewed the terrain. The sérac band we had abseiled was unstable and had obviously collapsed recently. The slope stretching down to the glacier was covered in debris. Paul arrived looking worried.

'We need to get out of here,' he said solemnly.

'You're not kidding. Let's get the ropes down and leg it.'

We hastily pulled the ropes, packed them into our rucksacks and sprinted down between huge blocks of ice lying in the snow. At the limit of the avalanche debris we threw down the sacks and rested. Hours of trudging up the Dusty Glacier followed until we called it a day.

Our last remaining gas canister provided breakfast and then expired. It left us in a serious position, but the weather was holding and I reasoned we would be back at base camp within a few hours. We set off for a col that we knew led to the upper Alverstone Glacier.

'Don't you think that col looks a better option?' Paul asked a little below the pass, pointing to another lower col further to the west.

'I'm not sure,' I replied, having not given it much thought.

We debated the change of plan and went with it. The col was further than it looked. The view from the saddle was not the one I had hoped for.

'We've gone too far west,' I told Paul. A lobe of the Hubbard Glacier lay below us.

'Oh man, I'm sorry,' he replied, viewing the disappointing panorama.

The slopes down to the glacier were unpleasant but the real penalty for our mistake was the climb out. A long, gently angled ridge led out of the basin, attracting the full force of the afternoon sun. Paul dug deep and broke trail to the watershed and the welcome sight of our tents. We finally reached camp, tired but happy, in the early evening.

Our descent, with the crossing of three watersheds, had taken as long as the climb and in some ways had been more demanding and dangerous.

I immediately made a satellite phone call to Andy at the airstrip.

'We're done here,' I told him.

'I'll be with you in the morning,' he replied reassuringly.

It was not to be. We woke to fog and had to call the airstrip again. Andy told us to call again once the weather improved.

❄ ❄ ❄ ❄

Four days later the storm began to clear. With two weeks' food and fuel remaining our situation was hardly desperate, but the whisky had run out. Two phone calls to Andy secured a well-timed exit. As we flew out, I looked down on the Wrangell-St Elias ranges in all their great emptiness and with virtually limitless climbing potential. It was that siren call again. Just as in Tierra del Fuego, I knew I would be coming back. We had been in the mountains a mere 11 days, yet it felt like many more.

Back at the Kluane Lake airstrip we celebrated our good fortune with some Yukon Gold Ale. The bottles carried the advertising slogan 'Melt the snow. Brew the beer. Life is good'. We drank to that simple but fine philosophy.

SIX

More Like Being Abroad

Sometimes events that seem small at the time get embedded in your psyche and go on to alter the whole course of your life. In 1991 at the end of May I gathered with a diverse group of climbing friends from Sheffield and North Wales in the Scottish west coast town of Mallaig. Our plan was to catch a ferry to Eigg – one of the Small Isles south of Skye – and to climb on a plug of volcanic basalt called the Sgurr.

On the ferry the mist slowly cleared and revealed the enchanted isle. The Sgurr was impressive, thrusting above the moor at the southern end of the island, but also of interest was a ramp-like hill at the northern end, fringed with vertically jointed basalt cliffs. To be clear, we did climb initially, but soon got diverted by the beauty of the place and the warmth of the islanders. The sun blazed from an azure blue sky and it barely got dark. We played in the annual inter-island football match between Eigg and Rùm, where half-time refreshments were cans of McEwan's Export and crab claws, and had a dinner party round a sandcastle table on the beach at Laig while the sun set in glorious bands of colour behind rugged hills. Then on our final night we pooled all our remaining money and spent it on booze at the island post office; the bottles and cans turned up at our campsite party on the back of a tractor and trailer with many of the locals in its wake.

Even now, 20 years later, when occasionally I run into someone who was there, they will invariably say, 'Do you remember that week on Eigg?' I go back to the island when I can and the locals still recall the time when the mad climbers paid a visit.

A year after our wedding in 1999, I organised an anniversary outing to the Isle of Arran. The destination was secret and Jane only guessed where we were going when we turned off the motorway short of Glasgow and headed for the ferry at Ardrossan. We left the car at the port and took our bicycles to the island. Over the following days we came to appreciate bikes as the ideal way of exploring Scottish islands. They are easy and cheap to take on the ferries and because a lot of islands do not have much road they are an efficient means of getting around. With the addition of panniers and some lightweight camping gear you can easily become completely self-contained.

Later that summer we cycled the length of the Outer Hebrides. More islands soon followed and slowly a grand idea crystallised – to visit all the inhabited Scottish islands serviced by regular ferries. It has proved to be a fascinating and time-consuming ride.

After Maisy was born we bought a cycle trailer so that we could take her along on our island tours. The Orkneys were next on the list, the last large group of islands we had still to visit. Our mission was proving infectious and Celia Bull was keen to join us with her young son Dylan. Celia had been one of partying climbers on Eigg in 1991 and shared our love of such places. After her sojourn in Whistler and becoming a mother, she had relinquished life at sea, sold *Ada* and bought a house in Puerto Varas near to where Woody lived so that Dylan could have regular contact with his father.

On a cold, windy and overcast July day we got up early, packed up our wild camp and cycled the short distance from Sandi Sand on the eastern edge of the Orkney mainland to the airport at Kirkwall. It was such a small airport that we were able to watch the plane land and see Celia with Dylan walk to the terminal building. It was an improbable place to meet given that Celia was now living in Chile. There was an emotional reunion before we moved on to the youth hostel in town.

In a frantic few days of cycling and ferry crossings we visited the nearby islands of Stronsay, Eday and Sanday. Dylan and Maisy played on empty windswept beaches, slept as I cycled them around in the comfort of the trailer and occasionally had their little tiffs. It was a lovely time. Then we returned to the mainland to take the short flight to the gravel airstrip on North Ronaldsay. The tiny plane was only in the air for about 10 minutes, flying low out over sea dotted with bright green islets ringed with white sand beaches. North Ronaldsay has the distinction of a perimeter wall around the entire island. Beyond the wall, 5,000 sheep of a breed unique to the island grazed seaweed on rocky promontories between the grey seals.

Then it was back to the mainland. After a final night together we waved a sad goodbye to Celia and Dylan as they caught a plane back to Aberdeen. Our remaining time on the Orkneys passed in a haze of continual movement between islands. More so than other islands we had visited, the Orkneys are defined by antiquities. Chambered cairns, burial mounds, stone circles and standing stones dot the landscape. Chief among them is the haunting mainland site of Skara Brae, overlooking the ocean, where an entire Neolithic settlement was discovered buried beneath sand dunes. The excavated houses looked like the occupants had just nipped out for the day and somehow failed to come back. On Hoy, the highest of the islands, we gazed out over Scapa Flow where the German fleet was scuppered at the end of the First World War and tried to imagine what this huge natural harbour had looked like when it was fortified to accommodate the Home Fleet in the Second World War.

Racing to get the ferry back to the mainland the trailer wheel clipped a large kerbstone in the centre of Stromness; Maisy's carriage flipped on to its side and slid down the road until I brought the bike to a halt. Maisy was safe as she was securely strapped inside, but there was no time to comfort her from the shock of the incident. I turned the trailer upright and continued the dash for the ferry.

Two years earlier Jane and I had cycled across the Shetlands, another group that provided its own particular charms. After making our way slowly up the islands we camped on a beach at Burrafirth and watched an otter dance along the shoreline in an attempt to snatch some eider duck chicks. Then we walked over moorland to Herma Ness and looked out from the cliff tops to Muckle Flugga – a small clump of rocky islets capped with a lighthouse – the most northerly point of the British Isles. In the nearby settlement of Baltasound we cycled by the legendary Bob's Bus Shelter complete with table, chairs, net curtains, telephone, computer and a microwave. There was even a pot of geraniums.

Shetland had its hottest day on record while we were there, the temperature reaching a balmy 23 °C, and despite it being late summer a constant breeze kept the midges at bay. We made our way back down the west side of the mainland, picking off islands en route, and took a ferry to Foula for the final stage of our Shetland journey.

Foula is the most remote inhabited island in Britain, sitting out to the west of the mainland. On arrival we were advised to go and camp by the airstrip in the centre of the island. A man arrived in a car and kindly gave us a large fish he had just caught.

'I live in that house over there,' he said pointing to a building in the distance. 'Come over for a drink later if you like.'

That evening Dell plied us with gin and tonics and talked about the night he had spent sheltering under a table as a storm blew in his windows. Next morning his garage had disappeared without trace, even though it had been bolted to a raft of concrete, and the valley above his house had been stripped bare of grass. Happily, the weather was a good deal calmer when Jane and I walked up the self-same valley, dropped down a chasm on to a beach then followed a grassy rake that cut up through huge sandstone sea cliffs. Fulmars circled over-head while puffins jumped from their burrows and flew out to sea, all in their comic-frantic style. The rake finished at the cliff top. 'The Kame' is arguably the largest cliff in the British Isles; peering over the edge from the highest point, I felt dizzy as I watched gannets going to and from their nests far below. As we walked back down the hill-side, a fat, furry white bonxie chick was sat in the heather and hissed and spat regurgitated fish as we approached – just as nesting seabirds will do to repel climbers on cliffs all around the British Isles.

Our Scottish islands quest is nearly complete. Shortly before set-tling down to write this book we ticked off Raasay, lying between Skye and the mainland, where we made a pilgrimage to Callum's Road, a poignant memorial to one man's toil. For years Callum MacLeod lobbied the local council to extend the road to his isolated home at the northern end of this forgotten island, but to no effect. Then one day he decided to take the matter into his own hands. Working mostly with just a wheelbarrow, pickaxe and shovel, it took him 10 years to single-handedly complete the three-kilometre road.

Here at the far edges of our crowded country is a rare commodity – space: space for the natural world to flower and flourish, but also space for people to dream, to think and act on their own.

I can clearly remember one special day on our first prolonged trip through the Outer Hebrides. We left Eriskay on an early ferry to South Uist (now there's a causeway) and in a single long day cycled all the way to Berneray off the northern tip of North Uist. It was sunny but with a stiff headwind. For kilometre after kilometre we pedalled past empty white sand beaches, huge tracts of *machair* – grasses and wild flowers fringing the coast – and lonely expanses of peat bog dotted with lochans stretching inland to distant hills. There were hardly any people and few cars. For much of the day the only sound was the wind blowing through the *machair* and the call of birds. Mostly we rode apart – taking in all these sights and sounds, lost in thought. Sometime during that beautiful day at one of our infrequent stops an odd comparison came to me.

'It's more like being abroad, than being abroad,' I said to Jane.

In early January 2006 I left home, bound for Montreal. World Expeditions were keen to roll out my lectures to North America and had put me in touch with their offices in Canada and the United States. Between them they had arranged modest three venue tours of both countries, but by following up on some of the college contacts I had made in New England a year earlier I managed to make it a little more expansive. The timing also coincided with the Mountainfest in Keene Valley where I was hoping to meet up with the British climber Andy Kirkpatrick who had been invited as a speaker.

The weather on arrival in Montreal was reassuringly snowy and bitterly cold, promising good ice climbing conditions in nearby New England. On successive nights I spoke in Montreal, Ottawa and Toronto and the following day flew to Boston. The drive north from the city turned into a protracted struggle through a snowstorm, overturned vehicles and plummeting temperatures. The automatic hire car was hardly up to the job and at times slid ineffectually on the icy roads. It was difficult to imagine driving conditions getting worse, but they did when I ran out of screenwash just as it got dark. For half an hour I struggled to see the road ahead through a frost-glazed windscreen. When cars came from the opposite direction I simply could not see at all. Eventually I spotted the welcoming lights of a remote gas station. In the middle of the brightly lit forecourt was a huge pyramid of screenwash bottles. The retailers of the USA are not shy when it comes to sales opportunities and for once I was actually glad of such blatant marketing. I bought a bottle and the rest of the journey to the Adirondacks was a much more controlled affair.

Over the following week I climbed beautiful Adirondacks ice with

Andy, moved leisurely between speaking engagements in pleasant college towns, then made my way back to Boston. It was time to get busy again. I flew to Seattle, arriving in the late evening, and the following morning decided on a whim to get a haircut. The barber made a good job of my hair but also snipped a chunk out of the top of my ear. It bled and would not stop. The poor man was soon seeing lawsuit, the end of his career and business.

'It was just an accident,' I had to reassure him. 'These things happen.'

'That's very understanding of you sir,' he replied, still not completely convinced I was for real. He was still thanking me when I left.

I got the haircut for free, however, the cut bled intermittently for the rest of the day. That night as I delivered my lecture blood dripped from my ear and on to the floor; I self-consciously shuffled sideways hoping the audience would not notice.

Next morning my early flight to San Francisco was delayed. It was hardly unusual – internal flights within the USA are often late – but this time it was annoying: Jane and Maisy were waiting for me and the delay was eating into precious time together. They were staying in San Francisco with an old friend, Tom Curtis, and his family, Tom having got a fellowship at Stanford University for a year.

Fortunately the delay was short and I was not too late for a happy reunion with Jane, Maisy and Tom who had driven out to the airport. We spent some time back at Tom's lovely house in Palo Alto, took a tour of the university campus, had lunch in a nearby diner and then Tom drove me into the city as I slept off the East Coast time difference. It was late when we got back from my talk at a downtown venue and there were tears in the morning when I was up early to take a taxi to the airport. Jane had travelled to San Francisco with Maisy so that they would get to see me in the middle of what had developed into a lengthy absence from home, but the snatched moment felt frustratingly brief.

That night I talked at Neptune's, a legendary outdoor shop in Boulder, Colorado. Boulder is regarded by many as the outdoor capital of the

USA so it was good to be well-received by an enthusiastic crowd. By a happy coincidence my old climbing partner from home – Sean Smith – was in town on a filming assignment and came along, making it a special evening.

❄ ❄ ❄ ❄

'It's a disaster,' Mono said, watching the boxes of wine being carried on to the *Mago del Sur* along with all the usual expedition baggage. 'This is too much wine. They will never drink it all.'

'I think they probably will,' I told him.

I was back in Ushuaia after a three-year absence, this time with a group of doctors and lawyers who lived around Guildford to the south of London. They were good company, liked a drink and were on holiday. They had also paid for the charter of Mono's boat, so I could not really understand his bluster. Still, the combination of Mono and the ebullient chaps from Surrey provided some entertaining moments during the course of the trip.

Mono took us to Caleta Olla where we spent a week in the Cordillera Darwin. Monte Francés unfortunately eluded us; we had to turn around close to the summit when white-out conditions made continuing upwards a hazardous proposition. It was a tired team that returned to the boat yet all were keen to get on with the next stage of the plan – to sail around Cape Horn. As if to mock us, the next day was fine and clear as we left Caleta Olla and motored east towards Puerto Williams. The outline of Monte Francés towered above the still water of the Beagle Channel with just a few puffs of diffuse white cloud hovering around its summit. It is the way of the Cordillera Darwin and part of its charm: from tempest to flat calm within a matter of hours.

Two days later we left the tiny fishing village of Puerto Toro and motored down the east coast of Navarino Island and out into open water to the south. Puerto Toro is the most southerly proper settlement in the world; those further south are all scientific bases. After crossing the Bahia Nassau we slipped into channels between islands that ran down to the Horn. The landscape was quite barren, mostly peat bog and tussock grass. Only leeward slopes leading down to sheltered bays held a few stunted, wind-sculpted trees. Lone pillboxes and other military fortifications scarred the bleak islands, a reminder that in the early 1980s Argentina and Chile came close to war over ownership of the inhospitable and uninhabited Isla Lennox at the eastern end of the Beagle Channel. I could not help but think what a grim posting it must have been for the soldiers.

After anchoring at Caleta Maxwell on Isla Hermite we went ashore and walked up to the high point of the island. The desolate panorama over the lonely archipelago was stunning, but also a little forbidding. It really did feel like the end of the world. To the south, partially hidden by a smaller island, stood the craggy outline of Cape Horn. My mind went back to our cycle rides and views in the Outer Hebrides, Orkney and Shetland at the other end of the Atlantic.

A calm sea greeted us as we slipped from the anchorage next morning and out into open water. Our passage round the Horn looked like being something of an anticlimax. Then a bank of dark grey cloud appeared on the horizon to the west.

'Quick,' shouted Mono, without telling us what he wanted to be quick about. Soon he was running around on deck with impressive agility for such a big man, barking out orders and hoisting sails. We all tried our best to help but really only seemed to get in his way. The cloud was approaching remarkably fast and as it came overhead the wind rose and the sails filled with a crack. It started to rain, the swell got up and the boat surged along heeling on to its side. At first the wind was unpredictable and squally but soon settled into a constant strong blow. What exhilaration! Everyone was on deck smiling and wanting a turn on the tiller. As we rounded the rocky promontory that forms the Horn itself we could see the white huts of the Chilean Naval Post on top. Simultaneously the radio crackled into life below deck; judging by the length of time the woman on duty spent talking to Mono she was seriously bored. It must be a lonely job monitoring shipping here, but at least it is now a posting for whole families. In the past the authorities had only sent groups of men, and predictably they often ended up fighting.

All too soon it was over and we were sailing northwards up the eastern side of the islands to an anchorage for the night. The wind dropped away, but the smiles remained. We all knew it had been a special day. As we motored back to Puerto Williams the following morning a pod of dolphins shadowed the boat for several hours, dancing through the bow waves; then as we entered the Beagle Channel the sun set in a blaze of reds to the west as the full moon rose above a bank of cloud to the east.

Early in the morning of 10 May 2006 our son Lewis was born. His birth was a little less dramatic than his sister's, but not without prolems and in the end he was delivered by emergency caesarean. He was big: just shy of five kilos and never looked like a newborn. A fourth member of the family added urgency to our efforts to move house. We had started the process the previous autumn however progress had been slow. We wanted to continue living in the same Eden Valley village near Penrith that we had settled in 13 years earlier. Eden is one of the largest local authority districts in England and certainly the most sparsely populated. Tourist literature sells it as 'England's green and pleasant land.' It is a very apt description.

In a small village such as ours there are never likely to be that many houses for sale at a given time. And first we had to sell ours. For years, prices had been going up and property had been selling quickly. Some folk had got wealthy on the back of a few shrewd house moves. It could not last and now people were beginning to question the ridiculous prices. The market was wavering. By the time we got an offer, several properties we had looked at had already sold. There were only three places available, two of which were unaffordable. We went and looked at the third. It was a 1960s bungalow with a block of ageing double garages and a small field at the back.

'It'll be good for the children to play in,' said Jane.

'Aren't we too young?' I replied.

We bought it. If someone had told me in my twenties or thirties that by my early forties I would be living in a 1960s bungalow, I would have laughed at them. I have grown to like the place and the absence of stairs has the long-term benefit of eliminating a further move in old age. Life takes some strange turns at times.

On the back of the lectures I had been doing for World Expeditions the company suggested I lead an expedition for them. They knew of my long-standing interest in Pakistan and between us we came up with the idea of going to Spantik. Situated at the western end of the Karakoram and 7,027 metres high, Spantik is best known for a huge pillar of marble that turns golden in the evening light when viewed from Hunza. The pillar was first climbed in 1987 by the British pair of Mick Fowler and Victor Saunders in what was widely regarded as one of the most difficult alpine-style ascents ever completed in the Himalaya. But we would not be going that way. I knew the mountain was climbed fairly regularly by commercial expeditions via its South East Ridge, which although long is not too technically difficult. For me, the other big attraction of Spantik was its location. I would get to see the Chogo Lungma Glacier, one of the few major glacier systems in the area that I had never visited. I was enthusiastic about going. World Ex' advertised the trip and managed to pick up five clients.

Early in July I flew to Islamabad and met with the group who were mostly Australians. The trip did not get off to a good start. Many days of bad weather had forced the cancellation of flights to Skardu in the mountains; a backlog of people had built up and we would be unable to fly. I knew the alternative all too well. We would have to go by bus up the

Karakoram Highway – a torturous two-day journey following the Indus Gorge.

The bus ride was so exhausting we needed an unscheduled rest day in Skardu to recover; then on reaching the roadhead at Arandu after a day-long jeep drive, a night of rain which continued into the morning put a dampener on the start of the walk-in. The porters – who were mostly from Arandu – were reluctant to leave the shelter of their houses. I called another rest day fearing a shambles if we tried to leave in the wet. We got away early next day, but the rain returned, making a misery of the walk along an ablation valley at the side of the Chogo Lungma Glacier. Thankfully our luck was about to change.

In the evening Spantik emerged from the lifting cloud further up the glacier and next morning we continued up the valley under clear skies. After crossing the moraine ridge, easy walking on flat ice led up to a more broken stretch of glacier and a final steep pull onto a grassy bank where we established our base camp. It was in a sensational position, perched on an airy promontory with amazing views back down the Chogo Lungma. Scree slopes behind the camp led up to the South East Ridge. A Korean expedition was in residence while a Spanish team had been already and gone home empty handed. Bad weather and deep snow on the ridge had been hampering progress. We paid off the porters and began setting up the tents.

Another day in camp was required to get sorted. I struck a deal with the Koreans who were happy to leave their fixed ropes in place if I traded them some of ours. This attractive arrangement saved me two days' work higher on the mountain fixing our own rope in place.

We soon reached the crest at the start of the ridge proper and from here the way ahead was obvious. Stretching out at a gentle angle, the ridge did not look technically difficult, but there was a lot of it – more than eight kilometres all above 5,000 metres. We put up the tents, stashed our personal climbing gear inside and dropped back down to base camp.

After returning to camp one for a night, we moved up to the site of our second camp at 5,400 metres in indifferent weather, and climbed a bit higher the following day. Our high-altitude porters Ali and Sikander meanwhile carried tents up to the site of camp three. After a further night in camp two the weather cleared and we dropped down to the base camp for two days of well-earned rest.

The Koreans made the most of the improving conditions and climbed to the summit. Soon we were ready to complete our game of camp chess. In one long day we reached camp two and the next day carried on higher, following the Korean rope to camp three at 6,300 metres. Leaving our top camp at 1.30 a.m., we made quick progress across a high plateau in darkness and reached the last section of summit ridge at dawn. The angle eased and led by Ali and Sikander we breathlessly ground our way up the final metres to a football-field-sized platform. There was no further to go.

I felt proud. Ten days after arriving at base camp we were all on the summit of a 7,000-metre peak. Each night during our climb the sky to the south had flickered with monsoon storms. I had expected the turbulent weather to move north, but it never did. My plan and our movement up the mountain had been seamless. This was rare moment of perfection in a sport where management of setbacks is often the norm. The view was ample reward for the achievement – peaks stretching as far as K2 in the east and to Nanga Parbat way to the south. I stood silently trying to take it all in, to figure out the geography and give names to some of the points studding the horizon.

Slowly everyone arrived on the summit. We shook hands and took photographs. There was little need for words. The panorama spoke for itself and we each absorbed it lost in our own thoughts.

'Time to go down,' I said eventually.

After a speedy descent of the ridge, the walk across the plateau was exhausting. The sun was high and it had become very hot; we sank to our knees in melting snow. Back at camp three the temperature was almost unbearable. Through the afternoon we lay listlessly in the tents in our underpants, sleeping bags draped over the flysheets in a futile attempt to keep cool. At 3 p.m. it was 38 °C inside the tents. It was a relief when the camp fell into shadow. Within a few minutes the temperature was below zero, ramming home the brutal nature of the climate in these mountains. Both the coldest and the hottest temperatures I have ever experienced have been in Pakistan.

It was a long and tiring day back to base camp and we needed two full days to recover before being ready to walk out. We planned to cross the Chogo Lungma Glacier to reach the Haramosh Glacier opposite base camp, then walk up this to the Haramosh La and descend into the Haramosh Valley.

First, however, there was some local politics to deal with. A few years earlier some Haramosh folk had come over the pass and been spotted by villagers from Arandu gathering crystals on their side of the watershed. A confrontation had ensued and shots were fired. Animosity still lingered between the two communities and no one from Arandu was prepared to come with us over the pass. Awkwardly, this included the two high altitude porters, Ali and Sikander, who were the logical choices to accompany us. Only the two cooks, who happened to be from different places, could make the journey, but they could not really carry much. In the end I found a solution. Ali and Sikander would come to the pass, stay the night there and then return to Arandu. Their extra carrying capacity would help us on the uphill leg and we would only have to carry one night's supplies after they left.

The crossing was remarkable. On the first day we made it to just below the pass at 5,100 metres and camped on the glacier. Then in the early morning we slowly made our way to the high point, a prominent notch formed between scree slopes and the side of the glacier, where Ali and Sikander transferred their loads and said their goodbyes. The valley below was filled with cloud with Haramosh towering clear on the far side. Then it was down into the cloud, negotiating a slope that was steep, loose in places and vast. The cloud burned off with the morning sun revealing the Haramosh valley. I could not believe how green it was; it was as if we were entering a lost world. At the bottom of the face we walked across lush meadows with glades of shimmering birch trees. It was unlike any other place I had been to in the Kara-koram: a lush oasis in an area that is essentially a high altitude desert. It took most of the day to get down and we stopped at the first village – Kutwal – to camp for the night.

Further down there were pine trees and we entered a gorge with steep granite walls pitted with improbable tunnels – the work of Haramosh crystal gatherers on their home turf. Lines of rope hung down rock walls to the workings and occasional explosions echoed round the valley.

We reached the road and after a short walk met the jeeps that would carry us away from the hidden realm of Haramosh and back to the dusty plain that is Skardu. We were further blessed with the chance of an early flight to Islamabad. Everyone was now keen to get home and with a hurried change of tickets we were airborne so swiftly that some of the Australians made an onward flight that evening for Lahore.

The rest of us returned to Islamabad airport next morning, checked in, cleared security and immigration and were waiting in the depar-ture lounge when it started to rain. The sky darkened and went a sickly green colour. Within minutes the apron and runways outside were under water; I had never seen rain of such intensity. Our plane could not land and was diverted to Lahore. Soon we were escorted back through immigration and our exit stamps cancelled. The taxi to the hotel barely made it through the deluge. It wasn't much drier inside: the hotel staff ran out of buckets to catch the water that poured through the ceilings and the floors were awash. More than 200 millimetres of rain fell that day and people were swept to their deaths in flash floods.

The rain stopped overnight and by morning only puddles in the road betrayed what had happened the day before. We were driven back to the airport and caught our flights home.

On a sunny August day friends gathered at our house and helped us move. A local farmer turned up with a small livestock trailer and shuttled our belongings the short distance to the bungalow, stacks of furniture went straight into new resting places and boxed items into the garage – some are still there. It was a social occasion, took only a few hours and we thanked everyone with a few crates of beer and a Chinese takeaway in the evening.

There was little time for settling in before I was packing my bags again, this time for South Africa. Through my web of contacts I had managed to secure a series of speaking engagements. The Mountain Club of South Africa were the principal hosts and a local outdoor clothing brand – Capestorm – offered to organise further dates and venues. I opened in Cape Town, though first I was taken climbing in the Cederberg to the north, on beautiful quartzite crags with ancient rock paintings at the base of some of the routes. Back in Cape Town I got to climb on Table Mountain during the day before racing down to give talks at night. I visited vineyards, stayed with nice people in stunning locations and in the evenings, beer flowed around the braai – a South African barbeque. Then it was on to Johannesburg and out into the bush again to stay at Waterval Boven, one of the country's premier rock climbing venues. I struggled with the harder routes, having touched rock only fleetingly over recent years, but to ease any frustration there was a climbing festival underway with a great social scene. Then it was back to Johannesburg for a final round of talks and a day hiking in the Drakensberg Mountains before heading home.

It had been a memorable trip. The country was beautiful and the climbing superb; but I never felt very comfortable. Apartheid may have ended but its passing has done little to alter the distribution of wealth. There is no disguising the fact that the whites still have most of the money and that this is divisive. I felt tension in places and the threat of violence. Houses in middle class and wealthier suburbs are small fortresses, ringed by high walls and razor wire, accessed through remote controlled gates. Each area has its own security company providing round-the-clock armed response teams ready to rush to any property on alarm. Murders are a frighteningly common occurrence and this in turn has hardened the attitudes of the law abiding. It was a nice place to visit and I am grateful for the hospitality that I received, but it is not somewhere I would chose to live.

Four days after getting home I was heading back down to Manchester airport en route to a mountain festival in Taos, New Mexico. The trip was so short I spent most of the three days away on planes and was so exhausted that I fell asleep on the train back to Penrith and almost missed my stop. Then it was into the lecture season nearer home and a tour that finally expired – and me nearly with it – at the end of November on a depressingly damp Irish evening in Cork. Such is the life of the itinerant climber-lecturer.

SEVEN

It Might Not Be the Hardest

I recognised the fine spidery writing on the envelope before the stamp and Chamonix postmark. Andy Parkin is one of my few friends who still occasionally sends letters. In an age dominated by email it is always a lovely surprise when something hand-written drops through the letterbox. Inside was a letter and a small watercolour painting. Andy has given me several paintings over the years: 'thank-yous', I guess, for organising our expeditions. These evocative sketches and watercolours have developed into a unique and precious collection, mementoes of our time in the mountains and special places together. There was also a map. Looking at it I soon recalled the wind and rain, peaks and glaciers, southern beech forest, shoals of sardines and pods of dolphins that had accompanied our slow cruise along the Beagle Channel on Celia Bull's yacht following our first successful outing to the Cordillera Darwin six years earlier.

Throughout that voyage, Andy had sat on deck, pen in hand, meticulously adding notes to the map. Gradually it evolved into a priceless document, detailing potential climbing objectives, features and hazards. Then one day in an ice-choked fjord a gust of wind plucked the map from Andy's hand and dumped it in the water. Celia turned the boat around and I managed to scoop up the soggy paper with a landing net, however, the dousing and subsequent drying left their mark. It was difficult to make out the tantalising notes: 'waterfalls', 'good pk snowy', 'face mixed' and 'looks good'. Soon we would be returning to Tierra del Fuego and while I had made two visits since our initial magical journey, this would be Andy's first time back. The prospect was obviously exciting him. The map seemed both a fitting reminder of times past and a herald of adventure to come. One small map – so many stories.

Buenos Aires International Airport: the Yateses stood patiently in the queue for immigration. It was our first big outing abroad as a family since Lewis was born and he and Maisy had coped well with the long flight. Not that it had been without problems. Being just nine months old, Lewis had shared a seat with Jane, but the airline placed both Maisy and I in seats well apart for the 12-hour flight from Madrid. How a two-and-a-half year old was supposed to sit in a full plane, on her own and surrounded by strangers, for that length of time nobody would explain to us. Fortunately, a kind passenger offered to move and Maisy was able to sit next to her mother.

We had not been waiting long when an airport official approached us. 'Come with me,' she said, leading us into an empty aisle and straight to an immigration officer's desk. We were soon on our way to collect our baggage, leaving the main queue behind. It was a very pleasant welcome and a courtesy that happily would be repeated many times during the following weeks. In Argentina, we soon learned, the elderly, disabled, pregnant women and families with young children have priority. For us it meant goodbye to queuing for the duration of our stay, and while I do not expect to be treated differently because of the children I cannot deny it was nice. What was even nicer was the response of ordinary people. Everywhere we went we were made to feel welcome and the children were fawned over. Such warmth is in stark contrast to the UK where the faces of proprietors and customers alike often drop the moment a family walks into a café, restaurant or pub. Sometimes I think it would be more helpful and honest if places simply put a sign in the door saying 'children not welcome'.

We caught a taxi downtown and found a hotel in Congreso, an old district right in the heart of the city, surrounding the Congress building. It was the children's first time in a big city. They were used to life in a rural hamlet where the background 'noise' amounts to little more than sheep, the mewing of buzzards and an occasional passing tractor. What would they make of Buenos Aires, a conurbation with around 13 million inhabitants? Wide, tree-lined boulevards led to massive plazas, some roads are six lanes wide in either direction and the roar of traffic is deafening. Baby Lewis seemed fairly oblivious to his new surroundings while Maisy was at turns excited, puzzled and amazed. She spent a long time staring at a family who were living rough on a plot of waste ground near the hotel; they looked to be eking a living collecting paper, cardboard and scrap.

'What are those people doing daddy?' she asked.

'That's where they live.'

'Oh,' she replied, obviously having a think about that.

The following day we went to La Boca, another old, but mostly working class district built by Italian immigrants, part of which had recently developed into a vibrant and colourful entertainment area. The district is also home to the famous football club – La Boca Juniors – a spawning ground for many leading Argentinian players over the years including Diego Maradona. Some of the many restaurants employ singers and dancers to attract customers. Lewis danced the tango with a very striking lady and Maisy was serenaded. It was all great fun. By now we had noticed that virtually every block had its own children's play area. These oases for infants came to life once the sun had set and the stifling temperature dropped. It felt strange to be playing with the children in the centre of a city at eleven o'clock at night, but for Argentinians it was normal. Early next morning Jane left with Maisy and Lewis to visit Celia and Dylan at their home near Puerto Montt in Chile; they would join me later. Meanwhile I headed to the domestic airport and caught a flight to Ushuaia. For now, I had clients to tend to.

A year earlier while queuing at check-in to take a flight home from Buenos Aires, I had got talking with a man and his wife waiting in front of me. Rob Gearing was a likeable character and we connected immediately.

'I might be interested in coming on one of your trips,' he said at the end of our conversation. True to his word, he was now about to join me for an attempt on Monte Francés. Rob was also bringing his 11 year-old daughter, Ellen, together with his friend Noah le Mare and Noah's son Jack. I had never taken children into remote mountains before; even though they would not be climbing, their participation presented a new challenge, one I welcomed but that also made me a little nervous. In recognition of this extra responsibility I bought a satellite phone. Obviously it could be helpful in any emergency, and it would also enable the children to talk with their families back home.

Ellen and Jack had a great time, my initial concerns soon turning to delight as I saw how much they were enjoying themselves. At our camp in the forest Noah kept them entertained with bushcraft lessons, woodland walks and nights sleeping around a fire in a nearby cave. The two youngsters brought a completely different dynamic to the trip, to such an extent that it almost seemed secondary when, with the other clients, Rob and I slipped away from camp for three days and climbed the mountain, while Noah stayed behind to look after the children.

Back in Ushuaia Jane had arrived with Maisy and Lewis and I began preparations for Andy's arrival and the next phase of the trip. We had hoped to attempt Monte Francés's unclimbed South Face, but I had looked carefully at the face while taking my group up the standard route – the South West Ridge – and seen that it was bare of the necessary snow and ice. Without that frozen mantle, climbing would be so dangerous as to be out of the question. We would need to find another objective.

There were other hitches. Mono was busy, and so I had to look for an alternative boat to take us to the mountains. With some difficulty I managed to find the *Zephyrus*, whose English owner Andy Whittaker kindly offered to help us out. This Andy was also a climber and was slowly making his way northwards through the channels and islands that stretch northwards up Chile's west coast from Cape Horn to Puerto Montt. He had generously offered to take us into the Cordillera Darwin for free on the understanding that we would all climb together. When I first arrived in Ushuaia, *Zephyrus* was out of the water and Andy was carrying out repairs to the drive shaft and propeller. Thankfully when I next visited him the vital work had been completed and he expected the yacht would be back in the water by the time the other Andy arrived.

To my relief everything seemed to have finally fallen into place and there was still time for a weekend out of town on a family camping trip with our friends Luis and Carolina and their children Marco and Luca. It was a joy to relax after the organisational demands of the previous weeks – but perhaps premature.

The weekend over, I telephoned Andy to make some final arrangements before our departure on *Zephyrus*.

'The gearbox has broken,' he said despondently. 'I won't be able to take you.'

It was devastating news and I sighed as he went through the details. The boat was going to have to come out of the water again and the repairs would take days, possibly weeks depending on how quickly he could get the parts. Andy Parkin was due to arrive from Chamonix in less than a day and I had only a little over two weeks left before my flights home. Now our plans were in tatters.

'I might have found you another boat,' Andy W continued.

'Yeah?' I replied, clasping at the lifeline.

'A Belgian guy called Marcel; if you come and see me in the morning I'll introduce you.'

Marcel de Letter was a tall, powerfully built man in his mid-fifties with an agreeably straightforward manner. Terms for the charter of his yacht *Iorana* were quickly agreed and I dashed to the airport to meet Andy. We were to sail the following day. There was no sign of Andy at the arrivals gate; my climbing partner was not on his scheduled flight. Suddenly, all bets were off again. When Andy telephoned Luis and Carolina's house later in the day and related how a delayed flight from London to Madrid had knocked on, I could only laugh. Having rearranged his flights he would be with us the following morning.

Luis kindly lent me his car to go to the airport; I was running late and arrived to find Andy sitting outside on one of his kit bags. He looked completely drained.

'Good flight?' I asked. He did at least manage a smile.

There was little time to relax. As we drove to the harbour I told Andy about my own problems and the lack of snow and ice on the South Face of Monte Francés.

'I'd be keen to go back to Seno Pía,' he said, untroubled by this turn of events.

'Sounds good to me,' I replied, remembering our previous visit. There was hardly a shortage of objectives in the Cordillera Darwin – only a handful of the peaks had been climbed after all – and we had Andy's map.

It was a struggle getting our baggage to Marcel's yacht. The rusting pier had been severed from the mainland by a road-widening project on the seafront and wobbly planks spanned the gap. Bags then had to be passed up on to a large abandoned motorboat that was riding high on the tide. Then they could be lowered down to Marcel on *Iorana*. The same process was repeated with the children.

'I've been talking to Marcel,' Jane said when I finally made it on to the boat. 'He asked me if I was coming along with the children. What do you think?'

The question threw me for a moment. Jane and I had talked about this possibility before leaving home, but I had then shelved the idea, *Zephyrus* would have been too small to take us all anyway. However, as Marcel pointed out, *Iorana* most certainly could. In the swirl of the previous days events I had failed to notice.

'I don't see why not,' I replied, coming to my senses at last.

The fine detail was hammered out in a matter of minutes. We agreed a price to cover Jane and the children and Marcel set about getting extra supplies. Jane and I would have to go back to Luis and Carolina's to pick up things for the children, and so we decided to all meet back at the boat in two hours. Andy was relieved, at least now he had time to take stock, have a coffee and do some shopping. Together we made an unlikely crew: two childless bachelors in their fifties and a family with two young children. It promised to be an interesting journey.

The sail to Puerto Williams was a relaxing interlude but it was late in the day when we arrived in the harbour. We were in Chilean territory now and needed immigration clearance, but after visiting another boat the officers decided to knock off for the day. Marcel was furious; he had hoped to steal a march on an approaching storm by leaving immediately and motoring through the night. It was not to be. The immigration officers did not come aboard until late next morning and it was lunchtime before we were able to depart. Back out in the Beagle Channel we soon ran into strong headwinds and were forced to take shelter in a small bay. Failure to leave the previous night would cost us dear.

On the fifth day out of Williams we woke to silence. The wind that had blighted our progress thus far had finally dropped. The morning was wet but still. We slipped anchor and motored west past the Chilean naval post at Point Yamana, and as usual a figure waved to us from the balcony. A little later we passed Isla del Diablo – Devil's Island – guarding the entrance to the north-west fork of the Beagle Channel. Tantalising glimpses of snow and glaciers above the northern shore offered hints of the mountains above. The rain teemed from a leaden sky and danced on the flat calm sea.

Later, I recognised the line of rocks – a submerged moraine ridge – that marks the entrance to Seno Pía. Marcel carefully guided *Iorana* through a gap in the rocks and entered the fjord itself. After all the delay and difficulties I found it hard to believe where we were and nervously expected the wind to return, but it stayed eerily quiet. As we crept further along, the rock walls steepened, dropping straight into the water in places. Clumps of trees clung on improbably steep ground. The place was just as dramatic as I remembered. Ice appeared and became denser as we slowly approached the head of the fjord, where two huge glaciers spill down into the water. We got out Andy's water-stained map and lit upon a 'face mixed' marked above the right-hand glacier. There was a suitable place nearby for a drop-off. However the cloud was low, obscuring the mountains. We needed more visibility before committing ourselves.

'We cannot stay here,' Marcel declared, pointing to the ice cliffs. Whenever great blocks broke off into the water, huge waves rippled down the fjord. We called it a day and went back to a beautiful anchorage in a tiny bay below a waterfall six kilometres back down the fjord.

That evening I was standing on deck with Maisy when a pod of dolphins entered the bay. A smile radiated across her face as they bobbed past the yacht before returning to deeper water. It was a fitting surprise – I had already seen a whale early one morning while holding Lewis in my arms.

We had been carefully watching the air pressure throughout the bad weather. That evening it climbed above 1,000mb – a very rare event in this place – but during the night it blew hard. The ensuing day of torrential rain made a joke out of the rising barometer.

A week had now passed. Up to now the trip had felt more like a boating holiday than a mountaineering expedition. We still had to find an objective, climb it and make the journey back. Time was tight. To add to our worries Marcel expressed concern about dropping us off near the head of the fjord. On a previous visit he had struggled to escape from our present anchorage due to the amount of ice in the water. If a lot of ice calved from the glaciers it might prove impossible to pick us up. As climbers, it was not a scenario Andy and I had even considered. We would simply have to trust our luck on this; and up to now luck had been a commodity in very short supply.

Next morning at least brought signs of hope. It was still, the rain had eased off and the cloud was slowly lifting. We slipped anchor and motored back to the drop-off. Nobody spoke. The atmospheric beauty of the place was overwhelming. At times I felt the hairs on the back of my neck rising.

Marcel grounded the yacht on a muddy stretch of the shoreline. Unloading our gear was easy. Marcel simply passed the bags off the bow of the boat and we waded them ashore. Jane brought the children on to the deck of *Iorana* and Andy and I stood on the beach with our gear and waved 'goodbye' as the boat left to wait at the anchorage.

'I'll see you in four days,' I shouted at the departing yacht.

'Call me when you need the pick-up,' Marcel yelled back.

In a hurried frenzy we set up base camp in a small clearing in the forest next to a stream. Then we left for a reconnaissance. The glacier nearby was relatively easy to cross, however, the moraine on the far side did not extend above the icefall as we had hoped. We tried to go higher on the glacier but soon found ourselves weaving up through huge, unstable séracs. The cloud had lifted enough now to reveal some good-looking faces on the peaks above.

'This is no good,' Andy said eventually.

'We could try the other side,' I suggested. 'I think we could get up that gully above the camp, which would bring us on to that shoulder above the icefall.'

We dashed back to camp and exchanged mountain boots for wellies. We would need them. There was bog in the lower section of forest, but it quickly gave way to steep, wooded slopes thick with undergrowth. Soon I could only make progress by swinging up through the branches and roots. I had never come across terrain like this, even in this densely forested part of the world. Then I realised why. There were no signs of guanaco. The inaccessibility of this place had kept out even these resourceful grazers. There were none of the faint trails I had become adept at following and in their absence the vegetation had grown unchecked.

Eventually I managed to force my way up to a steep gully. I had already left Andy well behind. The loose boulders in the streambed above provided a different challenge. Higher, a waterfall barred the way, the walls on either side coated in dripping moss. To continue this line of exploration I would have to climb the spout. Apprehensively, I took the plunge. On the steepest section a chockstone dislodged beneath my feet, leaving me hanging from a loose block by one hand. It was a relief when I pulled clear of the water, though there was still a series of mossy shelves to surmount before escaping the gully. The angle eased but pushing through the head-high beech as I neared the upper treeline was like wading through an uninterrupted hedge. Two hours after entering the gully I burst out into meadows covered in what I affectionately called cabbage daisies. The sun was shining, swallows were darting around feeding on insects floating above the flowers and the views down the fjord were stupendous. With time pressing, I tried to hurry across the meadows. The ground proved frustratingly awkward. The knee-high daisies poked through wet snow and the slope was steep. Snow slipped from the daisy leaves when trodden on and the stems broke off in my hands when I tried to use them for purchase. Staggering progress was regularly interrupted by barely controlled bum slides until I reached a shoulder and could look down on the glacier. The view was not encouraging. Although we could drop down on to the glacier it was still very broken and higher up there would be a further band of séracs to negotiate before reaching faces above. The approach was simply not safe and the lines on the faces looked bare of snow and ice.

I retraced my steps and met Andy just above the treeline. He looked drained and was dripping wet.

'You cannot be fucking serious,' he said angrily. 'How are we going to get up here with rucksacks on?' It was a fair point. They would snag on the vegetation and the extra weight might make climbing the gully near impossible. Slips and falls had made Andy's time in the gully even worse than mine. I told him of my observations beyond the meadow and with the day drawing to a close we set off down.

The descent of the gully was unpleasant – a series of barely controlled falls – but mercifully fast. Soon we were back in our forest camp discussing options. Should we try and approach the face and force a way up it, or go for a more modest objective? We wandered down to the beach and took turns looking through binoculars at a peak at the head of the fjord.

'I'm still keen to have a go at one of those faces,' Andy said.

'I understand that; but how do we get to them? Given enough time I'm sure we could find a way, but we've used up a day already.'

'This peak up here looks like it will go,' Andy said peering through the binos. 'There's a broken ridge above this lower buttress that leads up to a short face.'

'And we can get across the glacier.'

'Exactly.'

'It's got my vote.'

'Let's do it then.'

We might have decided on an objective but there were still potential obstacles – notably the forest covering the lower buttress. As we knew only too well, it hid unpleasant surprises.

A clear, cold night left a hoar frost on the grass and a skimming of ice on the fjord. The barometer remained absurdly high, but cloud was drifting in over the mountains. After a leisurely breakfast, we packed our rucksacks, recrossed the glacier and headed directly up the hillside. Initially we followed a streambed until it became too steep and forced us into the forest. It was slow going but at least we had gained height without having to fight through the denser under-growth found lower down. The forest soon became more broken, trees giving way to expanses of rough grass and cabbage daisies. Route finding was often difficult and Andy was struggling to drag his weaker left leg up such tricky ground, yet we continued to make pro-gress. Occasionally the sun broke through the cloud and cast shafts of light on to the fjord now far below, highlighting reflections of the peaks above its dark, still water.

At about 1,000 metres, rock slabs covered in deep snow formed a faint ramp line that we followed leftwards until the rocks gave way to the ice of a small glacier. Now I was able to move quickly for the first time in the day and soon reached a shoulder below a faint rocky ridge. I threw my rucksack into the snow and sat down on it to admire the views.

'This will do,' I shouted to Andy when he arrived. We chopped out a platform, put up the tent and began the laborious process of melting snow.

The ridge above ran up to another glacier split by a band of séracs. A ramp line led into a basin capped by further séracs below the sum-mit. It all looked reasonable and the weather, although not perfect, seemed to be holding.

Marcel had lent me a walkie-talkie, so I called the boat. It felt strange to be talking with Jane from such a location, knowing she was just a few kilometres away. She had only accompanied me twice before on my own climbing trips – the trips to Tierra del Fuego and

Pakistan I mentioned earlier – and then she had left us at base camp to get on with our climbing. In both cases I had not spoken to her again until the climbing had been concluded. Here we could speak whenever I wished, but I did not feel like I wanted to say much.

'Are the kids having a good time?' I asked.

'Yes, we've been on the beach most of the day. We made a fire and cooked some sausages.'

'We're at the shoulder,' I explained rather pointlessly, as Jane had no idea of exactly where we were. I could hear Maisy talking in the background. 'We'll try for the summit tomorrow. I'll call before we leave.'

The radio allowed us to talk, but it remained difficult to communicate across the divide of circumstances. The yacht was physically near yet I still felt we were incredibly isolated. I went to sleep happy, confident of a good day ahead.

❄ ❄ ❄ ❄

The alarm signalled the start of summit day and I heard Andy getting ready to light the stove. Yet again I found myself admiring his meticulous and tireless dedication to this crucial task. I sat up, slid towards the porch and opened the tent door.

'You're not going to believe it,' I said excitedly. 'It's crystal clear.'

Andy poked his head outside.

'Looks like we got lucky kid.'

The view was astonishing. There was not a breath of wind. In all my time in the Cordillera Darwin I had not seen a day like it. From our perch we were looking straight down Seno Pía to the Beagle Channel, Isla Gordon and even Isla Hoste at least 30 kilometres to the south. Both islands were covered in snow-capped peaks, offering limitless scope for new climbs and exploration for those with time, transport and an adventurous inclination.

We ate a leisurely breakfast, already savouring every moment of our special day. At nine-thirty I called *Iorana* and told Marcel that we were about to leave. He was astounded by our relaxed approach, but I assured him we knew what we were doing. We had already decided to leave the tent and go light, reckoning on return by nightfall. For once, we were so confident of the weather holding that we simply left everything inside the tent and set off.

Good, hard névé on a rocky rib led back to glaciated terrain where the rope came out as we crossed a series of snow bridges over deep, wide crevasses. We reached the sérac band and made for the most gently-angled central section. It was a strange feature – a colossal block of ice that had slipped down the mountain, with either side massively undercut. Andy made short work of leading a pitch up the front on 50-degree ice. Following on, I was about halfway up when a 'boom' sounded as I drove in my axe and a vertical crack shot through the ice. I realised my blow had split the block in half and I suddenly had the irrational fear that one of the halves could slide down the slope.

'Which side of the crack should I climb up?' I yelled up to Andy, who did not seem to be sharing my concern. I tried again and he gestured to my right. Personal crisis over, I climbed on to join him and continued up the snow slope above. We moved together, and though the snow was very deep in places the outcome was never in doubt. With just day packs on our backs and the sun riding high we could enjoy the moment and the ever expanding views. I led through the upper sérac to the summit ridge and another peak appeared to the west. It was higher.

'We should do that one as well,' I said to Andy as he joined me on the top, and so we did.

The second peak proved more of a grind. At one point Andy was sinking so deep into the snow that he had to repeatedly pull his left leg out of the post-holes with his right arm.

'I don't think I can carry on with this much longer,' he complained, but the ground improved and he cast the negative doubts aside.

'It might not be the hardest mountain I've ever climbed,' Andy said as we shook hands on the summit, 'but it's certainly one of the best.'

We savoured the views that had now opened out to the north and west, took endless photographs and pointed out potential future projects. It was remarkable to think that not a single person lived in all the territory we were now blessed with surveying.

As the shadows lengthened we made our way down, reaching the tent just before nightfall. By lunchtime the following day we had reached the glacier and I got on the radio to summon our pick-up. Later, as we ferried bags to the shore, we watched *Iorana* slowly advancing up the fjord through the ice. There was more high cloud today but it was still an idyllic scene. As the boat approached the shore we could make out figures on the deck.

'Hello stinky bum,' a child's voice echoed around the fjord. We laughed at Maisy who was smiling and waving frantically from the back of the yacht. The magical silence of the previous days was broken and now a different life beckoned.

'Which mountain did you climb?' Jane asked when we were back on the boat.

'Those two,' I replied, pointing to the peaks directly above.

'I told the children you were climbing that one.'

'How did you know?'

'I didn't, but it was the only one we could see from the anchorage.'

Marcel had a bottle of sparkling wine chilling on ice collected from the fjord. It was a nice touch. He had also caught and cooked a *centolla* (king crab), which was sitting on the table in the cabin.

'We're going to name the mountains *Iorana* one and two,' Andy told him.

'What does it mean, anyway?' I asked.

'It's Polynesian for "good day".'

It seemed appropriate. It had been a good day.

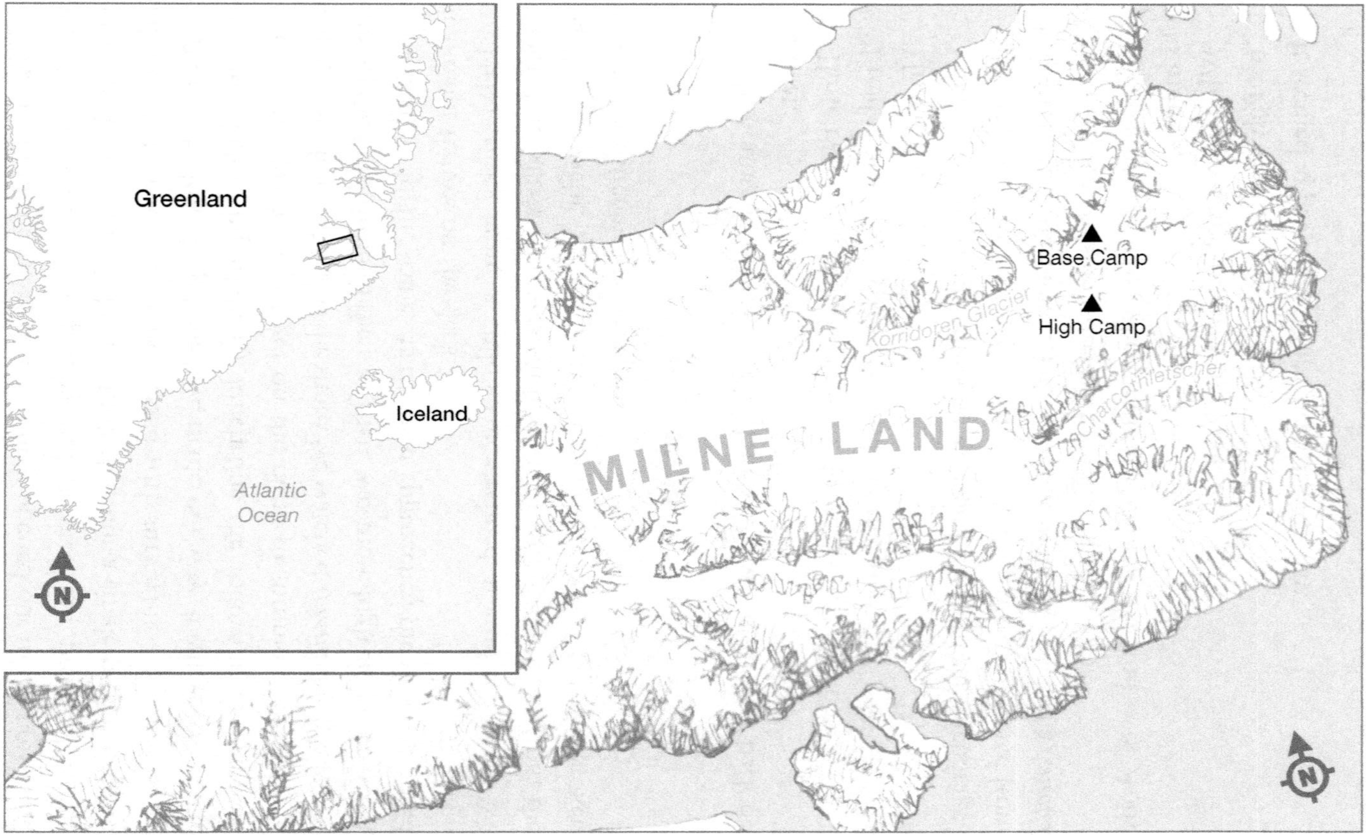

Milne Land – Eastern Greenland

EIGHT

A Plane Crasher

The trip to Tierra del Fuego had been an amazing adventure on so many different levels: I had enjoyed the professional challenge of taking youngsters into a remote wilderness setting and all that I learned from it; our own small children had had priceless experiences and who knows what seeds may have been planted in their receptive and rapidly developing minds; and then there had been our unexpected and unforgettable day on Monte Iorana. Time had gone quickly and so much had happened that on arriving back at Manchester airport it felt as if we had been away much longer than six weeks. When we reached home it was nice to be back, but the bungalow looked strange and unfamiliar – like we were just moving in. We had left Ushuaia at the end of a southern summer while in Cumbria the northern spring was underway. Ever since Maisy had been born, life had taken on a frenzied intensity that at times I struggled to cope with, but for the next few months my diary was less frantic. I was pencilled in to take another group to Spantik in the summer for World Expeditions and there was potential interest in a trip to Nepal for the late autumn, otherwise not much else. Having moved to live in one of the most beautiful parts of England, I paradoxically spent much of my time away. I resolved to take stock, relax a little and enjoy my favourite time of year at home.

Then the invitations and opportunities started cropping up; quiet periods tend not to turn out that way. The Alpine Club got in early.

I had been a member of the AC for many years, though perhaps only the blink of an eye in the club's long history. The AC was coming up to its 150th anniversary and was marking the occasion with a number of events held over 2007, the centrepiece being a grand midsummer gathering in the Swiss mountain resort of Zermatt. I was invited as a guest and happily accepted.

I contacted Andy Parkin who was also planning to attend. We agreed to team up and get in a few days of climbing around the weekend of celebrations. It would be a first for us both – my first visit to Zermatt and Andy's first return since his horrific accident on the Riffelberg more than 20 years earlier. Indifferent weather limited us to a couple of days of climbing, but that hardly mattered.

It was a lovely event – a time for meeting old friends and acquaintances and making a few new ones, and also a time for reflection. Zermatt was effectively 'base camp' for the Victorian pioneers during the so-called 'golden age' of mountaineering in the mid 19th century; quite right therefore that the municipality should want to enter so generously into this celebration of the rich contribution by British alpinists to the development of mountaineering over 150 years. Yet it's a contribution that seems somewhat unlikely, given the diminutive size of the mountains on our own small island. A sculpture was unveiled in the centre of the town: a Whymper-like figure pointing towards the Matterhorn and an inscription acknowledging Zermatt's ongoing friendship with British mountaineers. Later, during a dinner at the Hotel Riffelberg perched on an alp overlooking the town, the cloud lifted to reveal the Matterhorn soaring above the far side of the valley. There had been ideas of an AC ascent to crown the party, the Matterhorn being one of a score of peaks nearby first climbed by Brits. And Edward Whymper, whose triumph and tragedy on its first ascent really put Zermatt on the map, was an early AC member. But the mountain had been shrouded in cloud and its climbing routes buried under fresh snow. Only now did it emerge to offer a suitably dramatic backdrop to the evening festivities.

As the glittering proceedings unfolded, it struck me that I was one of the youngest climbers attending, and being in my mid-forties I was hardly young myself. The AC was ageing. Nor was, or is, it alone in this greying process. Many more locally based climbing clubs in Britain are similarly struggling to attract young and active members. In the past the collective approach facilitated the exchange of information for otherwise isolated individuals and allowed a pooling of meagre resources for such things as transport and accommodation. Today, car ownership, saturation coverage by guidebooks, magazines and recently the internet, coupled with increased wealth has enabled people to organise climbing trips more easily themselves. It is commonplace now for mountaineers to attempt even the most ambitious objectives in pairs or very small groups. If organisations such as the Alpine Club are to flourish they have to adapt their roles and outlook to rapidly changing circumstances. I am hardly alone in my observations, and maybe the AC is getting the message – a drive to attract younger members is already making an impact on the club's demographics.

While I was glad of a bit more downtime, I could not afford to be too relaxed about making a living. The lectures I had done so far around the UK had been reasonably attended and, so far as I could tell, had gone down well. I was keen to do more and noticed from advertisements in the outdoor press that the climber Andy Kirkpatrick was busy with presentations in theatres up and down the country. How had he made this happen? There was a simple way to find out. I gave him a call.

'A friend here in Sheffield called Becca has been helping,' he told me. I arranged to go the city and meet them both.

I did not know what to expect. Would 'Becca' be some slick agent in a fancy office? In fact Rebecca Varley turned out – in the nicest possible way – to be an ordinary and down-to-earth mother of three living in a terraced house just beyond the city centre. She and Andy had formed a fledgling company called 'Speakers From The Edge' and Becca had worked her contacts to get Andy shows in theatres. They were willing to do the same for me. I liked the idea of trying to make something work with people just starting up. We agreed to arrange a few dates to test the water.

❉ ❉ ❉ ❉

Spantik didn't attract enough clients for the trip to run, but World Expeditions did have a trekking group going up the Baltoro Glacier to K2 Base Camp and they offered me leadership of this instead. I was a little hesitant in accepting. I had never taken a trekking group before, preferring to focus on mountaineering. I agreed, but wondered what changes there might have been to the area since my last visit many years earlier? I did not want the trip to deliver an experience of paradise lost.

On the expedition to Spantik the previous year some of the clients had been surprised to find that their mobile phones worked in Islamabad. Now, just a year later, they worked in Skardu – the town deep in the Pakistan Karakoram that acts as a staging post for climbers and trekkers visiting the great mountains of Baltistan. Apparently work was already underway building masts to roll out coverage northwards into the Shigar valley on the approach to the Baltoro itself.

In five years, mobile phone ownership in Pakistan had increased from five to 60 million people. The world's media are currently fixated by the economic performances of China and India, but other developing countries, including Pakistan, have seen similar growth rates. The pace of change is remarkable, particularly in the mountainous areas, which until relatively recently were physically isolated and populated mostly by subsistence farmers eking a living from a harsh land in conditions of great hardship. Roads have been built to even the most remote villages, starting the development ball rolling.

1   The yacht *Iorana* at our drop-off at the head of the dramatic fjord – Seno Pía, 2007.
2   Andy Parkin on the slopes of Monte Iorana on a rare clear day in the Cordillera Darwin, with stunning views down Seno Pía to Isla Gordon and Isla Hoste to the south.

1 Back on the yacht after the climb with Jane and our – then young – children Maisy and Lewis.
2 Between Greenland's lengthy coastline and the icecap filling the interior lies an enormous of area of mountain wilderness. This is on Milne Land – an island at the western end of Scoresbysund, the largest fjord in the world, in 2008.

3 John Coward on the summit of one of the nine virgin peaks we climbed on Milne Land.

4 Out on the sea-ice of Scoresbysund on our return to the airstrip at Constable Point, the mountains of Milne Land behind.

5 Our first winter visit to the Cordillera was not successful in terms of completed ascents, but we had some good sport. Andy doing what he does best, climbing rime-covered overhanging ice during an attempt on Monte Francés's West Ridge in 2008.

1 Andy during our bush-whacking approach to Roncagli III on the moraine ridge at the side of the Dartmoor Glacier.
   After our failed attempt we walked easily straight back down the glacier.
2 The eastern aspects of Monte Bove, Monte Ada and the Roncagli Peaks.

3 Looking down the lengthy South-East Ridge of Spantik and the Chogo Lungma Glacier in the Pakistani Karakoram, while leading an expedition for World Expeditions in 2006.

4 At the end of the Spantik trip we crossed the Haramosh La pass with magnificent views of Haramosh peak to the south, before dropping into the Haramosh Valley lying hidden in the cloud below.

5 With a group on Peak Lenin in the Pamirs, Kyrgyzstan, 2009.

6 Life can take you to some unexpected places at times. Preparing to do my turn at Worthing Theatre – it was actually on the pier! England's south coast, 2008.

1   Paul Swanstrom departs, leaving Paul Schweizer and me in a suitably isolated spot below Mount Vancouver's
    enormous South-West Ridge, in 2009.
2   The view out of the tent porch on the first of six bitterly cold overnight camps. The steely background is the Seward
    Glacier and Mount Logan.
3   Our second full day of climbing Mount Vancouver – Mount Cook in the background.
4   Paul heading towards the bizarre rime-cloaked wall that marked the top of the ridge.

5 Paul Schweizer on the top of Good Neighbor Peak – the southernmost of Mount Vancouver's three summits, and the only one in Alaska.

6 One of the two finches that took shelter at our Mount Vancouver base camp in 2009 during the storm. Sadly, a warbler that also turned up did not survive.

7 At our base camp after the storm had cleared holding 'climber ted' in my hand. I forgot to take him on the climb, but did get this picture to show Maisy later. There were times during our ascent when I felt this mascot would have been comforting. The satellite phone – which we had deliberately left behind – could have been useful as well.

8 Our pick-up. Paul Swanstrom had primed us to be ready for this moment, but our gear is only half-packed and the tents still standing. Our laziness had life-threatening repercussions.

Day three on Mount Vancouver– a lot of space, Mount Cook and Mount Saint Elias.

Schools, health posts and electricity followed and now phones were on the way. Infrastructure that took generations of gradual build-up in the developed world had arrived over just two decades.

Welcome though this change is for the mountain people, it under-lay my nervousness about going back to the Baltoro. It is the honeypot of the Karakoram – a massive glacier that leads the awestruck traveller past some of the world's largest rock towers to the ice junction of Concordia overlooked by the greatest concentration of high moun-tains in the world, including K2. Its popularity as a destination for both climbers and trekkers is hardly surprising.

I had only been up the Baltoro once before, back in 1988. It had been a special experience shared with a group of friends and we had spent a lengthy time in a rarely visited side valley on the northern side of the glacier. I had intended to return, but the desire to tread new territory had taken me instead to other great glacial valleys, less fre-quented by tourists. While I had drifted into connoisseurship of the Karakoram's quiet and esoteric corners, processions of visitors were surely having an effect on the Baltoro?

As in all the Karakoram, places used as overnight camps on the Baltoro are near to clean water supplies, where streams or springs flow from the hillside. They are oases in what is essentially a high-altitude dessert – delicate islands of life amid a barren and rocky landscape. I wondered how they had fared with the passage of time and many feet.

In some ways I was pleasantly surprised. The beautiful oasis of Paiju, where several springs emerge from the base of enormous granite cliffs that soar to the peak of the same name, were much as I remem-bered them – shimmering ribbons of silvery green flowing down a steep, dusty hillside. Paiju is one of a few places where there are trees and one where porters historically have taken a rest day. Inevitably it has been subject to great pressure. The trees I expected to have been hacked to the ground were still standing and the streams that watered them remarkably clear and bright. Nor was there much litter. Government rules forbidding the use of firewood, which I had witnessed being regularly abused on my previous visit, had obviously been observed quite strictly. Two days further into the trek we reached Urdukas, a fan of alpine meadow above the glacier. It is the last significant area of vegetation before the route continues up the glacier itself and here too nature seemed to be surviving quiet well.

Nonetheless there were problems, chief among them being sanitation. Toilets had been built at the overnight camps and standpipes for water provided at some. The water pipes worked well, where present, but the toilets were so badly soiled they were a health hazard. Groups were digging latrine pits and erecting their own toilet tents above them, however a short walk out of any camp and a look behind bushes or boulders soon revealed where many were relieving themselves. Toilet paper blew in the wind and dried faeces was probably being carried in the airborne dust. In such circumstances it is difficult to maintain hygiene standards. Members of our group began to get intestinal infections.

Higher up the glacier we came upon squalid camps of the Pakistan Army – a legacy of the ridiculous high-altitude conflict over the Siachen Glacier. The Pakistani presence on the Baltoro is intended to counter that of the Indian Army on the Siachen Glacier to the east, beyond the disputed border. Fighting has broken out sporadically, though in this unforgiving terrain more soldiers have died from cold and altitude sickness than in battle. Thankfully, the escalation in hostilities since my first visit had subsided; but when armies fight they make a mess. Piles of unsightly debris surrounded the military camps and other installations.

In the developed world, where we have covered significant parts of our own landscapes in buildings and concrete, and where much of the remaining land is devoted to agriculture, we can get very precious about unsightly refuse. The refuse I witnessed on the Baltoro was not nice, but at the same time would be relatively easy to remove. We tend to forget the huge amount of day-to-day rubbish our own lives generate because it conveniently gets taken away, and while some is recycled significant quantities still end up being buried in holes in the ground.

At Concordia we had indifferent weather, though fortunately there were enough clearings to permit a breathtaking appreciation of the giant peaks around us. During our walk back down the glacier army helicopters seemed particularly active and we wondered why. We learned later that a survey of the upper part of the Baltoro was underway – to find the best sights for mobile telephone masts. Once constructed, the masts would provide maximum signal coverage for the Pakistani Army, tourists and no doubt within a short span of time the locals too. Like the mighty Baltoro Glacier itself, the human impact on the area was still a work in progress. As for the mountains – they towered above it all, aloof from man's tampering, as majestic as ever.

Three weeks after coming home from Pakistan I was once more on my way back to Asia. Earlier in the summer, an Icelandic climber and filmmaker, Ingvar Thorisson, had contacted me. He and a few friends wanted to climb Ama Dablam in Nepal. More interestingly, Ingvar also wanted to make a film of the climb. After my experiences in Peru I was in no rush to return to the mountains with filmmakers, but Ingvar was charming, funny and a climber, who planned to work on his own. I did not envisage his filming being particularly disruptive or intrusive and so happily agreed.

Once again life seemed to be going in circles: after returning to the Baltoro in Pakistan, now I was set to go back to Ama Dablam – a peak I had last climbed 12 years earlier. I arranged to work with my old friend Henry Todd who had employed me on my previous climbs of Ama Dablam and who had continued to operate on the mountain virtually every season since.

We all met up beneath the mountain in the village of Pangboche and after a couple of days moved up to the base camp at Mingbo. I knew that Ama Dablam had steadily become more popular but was unprepared for the sight of the extensive tented village that Mingbo had become. Recoiling at the growing numbers, Henry had found an alternative site a few hundred metres away. Here we were away from the crowds and had a little privacy, but I was well aware that we would be sharing the mountain with all these people – it was going to be busy.

Even though I had ceased working for Henry years earlier I often met him when I was in Nepal. I enjoyed his company and found it interesting to watch how his business grew and evolved. As someone who spent much of the year away from the UK, often organising one commercial expedition after another, he was more involved in the whole scene than I was and therefore a good reference point.

Once our camp was set up, I sought out Henry and found him in the mess tent connecting wires to a battery.

'You won't have seen this?' he said almost apologetically, showing me the solar panels on the tent roof, which charged the battery. Then he showed me some expensive gadgetry that gave access to the internet via a satellite link. For an hour or so each day we could join the rest of the world on broadband.

'The clients want it, particularly on the Everest trips.'

'I don't think I'll be using it,' I said. 'It's quite nice to come away from all that.' The tentacles of the online office groping ever wider did not excite me very much, though later in the trip Henry and I were able to make use of the technology for a suitably serious purpose – to follow the final stages of the Rugby World Cup.

Up on the mountain there was a carnival-like atmosphere with large numbers of people moving up and down the standard South-West Ridge. At the same time there was acute pressure for tent spaces at the cramped camps. It was a world away from the conditions I had experienced previously, when for much of the time we were alone.

More people also meant more politics. Most of the team leaders were in no hurry to get higher and seemed to spend a lot of time deliberating how to gain a tactical advantage over other groups and arguing over exactly how much rope each team should provide to be fixed on the route. Meanwhile the Sherpas working to establish a route and camps on the mountain were simply pooling resources, co-operating with each other and getting on with the job. The Sherpas' common effort made all the phoney games of logistical chess going on back at the base camp look like the irrelevance they were. I let it all pass me by without getting involved.

Our time on Ama Dablam was not without difficulties: Vidar Helgason, the other Icelandic climber, never really acclimatised properly and in the end went down and met up with his girlfriend, Hulda, who was making her way up the Khumbu; Tony Millechope, who had travelled with me from Britain, also struggled and decided against a summit attempt.

On a beautifully clear, but windy and cold day Ingvar, Pedawa – a Sherpa from Pangboche who I had known since he was a boy – and I left the high camp and climbed to the top at 6,812 metres. It was my fourth time on the summit and while it was not as aesthetically pleasing as my previous ascents, I felt a professional satisfaction at getting Ingvar and his camera to that point. He now had the raw material to make his film.

Later, back at base camp, Ingvar asked Pedawa how many times he had climbed Ama Dablam. Pedawa shrugged his shoulders dismissively and said, 'Maybe twenty-five.' Over the many years I have been working with them, I have come to recognise that the Sherpas of the Khumbu are special people on many different levels and Pedawa's reply reconfirmed not only their climbing strength and talent, but also their humility.

On arriving home I went straight into a short series of lectures around the Midlands organised by a friend – Mark Dann – from Shropshire. These were quickly followed by the appearances that Becca had set up, the handful of gigs proving sufficiently well-attended to find myself working closely with Becca planning a spring tour on a grander scale. When she emailed through the final list it ran from the beginning of March to early May. Sandwiched in the middle, I had arranged to take a small group to Greenland for two weeks.

First though, in January 2008, I had a group of paragliders to take to Aconcagua in Argentina. As with Ama Dablam, I was returning to a mountain I had not visited for several years. Rising to a height of 6,962 metres, Aconcagua is also one of the Seven Summits – the highest points on each continent. The fashion for bagging these prestige peaks had grown enormously and I expected the mountain to be busier. It certainly was, but being a less technical climb than Ama Dablam, and with roomy campsites, it did not feel so congested. It was a lovely trip with good-natured clients and the fact that they intended to fly from high on the mountain gave it an added intriguing dimension. That said, watching some of the group launch from a camp on a glacier edge at 5,800 metres was one of the most stressful moments of my life. I felt completely helpless as they took to the air and flew down the valley towards base camp or beyond, knowing full well there was nothing I could do to help them until they were on the ground again. I had taken a set of walkie-talkies for communication on the mountain, but their range and power proved inadequate and there were too few for each pilot to carry one. Happily, it all ended well, with one flier even managing to reach the roadhead and make his own way back to Mendoza, where we were all re-united several days later.

Back in Britain a steep learning curve awaited. Becca had done a thorough job setting up the lecture tour and now it was time to do my part. Andy helped to make my presentation slicker and I bought various gadgets to operate the laptop remotely, which was linked to a digital projector. There was a lot to master, at least for me. Then there was the logistics of travel and accommodation to arrange, books and posters to be ordered, plus promotion with national and local media as the start date approached.

On 3 March I began the tour by driving to Llandudno in North Wales. I would be doing a lot of driving over the coming weeks. In fact, it would come to define much of the rest of the year.

❄ ❄ ❄ ❄

'Hey, you'll never guess what?' It was Rob Gearing on the phone. I had been expecting him to call; our trip to Greenland was now only a few weeks away. He sounded very excited.

'What?' I replied, trying to match his level of enthusiasm.

'J.C. was flying that plane that crash landed at Heathrow the other week.'

I knew little about John Coward, other than he was a climbing mate of Rob's who was a British Airways pilot and that he lived in the south of France. I had heard about the crash though and had seen pictures of the prone aircraft with its escape chutes deployed and covered in foam. Fortunately, it had been a rare example of a plane crash with a happy ending: the passengers had all escaped and the pilots and crew had been lauded as heroes. Now I connected the name with the news reports. Soon we would be climbing together in Greenland.

'Bloody hell,' was all I could reply.

'I've been telling people I'm going climbing with a plane-crasher and a rope-cutter!'

Rob's tone indicated he planned to get as much mileage as possible out of the recent turn of events.

❄ ❄ ❄ ❄

My final lectures before heading off to Greenland were all on the south coast of England. It was handy that the venues were close to each other, but they were a long way from home in the north of Cumbria. We decided to tag a family holiday on to the gigs and based ourselves centrally in a caravan at a holiday park near Bognor Regis. It was a week of amusing contrasts: I'd spend the days with Jane and the children visiting attractions, playing on the beach and watching 'Rory The Tiger' shows at the camp, before driving off to speak to audiences hundreds strong. I somehow doubted that the people watching would expect I was returning to a caravan near Bognor at the end of each evening. Still, the place suited us just fine and I was pleased to see that caravans have moved on since my own childhood holidays: there were no sleepless nights spent waiting for our shelter to be blown from its mountings, nor were pots and pans covering the floor to catch drips from a leaking roof.

I woke two hours into the flight and looked out of the window to notice the stark line between open water and sea-ice far below. The horizon ahead was uniformly white and slightly forbidding, however, the lengthy Friday night in Reykjavik, only a handful of hours ago, had taken its toll. I drifted back to sleep. When I stirred again the plane was manoeuvring towards a strip of lights next to a clump of buildings in the whiteness below. It landed with a thump and came to a halt by a cutting chopped through the snow at the side of the 'runway'. We were ushered off the plane. It was windy and bitterly cold. The airport buildings at the other end of the cutting were bleak and functional. Parked outside were a clutch of skidoos and a couple of earth moving machines sitting empty, engines still running. There was also a helicopter. This was Constable Point airport – gateway to the nearby Inuit settlement of Scoresbysund and the start point for our visit to Milne Land – a mountainous island at the head of Scores-bysund Fjord. It looked like Ice Station Zebra.

In the warm terminal we changed into our mountain clothes and then met up with our skidoo team, three young Inuit men and their older leader, Magnus.

'Show me where you want to go?' Magnus asked bluntly.

I got out my map and pointed at the Korridoren Glacier, which cleaves through the island from east to west and, unusually, drains in both directions from a high point roughly in the middle. I pointed to the spot.

'Somewhere around here.'

'Huh,' Magnus replied. He was obviously a man of few words.

After picking up some freighted gear and food from one of the hangars we had a quick meal in the canteen, loaded the sleds and headed out on to the sea-ice. Flat-out driving soon dispensed with Hurry Fjord where the airport is located, however driving overland through hills to reach the main Scoresbysund was more time-consuming, even though we were following previous skidoo tracks. At the coast was a group of huts with a sled of fuel canisters parked outside one of them. Now I understood why we had been following tracks: the boys had obviously made a preparatory visit.

It was good to stop and walk off some of the cold stiffness that had set in while perched on the back of the skidoo, and to fully appreciate our surroundings. The huts were in a slightly elevated position above the crumpled ice that marked the shoreline. Beyond, sea-ice stretched to a horizon where mountains shimmered in the haze. It was a scene of stark beauty.

'Why do you come here?' one of the Inuit lads asked.

'I like mountains,' I said, pointing to the distance, 'and you have lots of them.'

He looked unimpressed with my answer.

'Why not go to the Caribbean?' I could only laugh at his impeccable logic.

A little later we reached the shoreline and paused to consult maps.

'Now we go to Milne Land,' Magnus announced after a cursory glance, driving our skidoo towards the buckled and broken ice marking the junction between land and sea. Once we were out on the flat ice he opened the throttle, the engine screamed and soon we were skimming across the snow-covered ice at 60 kilometres an hour.

After about an hour's driving I began to register the scale of our surroundings. The inlet of Scoresbysund was vast and we seemed to be making no progress towards the mountains of Milne Land to the west. Huge icebergs static in the frozen sea provided the only reference points. Now it was bitterly cold and difficult to stay warm on back of the skidoo. Time dragged.

Suddenly our whole caravan stopped briefly, then skidoos headed off in both directions, at right angles to the route we had been taking.

'Polar bear!' Magnus shouted.

The hunt soon focused on a large iceberg. The bear had circled it looking for seals in the fracture line between the berg and the sea-ice. We did the same looking for the bear. I was not disappointed when the hunt ended in failure. It would have been exciting to see a bear, but the guys all had rifles as hunting provides much of their food.

'You drive,' Magnus told me at the next stop.

At first it felt scary travelling at 60 kph over ice, and if I left the tracks of the vehicles in front it was a real struggle to coax the skidoo back into them. However, I quickly got the hang of it. Not only was driving more fun than sitting on the back, the real bonus was the heated handgrips. I soon felt the heat diffusing up my arms and warming my chilled body. We crossed two more sets of bear tracks, stopped several times to replace broken drive-belts and then near the edge of the sea-ice a skidoo engine failed. The boys did not seem phased – they simply abandoned the dead machine, saying they would pick it up on their return.

Having seemingly made little visible progress since coming on to the ice, we reached the Milne Land shore. I was amazed. Without closely consulting the map or travelling on a bearing, Magnus had hit the spot navigating by sight and intuition. Directly inland were hills and ridges of moraine left by a retreating glacier. We had come ashore at exactly the right place.

It was now early evening and getting noticeably colder. Magnus and the boys refuelled yet again and stashed an entire sled load of additional fuel next to a huge, unmistakable boulder. Skidoos are surprisingly thirsty beasts.

Locating the snout of the Korridoren Glacier proved difficult. The hills and moraine ridges were complex. On several occasions all three skidoos had to be tied together to haul single sleds up the steepest sections. Eventually we came to a shoulder and saw the glacier below. We dropped down to it and the guys turned on a final flourish of speed up to a drop-off point where a large tributary glacier flowed into the Korridoren. All around were stunning looking peaks, it was 9 p.m. and the temperature must have been about -30 °C – dangerously cold, in my judgement, and we rushed to get our gear from the sled while Magnus and the boys took a rest. One of them opened a Carlsberg and the beer froze as it foamed from the can. He tried sucking at it, then threw it into the snow.

'Let's get the tent up,' I urged Rob and John. The wind was blowing hard as we stamped down a platform in the snow. Within a few minutes the tent was ready and we hurled our mats and sleeping bags inside.

'Now we will go,' Magnus said once we had finished.

'Aren't you going to stay the night?' I asked, surprised at their change of plan.

'No. We will go to Scoresbysund.'

'Good luck.' This was their land and they were obviously adept at moving over it, but I knew if I travelled through the coming night I would end up with frostbite. With a wave they were gone and I dived into the tent to join Rob and John.

Our first night was cold and windy. Although it was only early April there was just a couple of hours of twilight. Within a few days it would be light continually, nights simply defined by lower temperatures in the early hours. We slept in until mid-morning, then in the afternoon skied up the nearby side glacier and returned to the camp.

I cooked late into the night and after dinner we stood outside the tent watching the northern lights shimmering directly above us.

❄ ❄ ❄ ❄

Over the next 11 days we climbed nine new peaks. For most of the time the sun shone low from the Arctic sky, producing exquisite light but little heat, and the ground remained firmly frozen. Some nights the wind blew hard off the icecap to the west, however there was hardly any fresh snow.

I guess we each have our own individual highlights. For me it was a three-day round trip when we moved our base camp to a high glacial plateau to the south and climbed four new peaks, two of which I named after Maisy and Lewis. It was a joy to be able to move so quickly through mountain wilderness on what was my first climbing trip conducted almost entirely on skis – typically the planks were only dispensed with for the final steeper sections to the summits. The mountains struck me as a vast, glaciated version of the Scottish Highlands; they presented little in the way of drama or danger but it took a few days to adjust to the scale and gauge what it was possible to achieve in a day. Horizontal distances were much further than they appeared and the vertical ones smaller.

A raft of regulations has to be complied with to climb in Greenland. As in the Wrangell-St Elias, the Danish authorities insist that you take a satellite phone, along with a host of other communication devices and a rifle in case of polar bear attacks. One day I made a pre-arranged call to a journalist somewhere in the Home Counties to promote an upcoming lecture. She seemed almost hysterically excited about having a conversation with a man stood on a glacier in Greenland.

'What is it like?' she demanded to know.

'It's cold and very white.' It did not sound like it was the answer she was after.

Later I spoke to Jane.

'The boiler has broken down,' she said. What I was supposed to do about it in my current location did not come to me immediately.

'I'd call the boiler man,' I suggested eventually. Sometimes remarkable pieces of technology can have disappointing results.

My lasting memories are of good company, amazing mountain vistas, superb compact summits, but more than anything silence – a silence not disturbed by calling birds, falling rocks or collapsing séracs. Even the simple sound of ice settling in the glacier below was absent. This was a frozen silence, only broken by the roar of the skidoos on their return. As the Inuits jockeyed the skidoos into camp on the prearranged date, Sean Smith jumped from the leading machine.

'Get the kettle on,' was his simple greeting.

Even though I had known Sean was coming, it was still a surreal moment. After all, what are the chances of bumping into an old friend on a glacier in Greenland 200 kilometres from the nearest human habitation? He was filming a group who were training to walk to the South Pole later in the year.

'Best go and do my job,' said Sean as he went off video camera in hand to film the party arriving. Having worked together on building sites many years earlier, we laughed at our changes of fortune.

'It's like going climbing, but with a bit more cooking,' he remarked after studying my current employment.

That evening we drank some of Sean's duty-free whisky and chatted. In the morning I was able to leave him our remaining food, which was lucky for him, the supply he had been provided with looked very lean.

The trip back to the airport was a much more casual affair than our approach, the temperature having climbed above freezing for the first time since our arrival. Out on the sea-ice seals lay next to breathing holes soaking up the sunshine, casually slipping into the water as we drew near. We had seen none on our journey into the mountains, although we knew they were present – hiding in chambers below the snow as the polar bears wandered in search of them. Now the snow-covered ice had thinned enough for them to surface. Their presence hinted at life in the ocean below and on the land still beneath the melting snow. It was this natural harvest that had brought the Inuit to this inhospitable place and that continues to sustain them.

A huge lead had opened up in the centre of the fjord and icebergs now floated free in the water. As we got closer to the airport we met hunters coming out from Scoresbysund, mostly older men with teenage boys, perhaps grandfathers teaching grandsons the Inuit way. The hunters moved gracefully, their noisy dog teams pulling perfectly crafted wooden sleds. Tufts of bleached grass poked from the rapidly melting snow. The arctic spring was finally underway.

❄ ❄ ❄ ❄

I stopped off for a couple of days in Reykjavik, helping Ingvar with some advance publicity for his film, which was still some way from completion.

'Why don't you come back for the premiere,' he urged. 'You can make a holiday out of it. Bring Jane and the kids. I'll lend you a car.'

'Sounds good,' I replied cautiously. 'When will it be?'

'I don't know. I'll keep you posted.'

❄ ❄ ❄ ❄

Back at home I completed my run of lectures, ending in Oxford on a sunny May afternoon. I did not expect to hear from Ingvar for some time. I knew from experience that nothing is certain in the world of film. We communicated periodically over the following weeks until finally he was ready. Jane and I booked flights and arrived in Reykjavik still not knowing exactly what to expect. Ingvar was very busy, rushing from one meeting to another, constantly on his mobile phone. In the small world he was operating in, it seemed like people did not sleep during the light summer months. Often, Ingvar would leave a bar or his apartment in the early hours of the morning to go and work. It was all a bit manic and I was relieved when he finally set a date for the film premiere and we were able to leave Reykjavik for the countryside. We left hastily and on the outskirts of the city stopped at a bank to get some money before heading into the wilds. The cash machine would not pay out. We tried the next bank we passed, with the same result. When we failed to get money in the town of Selfoss we began to get concerned.

'Maybe the bank has stopped our cards,' I suggested to Jane. It had happened before. One time after I returned from India I was left stranded at a supermarket checkout with a trolley full of groceries after my card payment was refused. When I telephoned the bank to see what the problem was the operative explained that someone had been using the card in India and that they had blocked it. They spoke like they had just thwarted some major international fraud. When I revealed I had been using the card myself they were a little more humble.

'Shall I give them a call?' Jane asked.

'You'd better I think.'

The call from Jane's mobile was protracted and, more disturbingly, because she was phoning the UK, horribly expensive.

'I'm in Iceland,' she pleaded at one point.

'What did they say,' I asked when the call was finally over.

'The woman thought I was in the store Iceland. She was telling me to go to the nearest cash-point and get some money out. Anyway, she assured me our cards are still working, so we'll be able to use them to pay for things.'

'It would have been nice to have some cash though,' I commented. 'The machines must be empty or unable to dispense cash for some reason.'

Later we would hear rumours about Romanian gangsters targeting the ATMs as the reason for the machines' meanness with money. It seemed strange to me, but I had already noticed how Icelanders did not use cash. This made for frustrating queues in shops as people paid with cards for minor items such as newspapers. We were obviously going to have to adopt the same approach.

For the next few days we based ourselves in a mountaineering club hut near Skaftafell in the south-east of the country and explored a rugged coastline backed by dramatic mountains and glaciers. On the way back to Reykjavik we took up an invitation to stay with Vidar and Hulda in the fishing village of Stokkseyri. It was a lovely reunion, recalling our days together on Ama Dablam, before returning to the capital to share Ingvar's premiere with the great and the good of the Icelandic film world. In the end, after all the sleepless nights, he had made an entertaining film laced with dry humour, with him as the suitably mad central character.

To round off our holiday we went to stay with Tolli, a successful artist, in his stylish lakeside house in the hills north of the city. It was a charming place and just a few steps out of the patio doors took you to the water's edge, where you could cast a line and fish for trout.

The Icelanders we met were all proud of their country's achievements, but they were also realists and sensed that the unprecedented boom they had been enjoying was over. 'There is a time of some unemployment coming', Vidar had told me.

Later that summer the Icelandic banks ran out of money completely and the tiny country became the first state casualty of a global banking crisis.

NINE

It's Like Pantomime

'It's incredible,' said Luis, looking at the TV and shaking his head angrily. A news channel headlined a multi-billion-dollar bid by the United States government to boost the country's faltering economy. Luis was incensed – the amounts of money to fund the stimulus package defied comprehension.

'In Argentina this sort of thing happens every few years and the government does nothing.'

I could understand his anger. An economic crisis was unfolding in the developed world. Reckless lending by banks and other institutions had pushed up property prices for far too long and now the bubble had burst. The response, it seemed, was to spend yet more borrowed money.

Later, Luis appeared with a shoebox.

'This is all the different Argentine money in my life,' he said, opening the lid. Inside were lots of different notes of varying denominations. 'This is the first one. Ten thousand of these became one of these.' He pulled another note from the box. 'I think a hundred thousand of these became one of these, but I cannot remember. My grandmother remembered exactly.'

It was a sobering collection that only reinforced what I had known for a long time: to be born in England is a fortunate start in life.

In the company of Andy Parkin I was back in Ushuaia on unfinished business. Thwarted in January 2007 by the absence of ice on the south face of Monte Francés, this time we had returned at the end of the southern winter; it was September and we were hoping the face would now be holding enough snow and ice for us to attempt the climb. We had also been told that the weather at this time was generally more stable and less windy than in the summer months. As usual, Luis and Carolina were being the perfect hosts and had given us the run of their *ranchito* – a small cabin built in the garden of their family home – while we organised ourselves in the city.

Not for the first time, I had had difficulty finding a yacht to take us to the mountains. The problem was that many of the charter boats and nearly all of the operators left Tierra del Fuego over the winter for warmer places further north. Then just a few weeks earlier I had learned that Luis planned to climb Monte Francés with his friend Wolf Kloss, a German who lived in Ushuaia and who owned two yachts. Wolf was happy to take us along on the *Santa Maria Australis* to Caleta Olla, however the detail of his itinerary remained unclear. We met over dinner. Wolf was an amiable man with a lively sense of humour, but he was also quite busy readying his boats for the coming summer charter season.

'I can leave on Friday but I must be back here by the following Friday,' he said.

'That gives us four day's climbing,' I said, knowing we had to allow for at least four days of sailing.

'It might be enough,' Andy commented.

'We'll need to be lucky,' I replied, 'and we'll need to see if we can sort some transport out for the rest of the trip.' Yachts making excursions in the channels from Puerto Williams must return with the full complement of crew they left with; this meant we could not be dropped at Caleta Olla even if we could somehow organise a pick up.

'You can try in Williams,' Wolf suggested.

Denis Chevallay was a Swiss living in Puerto Williams and a friend of Wolf's; he worked as a trekking guide and local historian. Though he moved among the tight-knit yachting community, we had not met before. Williams is such a small place we must have walked past each other on the yacht club pier or in the street on many occasions. Arriving in the port, we called on Denis and over dinner Andy and I told him of our transport dilemmas.

Denis offered to help. Despite not being a climber, or having even spent much time in the Cordillera Darwin, it turned out he was an enthusiast for the range and had amassed an incredible collection of books, magazines and reports about these little-known mountains. For Andy and I it was a great resource to stumble upon, and a place where we would both lose many happy hours on subsequent visits. Denis may, in fact, have the best collection of Cordillera Darwin-related material in the world.

We sailed from Puerto Williams next morning, still not knowing what would follow the outing to Monte Francés – not that it seemed to matter much as we motored west along the Beagle Channel on a calm and almost cloudless day. Snow lay down to the treeline and the forest, which had been a forbidding dark green in the summer, was now almost black. We reached Caleta Olla in the early evening, anchored the yacht and ran lines to the shore just as it was starting to get dark.

Luis and Wolf were up early and busy sorting gear when I came out from our cabin. They were in a hurry, intent on getting the most from their precious days away from work and families. We organised ourselves more slowly and then took Luis and Wolf ashore.

'Remember – you need to be back by Wednesday night,' Wolf said as they set off along the gravel beach towards the mountain.

A little later it was our turn; we followed the familiar track off the shoreline, through the fringing strip of forest and on to the peat bog beyond.

'It's frozen,' I said to Andy after the first few steps, barely able to conceal my delight. In the summer months the bog was very wet and walking over it was slow and laborious. It was a joy to move unhindered over the hard surface, though strange to be following a familiar route under such different conditions. Most of the trees were bare of leaves, but now I could appreciate the evergreen beech; it looked almost identical to its deciduous namesake in summer. The dense undergrowth had died back and even the grasses were burnt brown by the frost. Only the intricate beauty of the place remained.

We soon left the trail the others had made and followed the usual path up past my summer camp to rock slabs by a waterfall that drains a small glacial lake. We were making good progress thanks to the frozen bogs and a covering of firm snow over the tussocky ground. The lake was frozen. What in summer is a time-consuming detour up through dense forest to gain a moraine ridge would not be necessary. We simply walked straight across the ice in a few minutes. Above, the rocky slabs and waterfalls were hidden, banked out in snow. We zig-zagged up hard névé to reach the Francés Glacier and gradually approached the South Face. The sight was not encouraging. The coating of rime on the rock we had seen from far below, was just that – a thin veneer – and we needed more.

'The face isn't holding any ice,' I said, as we paused for a rest.

'I've noticed,' Andy replied wearily. 'Let's have a look further along.'

We traversed westwards but there was no improvement.

'We can't force a line up this in this condition. We're going to have to do something different.'

'But what?' Andy asked.

'We could always go and do Italia, I don't think it's had a second ascent,' I pointed west towards a peak first climbed way back in 1937.

'No. I want to do something harder than that. What about this ridge on Francés?'

I looked up to where the top of the South Face formed a ridge descending westwards. I had never really paid much attention to it before, but it certainly looked interesting and led to some imposing towers near the summit.

'Yeah, lets give it a go.' It didn't require much deliberation; the day was coming to an end and we were on a tight schedule.

We continued traversing, looking for a weakness that would enable us to climb up on to the ridge; eventually as we rounded a shoulder we saw a snow slope leading up to a col.

'Let's see if we can dig a snow hole in that bergschrund,' Andy said, waving at a fracture crossing the slope. The crack line had an over-hanging lip below which we soon excavated a small shelf. Light cloud that had drifted by during the day was clearing now and radiant star-light was beginning to pierce the sky. It was dark by the time we slid into our icy shelter.

It was not a good night. The hastily dug chamber was not large enough to sit up in and was also narrow, forcing us to lie end-to-end. Even in such tight working conditions, Andy, as ever, got the stove going and managed to produce drinks and hot food, which he care-fully handed to me. The platform sloped down and with little room to manoeuvre I could not get comfortable. I dozed the night away and as the grey light of dawn filtered inside noticed that a fracture line had formed in the floor beside me. The snow and ice platform we had slept on was dropping into the crevasse that lay beneath. It was a sobering start to the day.

Despite the cold, it was a relief to escape the shelter and begin. The slope steepened as we neared the ridge, our crampons biting on hard ice under a thin coating of snow. At the col a huge, wind-sculpt-ed bank of snow formed a wall on its northern side. I led up out of the basin, climbing where steep powder snow met the granite of a pin-nacle on the ridge. Suddenly there was sunshine and a horizon. It was a beautiful winter's day on the ridge, out of the long shadow cast on the south side of the mountain, though the sun lent little warmth.

I stopped, belayed and prepared to bring Andy up to join me. He climbed slowly, dragging his left leg through the deeper snow.

'Does your leg hurt?' I asked, the somewhat belated thought immediately embarrassing me. He seemed so accepting of his old wounds and handicaps that I never felt the need to probe.

'No. It's just stiff.'

I was selfishly relieved that the answer was not 'yes', as then I would have felt guilty for not having thought to ask years earlier. Still, it was reassuring to hear he was not in permanent pain.

Andy continued easily above and then I swung up a steep ramp line of rock and ice to reach the crest of the ridge. Above, gentle waves of rime-covered rock led to a frightening looking pillar near the top. The features were sublimely beautiful, but I was in no doubt that there was difficulty ahead.

'Good lead that,' Andy said, joining me at the stance and looking happy to be on steeper ground. We weaved our way higher following the line of least resistance through increasingly large rime-encrusted towers. The day was slipping by, and so were the easy options. I belayed beneath a corner splitting a huge tower, glad that it was Andy's lead. After studying the obstacle ahead, Andy took off his rucksack, clipped it to my belay, carefully racked the climbing gear on his harness and then moved up above me.

The climbing was straightforward for a short way, Andy pausing to put in an ice screw as the ground steepened. Soon after, he was flailing to remove feathery rime and expose the hard ice that lay beneath. As icy debris rained down I cowered beneath my helmet, while trying to snatch glimpses of what was going on.

Andy slowly gained height. I could tell from his body position that the ground had become overhanging. At times his feet slipped from the hard ice and he was left hanging from his axes. I could barely believe what I was seeing: here was a 54-year-old man, who would easily qualify for disability benefit and a car sticker if he lived in the

UK, wrestling his body up overhanging ice. It was a privilege to guard his ropes and watch.

There were moments when I thought Andy was going to fall; somehow though he hung on, carefully clearing away the rime before moving up. It was a Herculean effort and took a long time. Eventually he disappeared from sight. Now the wind was rising and I was beginning to get cold.

'Safe,' came the cry I had been waiting for.

A little later Andy reappeared over the top of the tower.

'Don't even try to climb it, just jug it,' he shouted down. 'I'll haul my rucksack.' Then he moved back out of sight over the crest.

I found the pitch difficult enough jumaring up the rope while freeing Andy's rucksack. It continually snagged in the trench created where Andy had chopped away the rime. By the time I joined him on the tower, the wind was blowing hard and it was dangerously cold. Next was an undulating section of ridge below a final tower. We moved along to the flattest bit of the ridge and frantically hacked out a shelf for a bivouac. It was in an incredibly exposed position and we quickly added a small snow-block wall to the windward side of the platform before getting into our sleeping bags. After dark the wind increased to a worrying intensity and it began to snow. The stove was not functioning well in the maelstrom and it took tireless coaxing by Andy to produce drinks and a meal. Then we settled down to a long, cold night. At times, I found the wind frightening.

By dawn the wind had dropped some, but we were in cloud and it was spitting snow.

'What shall we do?' I asked Andy.

'It only looks like one hard pitch.'

I felt uncertain. If we could get above the difficulty quickly, going up and over the top might be the best approach; but I knew the higher slopes of Francés were complex and that finding the way down the other side of the mountain in poor visibility would be difficult.

'I'll give it a go,' I said eventually.

We packed up and readied ourselves for the day. I walked down and across a narrow col to the final tower. A narrowing tongue of ice led up the buttress. The ice was good at first but it got thinner, until there was just rime on rock. I searched for cracks, probing tentatively with my axes. Without cracks I could neither get purchase for the axes nor place gear to protect myself against a slip. There was nothing. I was going to have to make a long series of difficult moves up this just-off-vertical ground, hoping it would get better. There was every prospect of a large and nasty fall should I fail. My confidence crumbled.

'I don't like the look of it,' I shouted to Andy. 'Let's go down.'

'Okay,' he replied sympathetically, without a hint of disappointment.

We made a series of abseils back to the glacier and started the long trudge down.

It was many hours before we reached the lake. Then it was on through the forest. We reached the beach at dusk and shouted to the yacht. Luis came on deck.

'Did you summit?' he asked, rowing towards us in the dinghy.

'No,' I replied. 'You?'

'Yes, yesterday.'

'Congratulations. The sixth ascent I believe.'

❄ ❄ ❄ ❄

Luis and Wolf spent one night in Puerto Williams before leaving early for Ushuaia. Andy and I settled into a hostel on the seafront and then went to see Denis.

'I think your best option is to go to Yendegaia,' he told us. 'I will call the ferry company in Punta Arenas.'

We scanned Denis's book collection while he made the call.

'All done,' he announced proudly, putting down the phone. 'It leaves on Saturday at 6.30 in the morning.' That gave us two lazy days in Williams, trawling through Denis's Cordillera Darwin library and topping up a few supplies from the supermarket. We agreed that once we got to the estancia we would move up to a camp below the Stoppani Glacier and concentrate our activities on the eastern side of the three Roncagli peaks, only one of which had been climbed.

Early on Saturday morning we relayed our bags down to the jetty. The rusty roll-on, roll-off ferry was similar to ones that hop between Scottish islands. It had even been built in Glasgow. There were three truck trailers of *centolla* on the boat with their refrigeration units running, a couple of cars and a handful of passengers making the daylong passage to Punta Arenas. We parked ourselves inside and promptly went back to sleep.

By mid-afternoon the ferry was making its way slowly down the Bahia Yendegaia, heading towards the clump of white huts that mark the estancia. The bow was lowered on a rocky bluff to the side of the buildings and we carted our bags ashore. We stood and waved at the departing craft.

'No!' Andy suddenly screamed.

'What is it?'

'I've left my small rucksack in the cabin on the ferry.'

'Shit!' Andy's passport, money and other valuables were now on their way to Punta Arenas. Then I remembered the satellite phone. 'I'll call Denis.' Hopefully our friend would be able to speak to the ferry company and retrieve the bag.

Denis listened carefully.

'Where is the ferry now? Is it past Dos de Mayo?'

I could see on the other side of the bay the isolated Chilean police post that guards the border with Argentina.

'No,' I replied.

'I'll call them then. They will be able to radio the ferry and get it dropped off there.'

We watched the ferry stop at Dos de Mayo and then carried our bags over to the estancia. There was no one at home. We sat on the veranda and gazed down the fjord. It was just as beautiful as I remembered.

Later we heard dogs barking as Jose, his girlfriend Annamie and a Dutch couple arrived on horseback. They dismounted at the old shearing shed and we walked over to meet them. It was fantastic to see Jose after so many years and to meet Annamie for the first time. The Dutch couple – Peter and Paula – were staying on a yacht moored nearby.

That evening we ate in Jose's cabin and shared stories from the past and present. Jose was happy to take us into the mountains and when we told him about Andy's rucksack he made a radio call to Dos de Mayo and confirmed that the sack had indeed been dropped there. His friend Oscar would bring it on his fishing boat. We pitched our tents overlooking the shore and went to sleep happy, knowing everything was back on track.

The following day we packed our bags and in the afternoon Oscar arrived with the rucksack. Oscar was also known as 'GPS' – a tongue-in-cheek name for it was a navigational aid he managed well enough without. He turned out to be quite a character and he and Jose drank the day away.

Jose was subdued in the morning; nonetheless he was up early saddling the horses. Before we left Peter and Paula kindly offered to take us back to Williams and on to Ushuaia on their yacht, *Pacific Blue*. This neatly solved our transport shortfall for the end of the trip.

It was a long ride to the camp – dubbed *Casa Gringo* – below the snout of the Stoppani Glacier. At a little grassy clearing marking the boundary between frozen bog and forest we ate lunch with Jose and Annamie then bid farewell. We had eight days before they would return with the horses.

Rain the first night flooded the camp with meltwater. In the morning we solemnly moved our tents to higher ground and then sat out a day of more heavy rain. Andy kept himself busy building a small wooden shelter while I read in my tent, only venturing out to fire up the stove to make drinks and meals.

The weather brightened the next day and after a windy, showery morning we decided to carry a load into the mountains. Moraine ridges along the side of the Stoppani Glacier led to its junction with a valley leading westwards to the Dartmoor Glacier. After crossing a large flat area – given the name the Guanaco Flats by a previous expedition – below the moraine ridges at the snout of the glacier, we followed another ridge for a while before dropping into the ablation valley at its side. It was hard work. Dense forest on the moraine ridge crest was difficult to push through and there was deep snow in the ablation valley. We made a stash near some beaver dams and returned to *Casa Gringo* for nightfall.

The following day we regained our stash by early afternoon and continued up the valley, sometimes in the forest and sometimes walking along the moraine ridge. There was no continuous path. Eventually we reached a small clearing known as Foxes Glade. Beyond this point the ablation valley blanked out, forcing us to descend the moraine on to the glacier. A faint valley on its southern edge led on up to a grassy platform that offered a good spot to camp. Here we spent the remaining daylight examining the faces above and discussed various climbing options into the night.

Out on the glacier the next morning, as we approached the Roncagli peaks, it became increasingly obvious that the most sensible and least dangerous route was up snow slopes and a face on the north side of the east ridge of Roncagli III. The slopes led up to the ridge proper, which we hoped to follow to a col between Monte Ada and Roncagli III, giving access to the peak's south ridge.

Rapid progress up the initial snow slopes was followed by two pitches of difficult mixed climbing. Then we wallowed up deep, sugary snow lying over rock to reach the ridge. It was demoralising to discover that we could have reached the same spot by using our previous approach line to Monte Ada, followed by a gentle climb up from the Bove Glacier. Luckily, we found a bergschrund that we enlarged into a snow cave. The night passed cold with spindrift blowing in through the entrance. By the morning we were stormbound.

It was a miserable day. We kept warm by enlarging the cave and trying to seal the entrance with blocks of snow. Even so, there was no disguising the fact that we were living inside a refrigerator. The snowfall intensified into our second night, but by morning the storm was blowing itself out.

We dug our way out of the cave and tried to dry our sleeping bags; despite the sunshine it was cold in the breeze. We started to move up the ridge again. Snow conditions were awful. I managed to thrash my way up to a crevasse fracture line, then as I tried to pull over the lip there was a huge boom as it broke, dumping me inside the crevasse. The fall, although short, really spooked me. I climbed out trembling.

'I'm going down,' I told Andy, who was moving to my right to try and find another way over the obstacle.

'We can get up over here,' he countered.

'No, I've had enough.'

The summit was a long way off and the terrain looked complex, our food was low and I felt that to continue would simply invite an epic. My mind was made up. Silently I walked back down the slope to the bivouac and Andy followed. We abseiled the face we had climbed up two days earlier and walked down to where we had left the tent.

Next morning I walked easily back down the glacier, off its snout and through a river valley that cut down through the moraine ridge to Guanaco Flats immediately below me, cursing at the time we wasted going up and down the ablation valley and moraine ridge at the glacier's side. I remembered how Carolina had described her and Luis's first visit here.

'We did not understand the geography,' she'd said, laughing at their naivety.

Sometimes everything seems to click and you move efficiently, a complex three-dimensional picture of the landscape forming perfectly in your mind. At other times the skill deserts you. On this occasion, the geography of the place had got the better of us too.

❄ ❄ ❄ ❄

'It must be difficult for you, not finishing a climb?' Luis asked, when we were back in Ushuaia.

'Not really,' I replied half-heartedly. 'I think we've learnt a lot and we can always come back and try again.'

However, the more I thought about it, the more disappointing it was. The uncertainty around transport had not helped us make clear plans and we had ended up tackling two separate objectives. On previous visits bad weather had cleared at crucial moments and bolstered our confidence to continue. This time the opposite had occurred, although the weather had not developed into the full-blown storm I feared. As is often the case in mountains, the real reasons for failure were more psychological. As life got ever more complicated I was finding it more difficult to compartmentalise, and the satellite phone meant that the world at home now came into the mountains with me. Another large speaking tour was organised for when I returned and my thoughts had drifted towards that, the children and home. I worked best in the mountains when my mind was clear. Then I could concentrate and connect with the terrain; that had not been happening on this occasion.

Whatever the exact cause, I had lacked the focus and drive needed for tackling such committing objectives successfully. It was a focus and drive that never seemed to desert Andy and I could not help but feel I had let him down. I went home, while he stayed, still keen to climb on his own in the mountains behind Ushuaia.

I knew the routine and over time had become comfortable with public speaking. In some ways it was easier talking to bigger audiences in theatres or large auditoriums. They were more impersonal and the people more distant than in intimate venues. The crowds also responded better and it is always heartening to hear people laughing, sighing and gasping at the right moments. Talking was the easy bit. The harder work lay in sorting out the logistics of travel and accommodation, getting together all the books, posters, screen, computer and a whole raft of gadgets and cables, ferrying them from one place to another, then setting everything up only to pack it all away again a few hours later. On top that was the constant driving – a lot of it done late at night. I took a roadie to help. It was nice to have someone to help carry everything, sell books and posters, share the driving, to talk to and, most importantly, drink beer with at the end of each evening. Like mountaineering expeditions, the tours were pleasantly mad.

The world of theatres is one that I landed in by chance and I found it all a bit odd. Theatre managers seemed to think I would want to spend most of my time cowering backstage in a dressing room. I preferred to be out and about meeting people and helping to set-up. I barely used them.

'Do you want to see your dressing room?' people would ask.

'No thanks,' I'd say. 'I only have to change my shirt and put on a pair of shoes.' I could do this at my car, which I usually managed to park at the stage door. At Birmingham City Hall the dressing room was big enough for an entire orchestra and had a white grand piano inside – sadly wasted on me. I did take a shower though, simply because they looked so swish.

One evening in Bedford, returning to our hotel for the night, I found the car park full. It was permit-only parking in the streets nearby – so that was out too. Then I noticed a small area between two cars with yellow hatching on the tarmac, left to provide access to a path leading to the hotel. I managed to squeeze my car into the gap, but it was so tight I had to exit through the boot. When I went back in the morning someone had left a note behind one of my windscreen wipers. 'You are an arsehole,' it read. A fair point maybe, but under the circumstances I had little option.

Becca had done a good job organising venues reasonably close together, but there were exceptions that meant insane drives between appearances on consecutive nights. Epsom on the outskirts of London to Stirling in Scotland was brutal, as was Barnstaple in Devon to Norwich. Maidstone in Kent to South Shields was not much fun either. In Swansea we were lost somewhere close to the theatre until we noticed a neon sign on top of the building flashing my name; a heckler in Leamington Spa was forcefully told to shut up by people sitting nearby; and someone ran into the back of my car on a wet evening in Inverness. Then there was a fantastic evening driving back from Arbroath, near Dundee, to stay with a friend in Edinburgh. We decided to go cross-country and went over the Tay Bridge to get on to the Neuk of Fife. Joe Pester clutched his TomTom GPS and like a co-driver in a rally called out the direction and severity of the bends ahead as I drove flat-out through the night. Some places were just plain out-of-the-way: in Lowestoft on England's east coast the locals joked that the nearest motorway was in Holland. The tour ended in Norwich and a memorable night out before driving wearily back to Cumbria.

Late that year, I managed to attract a group of clients for Monte Francés, but with another block of lecture dates looming the trip needed to begin in early January. The flight left Manchester before breakfast on New Year's Day. Life has treated me very kindly, but seeing in the New Year in a hotel at Manchester Airport does not rate as one of the highlights.

We had a few drinks and a meal in the surprisingly busy hotel bar and then took the children to bed.

'This has got to be the saddest New Year ever,' I told Jane.

I cannot even remember if we stayed up until midnight.

At five in the morning I got up, said my goodbyes to Jane, kissed our sleeping children, then dragged my bags from the room and went to the terminal to catch the first shuttle flight to Heathrow. The entire day would be spent in airports and on planes.

Ushuaia felt very familiar: it was only three months since I'd left. I met up with Luis, gave him some tents I had brought from England, and asked if he had been busy.

'Yes, I have been to do a rescue in the Dientes.'

Later, Luis showed me some photos he had taken and told me the story. A group of Israelis had gone trekking in the Dientes de Navarino – a range of peaks behind Puerto Williams – and had become lost as cloud and snow enveloped them. They had a satellite phone with them and called for help. Israeli diplomats in Santiago and Buenos Aires moved with remarkable speed. There is normally only a single helicopter on Tierra del Fuego, based in the Argentine part of the island at Rio Grande and used exclusively by an oil company. The Israelis somehow secured its use and learned of Luis's guiding company.

Luis received a telephone call telling him that his services were required and that a helicopter was waiting for him in Puerto Williams. He hastily arranged for another guide to accompany him, got some gear together and chartered a light aircraft to fly across the Beagle Channel.

In Puerto Williams they transferred to the waiting helicopter and flew up into the hills behind the town. They had a GPS location fix from the phone but the helicopter landed short, just below the cloud base. Luis and his colleague walked up the hillside through the mist for 20 minutes and found the 'lost' travellers. The trekkers were no more than a few hours walk from the town. They had simply sat in their tent and waited to be rescued.

'It's incredible,' Luis said in disbelief as he finished the story.

I doubted the British government would have been quite so helpful. But why should they be? I had always come to places like Tierra del Fuego expecting to take responsibility for myself and for my companions, and made provision accordingly. A big part of the area's attraction is its remoteness. There is no system in place for rescuing people from the mountains. I have always operated on the understanding that you have to deal with any incidents yourself. Now it seemed that some people who were not in great danger and had not even tried to help themselves felt they could abdicate all responsibility simply because they had a satellite phone. The device had encouraged a laziness of both thought and action.

Still, it had been a profitable start to the season for Luis.

We climbed Monte Francés within a week of arriving at Caleta Olla, made a rain-thwarted attempt on Monte Italia and dropped in on Jose and Annamie at Yendegaia before heading back to Ushuaia. It was a happy and successful trip and time passed quickly. All too soon I was back at home in the depths of an English winter.

❄ ❄ ❄ ❄

The gigs started again in a snowy Southend. My overriding memory of all the time on the road is of the many towns across England I ended up visiting. I have travelled quite widely around the UK over the years, mostly through climbing but also for work, but these were places I would have otherwise overlooked. I am grateful for having had the chance to visit so many unsung towns and cities. Most were very pleasant; some were not. In Stoke-on-Trent I spoke in a beautifully refurbished theatre adjoining the town hall, but the surrounding area – what should have been the city centre – was simply a wasteland. In the early 1980s a lot of Britain's manufacturing and heavy industry went to the wall, leaving large areas of dereliction in many cities. Over time much of this has been redeveloped. However, I found it shocking to discover places where this had simply not happened.

Aberdare, in the South Wales valleys, was not derelict but many of the shops and pubs in what once was a thriving mining town were boarded up. As always though, the people were warm and friendly.

'You're the only turn that I can remember helping to set up,' one of the technical assistants commented.

Nearing the end of the tour I played to a full house in Loughborough. It seemed fitting: Loughborough is the nearest town to Charnwood Forest, an area of hills and small outcrops where I spent many happy days honing my rock climbing skills while a teenager growing up in a village in south Leicestershire.

The final nights in Dunstable and Broxbourne, north of London, were something of an anti-climax; yet these two Home Counties towns seemed suitably anonymous places for it all to grind to a halt. Theatreland was an odd, and sometimes rewarding, world that I was pleased to have tasted, but it was not a world I was truly part of – just passing through. Now it was time to go home.

'It's like pantomime,' I told Jane after my performance in a theatre on the pier at Worthing on England's south coast.

And it had been.

TEN

I'll Never Do Anything Better

'Oh, hi Simon.' It was Paul Schweizer on the phone. 'We have more problems I'm afraid,' he continued in his slow, deliberate San Diegan drawl.

After our success on Mount Alverstone in 2005 Paul and I had kept in touch irregularly, hoping to do another trip together. We thought we had an objective. For the whole of the Alverstone climb we had looked across at Mount Hubbard and the compelling line of its West Ridge had lodged in our minds. Now, after four years crowded with commitments, we had at last found time for a return visit to the mountains of the Alaska-Yukon border.

My own involvement with the project to this stage had amounted to applying for a Mount Everest Foundation grant and booking flights to Whitehorse. Paul had focused on researching the route and already there had been a setback. The West Ridge of Hubbard had already been climbed – by a Harvard University group in the 1970s. However, following further research and a tip-off by the Wrangell activist Jack Tackle, Paul had quickly come up with a stunning alternative.

Good Neighbor Peak is the southernmost summit of Mount Vancouver, another of the peaks we had surveyed from Alverstone, and if anything the line of its huge South-West Ridge looked even better than that on Hubbard. Amazingly it had not been climbed or attempted before, or so we thought. With an objective finalised, Paul had turned to in-country logistics. We expected few problems: we would simply follow the same routine as on our first visit.

'Andy can't fly us in,' Paul said, sounding irritated.

'You what?' I was stunned.

'Neither can anyone else from the Canadian side of the border. We'll have to fly in from Alaska.'

Paul detailed the game of logistical chess in which he had become embroiled. Since our previous visit some misinformed bureaucrats had decided to clamp down on bush pilots over-flying the Alaska-Yukon border. The United States had made the first move, introducing regulations out of their paranoid sense of security, and the Canadians had simply reciprocated. To climb our route we needed to be dropped off by ski-plane in a glacier basin to the south of the peak, therefore nominally in Alaska. We assumed this would be no problem as Andy had dropped us on the Alaskan side of the border before. Now it was impossible. The nearest place we could fly in from within Alaska was Yakutat. However, we could not change our international flights to Whitehorse without prohibitive cost, nor could we access Yakutat overland from Canada as there are no roads into the place. Our only option was to cross the land border from Whitehorse in the Yukon to Skagway on the Alaskan coast, cross a fjord and fly in from a town called Haines. The cost of the extra ground transport and the lengthy (very expensive) flight from Haines hurt. We had become unwitting victims of the US 'War on Terror'.

❄ ❄ ❄ ❄

'Simon. Wake up. We've got to go,' Paul was shaking me. 'We need to go and catch the flight to Whitehorse.'

'All right,' I replied grumpily, trying to re-adjust to the surroundings. We were in a restaurant-cum-bar in Vancouver airport, and had been for most of the day.

'They were going to ask you to leave,' Paul said smiling. 'Said you were drunk.'

'Hardly,' I replied, though we had downed a few beers. 'It's the middle of the night for us.'

'Yes, I told them you were tired. It seemed to do the trick.'

By the time we arrived at Whitehorse it was the middle of the Yukon night and I felt like we had been travelling for days. Paul had booked a taxi in advance. It was a good call as there was none waiting speculatively to meet the flight. The driver was the same man who had ferried us around on our first trip. He dropped us at a guesthouse in town and arranged to pick us up to do the shopping the following morning.

In a frantic day we amassed food and supplies, packed and spoke to the driver in Skagway who would come to collect us. Driver Dave arrived the next morning, a huge man, with a larger-than-life character and a vehicle to match. We carried our now considerable pile of food and gear from the veranda of the guesthouse and stowed it in Dave's wagon. Even then there was room for plenty more. Despite all my visits to US, the size of vehicle that most Americans drive still had the power to shock me.

The Yukon has a total population of 35,000, of whom 26,000 live in Whitehorse, its capital. It follows that the rest of this vast territory is largely empty. The road to Skagway was no exception. We passed a few native American settlements and road ends that led to others, but mostly it was just trees, snow and frozen lakes. This was big, raw country and I gazed out of the bus window mesmerised, trying to let Driver Dave's running commentary drift over my consciousness. Midway through the journey we began to gain height. After completing our exit from Canada at a border post we headed up into the mountains. At the high point of the road was a simple wooden sign that said 'Welcome to Alaska'.

We dropped down more steeply on the seaward side of the pass, did the formalities at the US border post, then wound our way down into Skagway – a pretty little town at the head of the Taiya Inlet. Paul had arranged for a pilot to fly us into the mountains from Haines and Dave kindly called Paul Swanstrom on his mobile.

'He's coming to get you guys.'

'Good service,' chuckled Paul.

This was a bonus, as we had reckoned on taking a ferry on to Haines. Dave drove us to the terminal buildings of the small airport and after only a few minutes' wait a light aircraft appeared coming up the fjord. The red Bush Hawk over-flew the airstrip, did a tight turn further inland and landed neatly on the runway. After taxiing to the apron where we were waiting, Swanstrom killed the engine, climbed out of the cockpit and strolled over to meet us.

'Looks like you guys got lucky,' he said shaking my hand. 'The forecast is good for the next few days.'

'Will we fly into the mountains today?'

'Tomorrow looks better, but we can have a look at the latest satellite pictures back in Haines.'

We transferred everything into the plane, said goodbye to Dave and were soon flying down the Taiya Inlet a few hundred metres above the water, chatting to pilot Paul through the headphones. As we flew over Haines, he turned to approach the airstrip, tucked away in a river valley outside the town. Another tighter turn and we landed gently and stopped outside a smart new hangar. Paul went inside and shortly afterwards the main door opened to reveal a workshop along one side and two aircraft to the rear. Then he started a small machine that looked like a lawnmower and towed his plane inside. This was obviously a highly organised, cash-rich operation.

'You can leave your stuff there,' Paul said, pointing to the side of the hangar. The place was so immaculate that I was conscious of our pile of gear making it look messy. It was time for another mammoth packing session.

Later, as Paul drove us into town, he told us how he became a pilot. For many years he had worked as a rafting guide, then one day while struggling to drag a raft across a series of gravel beds he decided he'd had enough. Guiding had brought him into contact with bush pilots who flew people in and out of the more remote rafting locations; that was the way for him. Now in spring Paul flies skiers and climbers into the mountains; his busiest time, though, is summer when cruise liners call into Skagway during voyages up and down the Alaskan coast and he takes passengers on scenic flights. Judging by his set-up it is a profitable business.

In his downtown office Paul checked the weather and confirmed we would fly the following day. We paid for our flights and then went to find somewhere to spend the night. It was not a long search, the tourist season had not yet begun and only the Seward Hostel was open.

In the afternoon we wandered around Haines, weak spring sunshine lending warmth to the town's picturesque setting between a harbour of fishing boats and enclosing mountains. Later we ate the finest wild salmon steaks before hitting the Fogcutter Bar – a no-nonsense establishment we took to immediately. Numerous TV screens showed baseball and American football for the early part of the evening before switching to programmes that featured men in camouflage jackets shooting various large Alaskan mammals. While I hardly warmed to the content of these shows, I did admire the fact that they could be shown in a public bar without causing offence. Over the course of several visits I have come to the conclusion that Alaska is the freest place in the developed world. It still feels like a frontier, where an 'each to their own, anything goes' mentality prevails.

Paul picked us up from the hostel at 10 a.m. and drove us to the airstrip. The hazy high cloud of the previous day had cleared. It was such a radiant sunny day it seemed strange to be changing into fleece and Gore-Tex. We showed Paul our map and the spot where we hoped to be dropped off.

'I'll see what I can do,' he said cautiously.

The plane loaded, our final act of preparation was to put on mountain boots and gaiters. Then we buckled ourselves into our seats and sat back to enjoy the ride. As Paul fired up the engine I felt the accumulated tension of days of travel, shopping and logistical headaches begin to ease. We had done all we could and were almost there. Now it was Paul's turn.

We traced a river valley inland northwards, gradually gaining height over a wilderness of forest and lakes. Soon the horizon filled with the ice sheets that drain from the Wrangell-St Elias ranges, then the mountains themselves began to appear. The first big peak was the inappropriately named Mount Fairweather, standing proud to the west: it reputedly has more snowfall than any other mountain in the world. Next the Hubbard, Kennedy and Alverstone group appeared to the east. The Bush Hawk ate up the distance, giving little indication of the scale of mountainous land below or the physical effort I knew would be involved travelling overland. Mount Vancouver and its summits came surprisingly quickly, leaving me excitedly pointing at the basin where we wanted to land.

'Looks okay,' Paul said. 'Let's give it a try.'

I sat silently, not wanting to break Paul's concentration as he completed the final manoeuvres. There was a small thud followed by the sound of the skis on snow, then Paul revved the engine to taxi into the back of the cirque where he spun the plane around and brought it to a stop. We stepped outside. There was complete silence and for a moment I stood stunned, amazed that a machine could bring you to such a place. It was probably the first time that anyone had landed here. It was warm in the sunshine, the snow was reasonably firm and the base of our route on Good Neighbor was just a few hundred metres away. I could hardly believe our luck.

We unloaded the plane casually and decided on a camp further out into the glacier, safely away from any avalanche that might fall from the mountain's enormous South Face.

'I want the gear here for the pick-up,' Paul said, pointing to where the plane was standing. We nodded our agreement. Then we stood and chatted for a while until Paul decided it was time to go. He shook hands and wished us luck. The noise of the engine restarting was deafening, then the plane accelerated down the glacier, took off after just a few hundred metres, and was gone.

The minute we had erected the tents, the journey caught up with us. We both felt drained. The travel and time difference from home could no longer be ignored.

'I've got to crash,' Paul said.

'Yeah, we can sort this lot out tomorrow.'

We left the gear and food lying in the snow. Inside the tent I shed a few clothes and slid into my sleeping bag. Within minutes I was asleep.

The next day proved frantic. The sun continued to shine, adding urgency to our actions. Good weather here is too rare to squander. We examined the South-West Ridge through my binoculars and were pleased with what we saw. There would be snow, ice and mixed climbing, and the overall angle was not too bad. At about three-quarters height up the ridge a steep tower was obviously going to provide a decisive stretch of climbing. Our biggest concern, however, was the strangely beautiful headwall of rime and flutings right at the top. We would be in a committing position by that point and it would have been reassuring to see a line through. No such luck; the headwall was impossible to fathom from such a distance.

We agreed on a minimal rack of climbing gear and a week's food and gas.

'What about the phone?' I asked.

'Dunno. Do you want it?'

'Not really. The weight is not insignificant, but it's more of a commitment thing.'

I had given the business of the phone some thought and knew that I needed to focus completely on what we were doing. The ridge was a large and serious undertaking. Talking to the children from precarious bivouacs each night would distract from that.

'We'll leave it here then.'

Finally we packed. After dinner I made a satellite phone call home.

'The route should take four or five days,' I told Jane.

'Will you take the phone with you?'

'No.' Jane did not ask for any explanation. 'I'll speak to you as soon as we get down.'

The 4 a.m. alarm signalled the start of our climb. We had a quick breakfast and trudged silently across the glacier into the back of the cirque, where a broad couloir led up to the ridge proper. After only 30 minutes' walking we reached the bergschrund. The snow wall above the fracture line overhung. We quickly roped up and I made an acrobatic pull-up to clear the lip. Paul followed and we dispensed with the rope to climb solo simultaneously. The previous day we had watched sporadic rockfall raking the couloir and knew that the next few hundred metres would be a race against the sun and stones. We climbed as fast as our lungs and legs would allow. Paul pulled ahead approaching the narrowest section, while high above I could see the sun's rays already hitting the ridge. Inevitably the warmth would release rocks from the ice. I had just cleared the constriction when a familiar clattering sounded and a salvo of stones buried themselves harmlessly in the snow slope above. Paul was now moving rightwards in the widening upper slopes of the couloir. I followed him with some urgency as more debris rained down until we reached a point safe from bombardment. Then the sun penetrated the couloir, softening the snow underfoot and drawing precious water from our skin. The day became hot, and as the angle eased towards the ridge we struggled in deepening snow.

It was a relief to finally reach the col, take a rest and marvel at the panorama that had opened out westward over the Seward Glacier flanked by Mount Saint Elias and Mount Logan. From this angle our ridgeline looked even more compelling.

We had plenty of time to consider the way ahead as we slogged slowly up the initial undulating section of snowy ridge. It was the last obvious place for a tent platform, but it was only 1 p.m.; we would have to take our chances further up. I halted at a small buttress and waited for Paul. We roped up and he led off, following surprisingly exposed mixed ground on the western side of the crest. Pitch followed pitch in swift succession. As the day wore on the heat and dehydration began to tell. Our pace slowed and we began to cast around for a place to pitch the tent. Nothing was evident and we rejoined the ridge. The temperature began to drop; soon it would become seriously cold, adding urgency to our search.

'I might be able to do something here,' I called down to Paul as I reached a notch of shattered rock. I moved some blocks around trying to shape a platform; it was only going to provide sitting room at the most. 'I'll have to try a bit higher,' I yelled, barely able to hide my frustration.

Above the rock I followed the ridge crest on steep snow. Then, nearly out of rope, a small shoulder appeared.

'This will do,' I shouted triumphantly, before anchoring myself and bringing up Paul. We hastily hacked out the first of what would be a succession of precarious tent platforms, into the knife-edge snow ridge.

We were soon established in the tent and sat contentedly with the stove purring. The sun dropped beyond the Seward Glacier in a myriad of red, orange and yellow hues, meanwhile the glacier and mounts Logan and St Elias turned shades of icy blue, The enormity of the landscape and the fact that not a single person lived here was mind-boggling. With the sun gone the cold started to bite.

Morning brought another fine day. The sun hit the ridge early and tracked us as we made a rising traverse on the western side of the crest to outflank a steep rock buttress. The climbing was not difficult but the hard ice made for slow going. Each ice-axe had to be carefully placed, sometimes taking several blows, before the steps up and across could be made. The angle required continual front-pointing on crampons, making our calves burn. We were moving smoothly, but not gaining height at the speed of the first day.

Whenever Paul led there was time for me to view the terrain. This was important: I wanted to build a three-dimensional mental picture of the ridge and this side of the mountain, both to figure out the route ahead and, just as vitally, to know potential lines of retreat. I found my gaze continually drawn to the flutings at the top of the ridge. They were simultaneously alluringly beautiful and a nagging concern.

At times I heard strange sounds moving around me and was amazed to see flocks of small birds flying above us, twittering their way northwards.

In a repeat of the previous day we rejoined the ridge in the late afternoon and found a sensational campsite just before a stretch of ominous looking cornices.

'This is going to take longer than we thought,' Paul said once we were comfortable inside the tent.

'You're not wrong.'

I was uneasily aware of how far the flutings still were above us. We had been hoping for a repeat of the Alverstone climb where we blasted 2,000 metres of climbing in just two days. Here, the complexity of climbing on a ridge, plus the height gain and distance involved, meant Good Neighbor was going to be an altogether more ambitious undertaking. It was sobering to think that after two very long and demanding days we were probably not even halfway up.

Paul led off in the morning. It was a scary pitch and I was happy to be following. Parts were right on the ridge crest with huge drops on either side. I tried to push the exposure from my mind by concentrating intensely on each step. When I reached Paul he was sat in a hollow, legs astride the ridge.

'It's an Alaskan belay,' he said.

In fact it was no belay at all, since no anchor was available. Paul was watching me closely; should I fall, he intended to roll off his perch down the opposite side of the ridge. Even in theory it's an unsettling plan and I was relieved we did not have to put it to the test. We continued up relatively easy-angled slopes to below an imposing rock tower that we already had marked down as one of the keys to the climb. It was obviously going to be difficult and time-consuming, and with nowhere to bivvy it would not be wise to start on it late in the day. We set about chopping a platform in the last good spot below the tower. It had been our easiest day so far. Unfortunately, there was nothing easy about digging a notch sufficient for the tent. The task took most of the remaining afternoon, though we were able to get the stove running and rehydrate as we dug.

A small cap of cloud – sometimes a precursor to bad weather – had formed over Mount Logan during the day. Though it dissipated during the evening, it had set me thinking. Having already done a long traversing section on the ridge, a retreat was looking tricky. The steep east side of the ridge – the most direct way to reach our base camp by abseil – was a no-go zone, threatened with icefall from a band of séracs high on the South Face. The western aspect offered little more comfort: its relatively gentle slopes dropped into an incredibly chaotic glacier and a huge hike around a group of lesser peaks would then be required to reach our base.

The night passed cold and crystal clear and dawn brought another perfect day. The weather seemed to be holding, but we were both tense: there was no obvious way of overcoming the tower above. The prow directly above the ridge where we were camped was not an option. A blind-looking couloir to our left appeared to offer the only feasible way through.

Paul soon completed the first pitch. Then I traversed over steep, hard, black ice into the base of the runnel. It looked no better from this closer vantage point. You get a feeling for places like this over time. I was sure it was going to blank out, forcing us into some very steep and possibly difficult aid climbing that would be tricky with our minimal rack of gear.

Paul arrived and viewed the terrain above. He did not look optimistic.

'If we'd brought the satellite phone with us,' he said with a smile, 'we would have been able to call for help in an emergency.'

'Well, we wanted the commitment.'

Paul's casual mention of the phone reflected a shared understanding. We had reached a point where the only practical way off the mountain lay up and over the top.

Paul slowly and deliberately took the climbing gear from me and clipped the pieces to his harness. Then he began to climb. A short section of steep ice led to a narrow rock band that guarded the entrance to the couloir above. Paul spent some time clearing cracks of ice before placing a nut into one. He clipped the rope into it and looked down at me.

'Watch me here.'

I nervously fed the rope out as Paul hooked his axes on the shattered rock and made a series of bold, strenuous moves until he was able to get better purchase in the ice above. He rested, breathing deeply, then continued up into the ice chute and out of sight. The rope inched up slowly and I felt a sickening tension building inside. At last, with the rope nearly out, an unmistakable yelp of joy boomed down from above. It could only mean one thing – there was a clear way ahead.

I eagerly followed, after the difficult moves the ice chute led into a widening basin that curled round to the left. It was enclosed by rock walls streaked by ribbons of ice that petered out into steep cracks. Paul was standing on a small platform chopped into the back left corner of the basin; a sliver of ice ran off up a corner behind him.

'Our asses are saved,' he said, only half jokingly. The ice ran continuously up to broader slopes.

I grabbed the gear from Paul. The moves were thin at first and I had to be careful not to cleave the ice from the rock. Soon, however, the ice was accepting first-time placements for my axes and I relished being able to move quickly over what was the best ice we had encountered so far. It did not last long. Out on the open slopes and into the sun, the ice became harder again, decent axe placements required several blows and occasionally a crampon would slip before biting.

The weather was holding, but only just; large lenticular cloud caps had formed over both Mount Saint Elias and Logan and the air was hazier than on previous days. Now the rime headwall hung above, tantalisingly close, yet menacing. Tension welled within me once again.

The hard ice eventually ran into snow that increased in depth the higher we climbed. By late afternoon we had slogged our way up to a shoulder where the angle lessened and we dug out what we hoped would be our last tent platform on the climb. At least at this height it was cooler and we were not suffering from the daytime overheating of lower down. It was not so steep either and for the first time at a camp we were able to untie. Such freedom of movement was a relief and made getting organised for the night much easier.

Next morning we quickly broke camp and regained the ridge crest, moving with real urgency, still not knowing how difficult the final headwall would prove to be. The approach along the ridge took longer than expected. Once again the sheer scale of what we were doing was deceiving us. Far below, a thin layer of cloud had drifted across the glaciers and the peaks now hovered above it. The weather was changing.

Paul led the final pitch of the ridge and was sat astride a cornice fracture line when I reached him. Continuing up the slope I could see a massive wave of snow and ice had peeled off and wedged above a gully. Only two small points of contact seemed to be holding it all up. Paul looked tiny and vulnerable on his airy stance.

I belayed below a couloir of hard blue ice and as Paul started to climb I studied the headwall now just above me. It was a bizarre and frightening feature: a mass of strange feathery wind-blown formations, some improbably overhung. Luckily there were lines of weaknesses, although it was impossible to see if any led cleanly to the top. The line directly above us looked the most promising.

Paul tackled the thin couloir. As the angle steepened he began to labour. Each axe placement was taking several blows and there was no rest for his legs; he was continually on his front-points and breathing very heavily.

'Why don't you take a belay?' I called up. 'It might be better to lead this without a sack.'

'Yeah, good plan.'

It took some time for Paul to place two ice screws, but it was reassuring to know that the belay was sound. I joined him directly beneath a wave-like formation spilling off the left wall of the gully. It was an intimidating spot. I removed my rucksack, clipped it into one of the anchors, grabbed some gear and set off. The ice was steep at first but with no weight on my back I was able to climb it quite fluidly. Soon I entered an almost enclosed tube of ice and rime. At its narrowest point I was actually able to rest with my back on one wall and my feet on the other. It felt more like caving than mountaineering. The tube opened out into a small basin below two steep, narrow, parallel runnels. I placed an ice-screw. The left-hand runnel appeared to offer the best route to the top but was overhung at its base, so I started up the other. The climbing was wonderful, perfect ice taking first-time axe placements until I reached a point where I could make a pull into the other runnel. I planted an axe and swung across into an overhanging groove. With a few frantic moves I cleared the overhang and established myself in a broader gully topped by a small wall. I placed another screw then wobbled my way up the wall of rather hollow-sounding rime ice and made a final pull on to the summit plateau. The central and north summits of Mount Vancouver lay directly in front of me. I let out a scream. Five long, arduous days of climbing had led to this point and somehow our route had saved the best until last. The rime headwall was quite literally the icing on the cake.

It was a sublime moment and I basked in it; alone on top of this huge peak, surrounded by pure mountainous beauty. There was cloud below, thicker than earlier and a cause of concern, but for now it could wait.

Eventually, I set up a belay, pulled up the slack rope and shouted down for Paul to start climbing. I got no reply and for a while I could not figure out which rope he was climbing on, or which had the ruck-sack attached to be hauled up. Then the sack got caught in the overhanging groove and I had to wait until Paul could free it from below. However, the miscommunication hardly mattered; Paul's face was filled with joy as he came into view in the top gully.

'I'll never do anything better,' he declared, pulling over the top to join me. I had been having the same thought. It was 4 p.m. We shook hands and wandered around on the plateau for a few minutes savour-ing our achievement and the astonishing views. A total silence complemented the immense feeling of space and freedom. Content, we made our way to the actual summit of Good Neighbor Peak, a knoll of rime just above our finishing point, and took photographs.

'Right, let's get the hell out of here.'

My pragmatism had returned. We set off down gently angled slopes and found the East Ridge. A col on the ridge a few hundred metres lower looked an obvious place to head for. Initially we followed slopes on the northern aspect, until forced on to an exposed section of the ridge itself. Lower down we had to negotiate a chaotic icefall before arriving at the col and calling it a day.

It felt good to be able to put up the tent without time-consuming excavations and just collapse inside. Through the evening the wind got up, buffeting the tent with increasingly savage gusts. It made cooking on the hanging stove a prolonged affair; each blast shook water from the pan and extinguished the flame. We took it in turns to hold the stove steady, which helped, but spillages still occurred and sometimes it was very difficult to relight the stove. The bitter cold forced us to wear down jackets inside our sleeping-bags. Despite being utterly beat, I found it difficult to sleep. A storm was coming in.

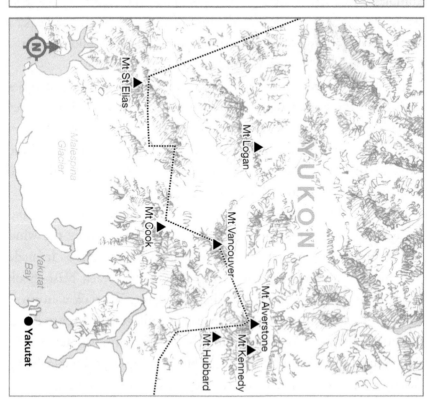

ELEVEN

Not for the Faint-Hearted

I woke to the sound of snow hitting the tent fabric. Frozen condensation had built up around the mouth of the hood of my jacket and more was falling from the ceiling of the tent. Our sleeping bags were dusted in ice crystals. I opened the tent flap a fraction and sneaked a glimpse outside. A fierce, gusting wind was driving snow over the col, enveloping us in whiteness. My movements had woken Paul.

'We're not going anywhere,' I told him. 'At least not for the time being.'

'Huh,' came the muffled reply.

I was acutely aware of our vulnerability. We were stormbound high on a huge and complex peak in the middle of a mountain wilderness, with little food, marginally more gas and no way of summoning help. People often ask if I carry a GPS in the mountains, implying that the device somehow guarantees you will make it safely down. Paul and I knew better. In remote and uninhabited mountains, the only available maps are often poor, due no doubt to the difficulty of surveying such places and the lack of demand for the finished product. I have found it best simply to take a sketch map marked with spot-heights, peaks, ridgelines and an outline of any glaciers. Our proprietary map of the Wrangell range was cluttered with contour lines which at best were approximations of features but often bore little relation to the relief on the ground. Nor did it mark the boundaries between glaciers and mountains. The only way Paul and I were going to get off this peak and navigate our way back to base camp through vast, complicated glacial terrain was by sight. And while we remained cloaked in cloud there was not sufficient visibility to find our way.

We made tea, ate a cereal bar each and went back to sleep. Thoughts of Jane and the children back at home mingled with dreams. I was struggling to reconcile two very different worlds: I knew Jane would be expecting a call and getting increasingly concerned, yet for now the link seemed tenuous. Throughout the day the snow gradually piled up around the tent.

'I've thought I've heard voices at times,' I confided to Paul, knowing the notion was fanciful.

'Yeah, me too. Strange isn't it?'

It was reassuring to learn I was not losing my grip on reality, or that at least we both were together. In all likelihood there were probably only a handful of people in the entire Wrangell-St Elias area and we knew of none anywhere near Mount Vancouver.

That evening I ventured outside to go to the toilet. The cloud was clearing and I was pleased to see the Alverstone, Hubbard and Kennedy group to the east, but the sky was pale and still streaked with high cirrus. Later we ate a single leftover packet of mashed potato for dinner and went to sleep with the wind blowing hard. The night passed bitterly cold.

'Hey Simon! Wake up!' Paul was calling with urgency. 'The storm has cleared. We need to get out of here.'

I sat up and immediately noticed sunlight filtering into the tent. The wind had gone. We quickly prepared tea and ate a couple of cereal bars each – the last of our food – then hurriedly packed. By eight we were ready to move.

We hoped to descend via the *Centennial Route* that follows a south-facing spur from the shoulder we had camped on the east of Vancouver's huge South Face. However, this was unseen ground for us; the speed of our approach to the climb had not allowed time for a proper reconnaissance. We would have to rely on sight, judgement and feel.

Initially the way was obvious and we moved swiftly down easy-angled snow slopes towards the spur. Soon the terrain became more broken and open crevasses forced us into lengthy traverses. Then we spotted a large band of séracs that appeared to dissect the whole spur. We cast around for an alternative. More open slopes led east towards a gently angled ridge. We followed our noses and went with those. We were moving quickly again now, and needed to – cloud was beginning to build.

Suddenly my left foot broke through the snow crust and I fell very heavily. A searing pain ran from my ankle up my leg.

'Shit!' I shouted, lying motionless in the snow. I knew all too well we could be screwed if I had broken my leg.

'Are you okay?'

'I don't know.' I replied pathetically.

The pain was beginning to subside, but it was hard to gauge what damage I had done because my foot was still post-holed in the snow. I pulled myself into a sitting position and noticed a faint depression stretching across the slope. It was a crevasse line and I cursed myself for having not spotted it sooner. We were getting tired now; I would have to be very vigilant about getting down without further mistakes.

I managed to pull my leg from the snow, revealing a black hole where it had broken through into the icy chasm. I carefully stood up and gently weighted my foot. It hurt, but felt like the injury was not too serious.

'I think it's okay.'

'Good, that was quite a bad fall.' A look of relief spread over Paul's face.

I delved inside my rucksack, found my first-aid kit and took a couple of ibuprofen to ease the immediate pain and counter any swelling. Then I shouldered my rucksack and carried on. The ankle was sore for a while but soon loosened up. We walked silently down to the ridge then followed its crest as patches of cloud drifted by. Once below the cloud base the weather began to improve, dispelling worries about a further storm. We were exhausted, but now it was surely just a matter of putting one foot in front of the other and grinding it out until base camp.

The ridge became more pronounced as we got lower, with a steep rocky face on its southern side and gentler, snowy slopes above a glacier basin on the northern aspect. Then it terminated abruptly in a rock tower. I followed the line of least resistance down towards the basin, hoping to pick up a continuation to the ridge lower down. The glacier itself tumbled off into a large icefall that offered no way down, so I contoured below the rock tower to where I hoped the ridge would start again. I was beginning to get a bad feeling about this place: the ground simply did not look like it was going to provide the walk down we wanted. Soon we were in a heavily crevassed area that ended in a drop-off. I climbed on to a crest and cautiously approached the edge. The view was horrifying. I was standing on the lip of a sérac perched above a rock wall. Hundreds of metres below, a snow slope fell away to a glacier covered in avalanche debris. The sheer precariousness of it all unnerved me and I hastily backed off the crest; it was simply not safe to descend here, even by abseil. I passed Paul without saying anything and began contouring some more, following an in-filled crevasse. After maybe 50 metres it too ended at a sheer drop into a very steep couloir at the edge of the sérac. I toyed with the idea of abseiling and even located a place to put an ice-screw for the first anchor, before I calmed down and reasoned it was madness. I turned around and made my way back up to Paul.

'We're going to have to go back up and find a way off the other side of the ridge.'

'Good,' he said. 'Now we are communicating again.'

I felt a little stupid. In my panic and haste, coupled with the dread of having to back track, I had omitted to share my knowledge and concerns with Paul.

'Sorry,' I replied. 'There's a huge, unstable sérac band over the edge. There's no safe way down.'

With a resigned sigh I retraced our steps towards the ridge. It was energy-sapping and demoralising, but without risk. Within 30 minutes we were back on the crest. A col below the rock tower dropped into a steep gully running some way down the South Face. The rock was shattered and it was obviously a fall line, but it was significantly safer than the death trap we had returned from. I wound a screw into the hard, wind-blasted ice and set up the ropes to abseil.

The top of the gully was jammed with loose rock that would be difficult to avoid knocking down on each other. Below were less-confined slopes, however, we were now bathed in fierce sunlight and the snow was pitted with rocks that had fallen from above. We tried to move as quickly as possible, even so time ticked by. The ropes would not slide when thrown below us; whoever went down first would have to free them while wallowing up to the knees or deeper in heavy, wet snow. Occasionally, rocks came from above. Some were moving at speed and made a high-pitched whirring sound before striking rock or snow; others literally slid into view and then gathered speed in a series of increasingly large and erratic bounces. This was our way off the mountain and we knew we had to make it work. We shouted warnings whenever rockfall threatened and tried to make ourselves smaller targets by bunching up under our helmets and ruck-sacks. Beyond that, all we could do was trust to luck.

The final abseil was the scariest. From the base of the last rock buttress in the snow slope, Paul went down a prominent runnel and disappeared from view over the lip of the bergschrund at the edge of the glacier. As soon as his weight came off the rope I followed. I felt vulnerable the moment I moved away from the rock and once in the runnel was acutely aware that it was the natural drainage line for the face above. I descended as fast as I could, pausing only on the lip of the bergschrund, which was huge and massively overhung. I took deep breath and went over the top. The first move was awkward, and then I was in space, slowly spinning as I slid down the rope towards Paul.

'Nice one,' he said as I landed beside him. We pulled the ropes down, coiled them and made a dash down a short slope into the glacier.

'I think we're safe here,' I said once clear of the avalanche and rock debris that had fallen from the face.

It was nice to rest for a while in the warm spring sunshine. I felt happy and relieved but knew that we were not yet completely out of the woods. We had landed in a different glacier system from that of our base camp and would have to cross another watershed to reach it. There was little need for debate about the way to go; further down the glacier on its opposite side, gently angled slopes led up to a pass. We packed away the ropes, removed our crampons and set off.

It was good to move independently again, free of the rope and each able to set our own pace. I was soon across the glacier and on to the slope. Though the snow was softer, I broke trail strongly up to the pass – only to find a cliff plunging away on the south side.

'We're going to have to abseil again,' I told Paul when he arrived, barely able to hide my disappointment. I wanted this to end now: to simply walk back to the camp, to eat and to rest. We dispensed with the obstacle in two long abseils.

'We won't be needing them again,' I confidently predicted, packing the ropes away for a second time.

I set off again over gently undulating ground, contouring around a spur and into a valley below an icefall that guarded the way to the upper section of the glacier and our camp. It was not steep and did not look serious. I weaved up through it, my mind on autopilot as the sun dropped behind our ridge on Vancouver. Higher, I was able to look back at the *Centennial Route* in profile and discern a clear way around the sérac that had diverted us down the East Ridge. But it no longer mattered. We were almost back now and I was not going to beat myself up over a minor route finding error.

Then suddenly I came to a large crevasse running right across the slope. I moved leftwards, which looked likely to offer the best way across.

There was a way around but it was going to involve a lengthy walk back down the glacier and we had walked enough. I dropped my rucksack where the crevasse was narrowest and went to meet Paul.

'You're not going to believe it. There's a huge crevasse splitting the entire icefall. We're going to have to jump across.'

Paul followed me back and inspected the crevasse. His face dropped as he peered into the abyss. It was maybe two metres wide at this narrowest point and about 50 metres deep; the sides were glistening smooth and vertical. It was the classic chasm of a movie sequence.

'Are you sure there's not a way further to the left?' Paul's tone suggested he already knew the answer.

'Yes.'

'Huh, okay. I'll go first if you want.'

'Be my guest.'

It was a generous offer. I had had enough for this day and perhaps it was showing. I got out a rope, booted my axe into the snow and firmly anchored myself; meanwhile Paul inspected his launch point and stamped down the snow. Then he tied into the rope and walked to and from the edge a few times, measuring his run-up while I calculated how much slack rope to give him.

'All right,' he said finally, and started to run. He cleared the gap easily and landed gracefully on the far side. Then he hauled the rucksacks over and I took the leap.

'This is becoming farcical,' I said, picking myself up from a clumsy landing as we dissolved into fits of tired laughter. The days of accumulated tension were finally lifting. Surely now we were safe? We laughed at ourselves and at the slightly insane situations that our chosen sport sometimes drops on you.

The glacier held no further surprises on the short walk back to camp. It was 10 p.m. and we'd been on the move for a full 14 hours. The tents had sunk into the snow over the previous days of sunshine; otherwise the camp was just as we had left it. We fired up a stove and began melting snow before digging out some food. There was plenty to go at that did not require preparation, starting with cheese and salami on crackers.

I knew it would be early morning back in Britain, so retrieved the satellite phone and made a call.

'Simon,' Jane said, in the same surprised way she always did when I called home, like she could still not quite believe that the technology actually worked.

'We've just got back. It took a bit longer than we thought it would.' There was silence for a moment and then I could hear the unmistakable sound of sobbing.

'Are you all right?' I asked, feeling rather guilty.

'Yes, I just didn't know what to do. You said you'd be on the mountain four or five days.'

'Sorry,' I replied rather feebly. 'It was a great route. One of the best I've ever done.'

Jane's sobs gave way to relieved laughter as she explained her dilemmas. She had started to get concerned after the fifth day, which had turned to worry as day six still brought no news. There was nobody living locally that she felt she could turn to for support and advice and so had texted Tom Curtis, a long-standing friend and ex-climbing partner who lived a little over an hour away in Newcastle. He called her back immediately, even though he was actually working in Norway, and offered his help if needed. Jane wondered how long to wait before instigating a search and rescue operation, but the immediate question was not 'when?' but 'where?' As Paul had taken care of logistics for the trip, Jane had little idea of our exact location or who had flown us to the mountains. On the evening of the sixth day she managed to arrange some childcare and went to my office in Penrith to trawl my emails. From these she was able to deduce that we had flown into the mountains from Haines. A search of the web provided the email addresses of three pilots in the town, one of whom was Paul Swanstrom.

Jane emailed them all and Paul replied saying he had flown us in but had heard nothing. A little more reassuringly, he was able to report that the weather had been fine and settled. He also told her he would fly in and look for us the following day. She was waiting to hear back from him before making her next move – a full-scale search operation.

'I think it was easier in some ways when I didn't hear from you,' Jane said at the end of her explanation. I understood what she meant. Before the communications revolution I would send a letter when I left for the mountains and then contact her on my return. There would be no information in between, which in this case would have meant no worry: Jane would have been unaware we were overdue.

'Maybe you should carry the phone in future. You wouldn't have to call every day. Just keep it in the bottom of your rucksack for emergencies.'

I have thought long and hard about this since, but in my mind the arguments both for and against are strong and their polarisation allows for no compromise solution. In the end our decision had boiled down to gut feeling, like the multitude of decisions taken during any big climb. I still remain undecided about taking a phone on similar projects in the future.

We were tired and dehydrated, yet at the same time our minds were still racing, filled with the heightened awareness that comes from many days on a mountain. I opened a bottle of single malt whisky bought in the Heathrow duty-free in hopeful anticipation of this moment. We used the first of the melted snow to dilute the liquor and saluted our success. Then we gorged ourselves on peanuts, fig bars and tinned fruit before finally calling it a day.

I slept long and deeply and woke to hear, once again, the unmistakable sound of the wind and of snow falling on the tent. There were also less familiar noises: the fluttering of wings and a persistent high-pitched chirping. At first I thought my mind was playing tricks again, like the stormbound day at the col, but soon realised there was a bird nearby. I unzipped the inner tent and peered into the porch. A small bird was flapping around in the space between the inner and outer tent. I had been amazed to see flocks of birds flying over us whilst on the climb, but this was even more startling. Somehow, in the middle of this vast glacial wilderness the bird had chanced upon our tents and taken shelter from the storm. I wondered how many others of its kind were right now dying, having been forced to land in less accommo-dating locations; we were, after all, surrounded by hundreds of square kilometres of utterly unforgiving terrain. Just like us with our climb-ing, the birds needed a touch of luck in timing their migrations. Those that had flown over us on Good Neighbor would by now be resting and feeding in forests to the north and west, while those attempting to clear the same barrier today would be having a grim time. At least we had been able to carry our own shelter and had a week's worth of food and fuel to sustain us while on our climb.

Two more birds soon arrived, probably drawn by the other's call-ing. Although I did not know the precise species I recognised the first bird as some sort of finch, and one of the two newcomers was the same; the third appeared to be a warbler. Confined to camp, we spent the morning eating, drinking and feeding biscuit crumbs to our guests.

Aware that Paul Swanstrom knew we were overdue, I made a call to him in Haines.

'You guys okay?' he asked.

'Yes, we're safely off the mountain and back at camp.'

'The weather's not looking so good for the next few days. What are your plans?'

'We've got a couple of bottles of whisky and are not going anywhere.'

'Good to hear that,' replied our pilot, laughing.

'I'll call again when the weather improves.'

In truth we were grateful for the rest – our first since leaving home 12 days earlier. The birds flitted from tent to tent and occasionally perched on a kit bag under an upturned sled. The storm continued.

On the third morning the weather improved, but it was too late for the warbler. Unlike the finches, which were still with us, it had refused all our offerings of food. I found it lying on its side, dead in the snow under the upturned sled. Later, in a surge of optimism, I called Paul, who advised a 'wait and see' approach. Then the cloud returned, bringing with it large amounts of fine powder snow.

Next morning all was silent. I banged the inside of the tent to clear it of snow and the light and heat of sunlight crept through the fabric. It was a beautiful day and we soaked up the sun while making breakfast. The finches had already gone. It was time for us to leave also. When I called Haines, Paul was cautious about the pick-up, so I was surprised when I called again at 11.30 to hear he was on his way.

'Be ready for when I arrive.'

We were outside the tents still packing when the tiny red plane came into view. Moments later it touched down on the glacier in a plume of snow; the roar of its engine grew ever louder as it bounced up the ridge behind our camp before spinning around and coming to a halt. The engine stopped and silence resumed as Paul climbed down from the machine.

We dragged several loads over to the plane, shook hands and then returned to collect more kit. The tents had to be collapsed and packed away. It took time. Patches of misty cloud began to drift by.

'Hurry up,' Paul shouted from the plane, pointing down the glacier. With perfect bad timing a bank of cloud was billowing up the valley below, heading for the icefall where we had jumped the crevasse on our way back to camp. We ran for the plane dragging the remaining gear, but it was difficult to move quickly in the knee-deep snow and we both arrived breathless, lungs screaming with exertion. Paul frantically stowed the last of our gear and we climbed aboard; then he quickly started the engine and gunned it for take-off.

Nothing happened.

Paul lowered and raised the revs several more times but the plane would not budge. One of its skis was stuck in the snow. A burst of digging and some well-placed kicks soon freed the ski, but by the time Paul had returned to the cockpit, re-started the engine and lined the plane up for take-off the moment had been lost. The cloud was now upon us.

'God damn!' Paul shouted, as we climbed from the plane.

I felt deeply embarrassed and uncomfortable. We should have been ready earlier and now we were stuck. More importantly, Paul's plane was stuck. We were sat on a glacier in the middle of nowhere with hundreds of thousands of dollars worth of shiny new aeroplane, which was effectively useless while we remained in cloud. It was obvious that Paul took great pride in the Bush Hawk; it was central to his livelihood and the lifestyle he had fashioned for himself. Our laziness had, however temporarily, put that in jeopardy. It was hardly surprising he was angry. We both felt incredibly stupid and tried to make polite conversation while silently praying for the cloud to lift.

Mists drifted around the cirque for more than an hour, occasionally offering tantalising glimpses of clear sky above. I consoled myself with the thought that at least the weather was not getting worse; even so it was a huge relief when the cloud eventually began to part.

'Right. Let's go,' Paul said.

We climbed back into the plane and strapped ourselves in. The engine fired into life and Paul meticulously completed a series of checks before concentrating on the GPS mounted in the centre of the control panel. He scrolled through the menu several times as I watched nervously from behind. Preparations complete, he increased the engine speed and released the brakes. The plane began to move down the glacier, but much more slowly than I was expecting, having watched Paul's first take-off from the same spot. The machine was struggling to accelerate with our extra weight and the softer snow. Slowly we began to gain speed, but we were covering a lot of distance. I felt a growing wave of anxiety; we were heading inexorably towards the icefall, and by now we were going too fast to stop. We were committed to the take-off, or at least its attempt. It was do or die.

The Bush Hawk became weightless just as we entered the zone of crevasses above the icefall. It skipped one slot and then took-off, the icefall gaping directly under us. I breathed a sigh of relief: we were airborne. However the easier feeling did not last long. A high-pitched screaming was coming from the instrument panel and more cloud was advancing up the glacier. Paul banked the plane sharply to the left and made a full 180-degree turn back into the cirque we had just left.

'He's going to land the plane,' I told myself. 'Let the cloud clear and try again later.' Then we hit the ground, bounced and were immediately airborne again, heading up into the back of the cirque. Clearly another turn was coming up. Paul waited until we were in the back of the basin before putting the plane on its wingtip. I could scarcely believe what was happening: instrument panel screaming, we completed the turn with the tip of one wing just metres above the snow. It was a moment of madness, but a very special kind of madness. In a way it was like climbing, but we were in a machine – a machine that nonetheless was still governed by the natural forces of gravity and the elements. It was frightening and exciting in equal measure. The moment felt surreal. Time slowed.

After what seemed an eternity, but could only have been a few seconds, Paul righted the aircraft and came out of the turn. We flew straight down the glacier gaining speed and height. The instrument panel fell silent. Our moment of danger had passed. Paul had made the whole series of dramatic manoeuvres to gain extra height and avoid flying through the cloud that was advancing up the lower glacier. It had been an incredibly brave and committing piece of flying.

'That take-off was not for the faint hearted,' Paul said dryly and we all managed a few chuckles of nervous laughter.

'What was that screaming noise all about?' I asked.

'That was the stall warning indicator.'

It was a sobering thought that throughout the aerial acrobatics the plane was in danger of dropping from the air. Paul Swanstrom had certainly earned his money on this trip and his bold flying seemed to mirror our efforts on the mountain. I'm sure in pure business terms the potential risks of flying to and from such places must outweigh any gain. The main motivation must simply be the challenge and excitement. I felt very grateful that Paul was willing to risk it all to help us realise our dreams; in a strange way it seemed a fitting finale to what we knew had been a very special adventure.

Stepping from the plane, I felt like an astronaut returning to earth. For nearly two weeks we had been living in a sterile world of ice, rock and snow, our only contact with other visible living things our chance encounters with the birds. It felt strange to walk on concrete, to feel the heat of the sun and to be bombarded with smells. Spring comes quickly to this part of the world; now the grass was growing and the trees were sprouting leaves. The air was rich with the fragrance of new growth. I savoured each lung full and then as I took off my jacket other smells permeated the air. I badly needed a shower.

Two months after returning home an email landed in my inbox from Paul Schweizer. The news it brought was stunning. I immediately telephoned Paul for confirmation. It was a fact – 'our' route had been climbed way back in 1968 by a Japanese team.

After the climb we had alerted the usual climbing magazine and journal editors to our success. One – Lindsay Griffin, an associate editor of the *American Alpine Journal* – asked for precise information on the line we had taken. I explained how we had not seen a single trace of the passage of others. With his usual thoroughness, Lindsay had then exchanged information with a contact in Japan who had unearthed a magazine article detailing the ascent. The map attached to the email clearly showed their route and ours to be the same.

'A bit of a blow,' was Paul's downbeat take on the news.

'I suppose so. But it was still a damn good climb. And ours is the first alpine-style ascent.' My words sounded a little hollow; we had thought it was a first after all.

We soon learned the detail of the previous climb. A 10-member team from the Osaka-Fu Mountaineering Association had tackled the route siege style over 13 days in May and June 1968. Starting from the Canadian-Yukon side, they had fixed a line of ropes and dug snow cave camps. Two climbers reached the top and on that same summit day three others had died in an avalanche. It must have been a remarkable climb at the time, but it was from another era on almost every level.

I could see there was little reason to feel disappointed. The 41 years that had elapsed since the original ascent meant that in essence we had done two different climbs. Only when confronted with such stark differences do you realise how things have moved on. Mountaineering in this sense is no different to anything else. It is a product of time and place, of cultural values and the technology of the age.

I could never envisage climbing Good Neighbor Peak as part of a 10-man team. Even when I first went to the greater ranges in the 1980s I usually only climbed as one of a pair, even if more climbers were sharing the same base camp. The use of fixed lines and established camps is similarly alien to me, while the logistics of travelling with such a large team with all their supplies and equipment is incomprehensible. It was hard to believe such an expedition had occurred within my own lifetime. Yet it is a fact there are still teams, particularly from the Far East, climbing Himalayan peaks in this fashion today.

Conditions on the mountain for the Japanese also sounded dramatically different from those we had encountered. Even though climbing later in the season, they had found the ridge so plastered in snow and ice that they were able to sleep in snow caves, whereas for us even finding and excavating tent platforms had been a struggle at times. Features we had climbed would have been buried beneath snow and ice.

Since 1968 this mantle had melted back to the underlying ice, rock and névé that characterised our ascent.

The most striking difference was that of speed. We had completed our climb in a mere five days and descended in two, including a full day of inactivity in the storm. Technology had played a part in this: Paul Swanstrom had been able to fly us right to the base of the route, and better, lighter clothing and equipment meant we began our climb carrying much less weight than the Japanese. We could even have taken a satellite phone had we wished. Mostly though the difference in our times reflected a difference of approach – a seismic shift in mountaineering culture to one that advocates doing more with less. Both Paul and I had embraced this notion over decades of alpine-style climbing around the world, giving us a clear idea of what was possible. We had followed that vision and on this occasion the interplay of chance, experience, determination and skill produced something special. The knowledge that others had done the route before did not alter that understanding.

Life quickly moves on, yet I still find myself thinking about our precious days on that perfect ridge, surrounded by an arctic vastness. I remember the first long day racing the rising sun to the ridge and later watching it set in splashes of red and violet beyond the steely sheen of the Seward Glacier. Then there were the days on the ridge itself: I see Paul, a tiny and vulnerable looking figure adrift on an ocean of ice and snow, his key pitch that unlocked Good Neighbor's upper slopes, the calm waters of Yakutat Bay at the far curvature of the horizon, and the magical final rope-length through the ice runnel and flutings to the summit plateau.

Deep down, I know that it was a moment of mountaineering perfection and that I will do nothing better, but the passion remains – I still want to try.

Epilogue

Nepal, October 2009

The Twin Otter turned off the runway and taxied on to the apron of Lukla airport. It is a busy spot. Lukla is the gateway to Nepal's Khumbu region. About a week's walk up-country rise some of the world's most impressive mountains – Mount Everest among them. Every day throughout the spring and autumn seasons dozens of flights ferry trekkers and climbers between Kathmandu and this improbable mountainside airstrip. My work running commercial climbing expeditions had brought me to Lukla most seasons for the last 15 years. Once again it felt like a homecoming.

The plane stopped outside the small terminal building and I watched the pilots complete a series of checks before killing the engines. There was a moment of silence before ground staff rushed forward to open the door. As I stepped on to the tarmac, kit bags were already being emptied from the hold while a trolley full of outgoing gear was being pulled towards it. Departing passengers were being hurried from the terminal to board as we were ushered in the opposite direction. It is the same scene every trip. It looks chaotic but works surprisingly well.

I made my way towards the rudimentary baggage reclaim, all the while looking into the crowd of would-be-porters, local guides and spectators milling on the far side of the perimeter fence. I was hoping to spot a familiar face. A policeman near the gate was waving and blowing a whistle in a vain attempt to keep the crowd at bay. Bolder individuals walked straight past him and into the airport.

Then there was a tap on my shoulder.

'Hello Simon.' Nima's face was radiating a smile that said more than any greeting. I thrust out my hand and he clasped it with both of his.

'I couldn't see you,' I said apologetically.

Nima is such a small and unassuming man I had failed to pick him out in the sea of faces. It was hard to reconcile his slight appearance with the strength and stamina I knew he possessed; as a young man he had climbed Kangchenjunga, working as a high-altitude porter. We had first met many years earlier in his home village of Pangboche when I was working for Henry Todd's company, Himalayan Guides. For more than 10 years Nima had worked with me in Nepal and India as my sirdar – that is a foreman/organiser. When called upon he also acted as guide, cook, porter and yak man. Off the mountains Nima owns three tourist lodges in Pangboche and nearby Dingboche, as well as farmland and livestock. He is a talented and industrious man, but like many Sherpas is calm, reserved and modest. Over the years I have come to admire and respect him enormously.

I introduced Nima to the group and moments later he was about his business, calling to a gang of porters beyond the fence to come and collect our kitbags. At the final count four bags were missing. A plastic barrel containing our hill-food had also failed to show. It was not an unfamiliar situation. The planes are small and sometimes it is impossible to load all the baggage on the same flight as the passengers. I knew it would arrive piecemeal on later flights. A large part of running expeditions is dealing with problems, trying to smooth the way.

We regrouped over cups of tea at the Paradise Lodge on the far side of the runway, next to Lukla's main street. Nima's son, Sonam, came inside and shyly said 'hello'. When I had last seen him, Sonam was still a schoolboy. Now he was a 21-year-old man and would be working alongside me as a high-altitude porter. It was satisfying to be able to give him a job.

'I'm going to stay and wait for the missing bags,' I told the group. 'I'll catch you up in Namche tomorrow.'

It made sense for me to remain behind. The other staff and yaks would be waiting up the trail in Namche Bazaar where we would pick up the bulk of our food and supplies. Nima would organise things while I waited for the bags. Then I could roll the two days of gentle walking into one and rejoin the group in the town the guidebooks call 'the Sherpa capital'.

After everyone had left I checked at the airport and was informed the missing gear would arrive next morning. Off duty, I walked around Lukla and marvelled at how the village had changed over the years, buildings extending haphazardly away from the airport. Recently, the pace had accelerated with new lodges, bars and restaurants springing up. A clutch of internet cafes had opened since my last visit two years earlier. It was strange to see the locals walking around with mobile phones pressed to their ears. I remembered how not long since I had stood knee-deep in water in a corrugated iron shack, calling home on one of the town's few landlines. I had wanted to tell Jane that I was safe; there had been days of torrential rain, it would be falling as snow higher up and people would be dying on the mountains. Now under similar circumstances I could simply send a text.

The bags arrived sporadically next morning and I sent them up the trail. The barrel of food did not, but I could wait no longer. I made arrangements for it to be portered directly to base camp and set off for Namche on a trail busy with tourists and porters. It was noticeable how the volume of traffic – all pedestrian of course – had steadily increased year-on-year. There were other changes too. Most of the trekking groups had Nepali leaders whereas previously they had been led by westerners. Recently Indians had joined the slow procession of Europeans, North Americans and Australasians making the pilgrimage to the base of the world's highest mountain.

After a slow start I settled into a comfortable walking rhythm. I soon started passing groups labouring with the unaccustomed exertion and rarefied air. It began to rain and I stepped up my pace. This was how I liked to move; I relished walking at a speed just below breathlessness, knowing that the coming days would have to be taken slowly to allow my group to acclimatise. The trail of people, livestock and landmarks passed in a hypnotic blur and I reached Namche in a mere five hours.

Despite the weather, the group were in good spirits and content to have a rest day, as is customary at Namche, allowing the body to adjust to the thin air at 3,500 metres. Meanwhile Nima and I shopped for food and other supplies and then packed loads to be taken directly to our base camp high in the Gokyo valley. For the group, I planned a more leisurely and scenic route via the village of Thame, with its cliff-side monastery, and over the 5,400-metre Renjo La pass.

'Where will you stay in Thame?' asked my friend Pasang who ran the Kalapatar Lodge, our billet in Namche.

'We'll find somewhere when we arrive,' I replied casually.

'You need to book, I think,' Pasang said, pulling a mobile phone from his jacket pocket. 'I talk with my friend. He has lodge in Thame.'

Calling ahead? Booking? This was all new to me.

'You don't have phone?' Pasang asked after finishing on the mobile. 'Not here.'

'Next time you bring. You buy local SIM card, only 500 rupees.'

'Okay,' I replied laughing, recalling a time when Namche did not even have mains electricity.

The next three weeks passed quickly, trekking over the Renjo La and attempting a peak called Hungchi, a 7,036-metre summit at the head of the Gokyo valley on the border with Tibet. It was not difficult to get away from the crowds. We simply went up a side valley off the main Everest trail. Above the last settlement of Gokyo we were on our own.

Large amounts of fresh snow deposited by the year's heavy monsoon made for slow going on Hungchi. We were unable to summit, but the group seemed happy, sensing, perhaps, that we were lucky to be able to spend time in such a place.

At the end of the trip I walked down to Gokyo a day ahead of the group to join Jane and the children who were trekking up to meet me. I had previously sent three porters down to Lukla to carry their bags, plus Maisy and Lewis. If all had run to plan they would be waiting in Gokyo. I reached the trekker settlement in a state of excited expectation, only to find they were not in the lodge where Jane and I had arranged we would meet. Having established they were not in any of the other lodges either, I settled down to wait, anxiously studying people coming up the trail with my binoculars. By mid-afternoon the last group of trekkers had arrived and still there was no sign. I asked around the recent arrivals but no one had seen them. Mobile phone coverage had not yet reached Gokyo, however, I was able to use a landline to call a lodge in Machermo, the next settlement down the valley. Nobody had seen them there either. I began to get worried and hoped the children had not been stricken by illness or altitude sickness.

Later, as I was having dinner in the lodge, a local stumbled through the tables of guests and stood in front of me.

'Mr Simon?' he slurred, very drunkenly.

'Yes,' I replied, somewhat bemused. He produced a folded piece of paper from his pocket and nearly fell over as he handed it to me. It was a letter from Jane who was waiting in Machermo. All was fine; they had walked in more slowly than expected and had decided not to come any higher. I chuckled to myself as I digested the information, thinking about all our meticulous planning, the satellite phone calls home, the interrogation of trekkers and the call down the valley. In the end, the communication had come by letter, delivered by a drunken porter. This was more like the Nepal of old.

I rushed down to Machermo next morning. By chance Jane and the children were outside their lodge as I crested the last hill above the tiny settlement.

'What are you doing, Daddy?' Lewis asked, as I ran down the

rock-strewn trail to join them. It was a good question, and one that I often ask myself.

'Coming to see you.'

Back in Kathmandu I arranged a farewell meal for the group. Later we moved on to a bar and I sat talking with the wife of one of the clients. While we were on Hungchi, she had been trekking with friends.

'John and a friend had to be rescued recently,' she confided to me. John was her 60-year-old husband and he'd been climbing for 40 years. I could tell from her hushed tone she didn't want to make a big deal out of it, or for John to overhear.

'Where was that?'

'In the Alps; they got caught out in a bad storm. Once they had been overdue for a couple of days I called out the rescue. They did not have a phone.'

'Were they all right?'

'Exhausted, cold and a bit shaken-up; but nobody could understand the phone thing.'

'I can,' I replied sympathetically.

John had been going to mountains since long before it was possible to carry a phone. He enjoyed the challenge of climbing and of being self-reliant. Perhaps he was worried that the phone might take some of that feeling away, or had simply not thought to take one. To me the reasons for the decision were unimportant. It was his choice, in the same way as deciding what clothing, gear and food to take.

❄ ❄ ❄ ❄

On the way home we stopped in Delhi for a few days. I had not been to India for more than 10 years. The city's astounding development was immediately obvious: a new airport terminal was being constructed along with a metro system, new roads and all manner of fancy buildings. New vehicles choked the highways; the smoke spewing tuk-tuks had been replaced with models that ran cleanly on LPG. For us, coming from a Britain mired in recession and self-doubt, such energy was refreshing to see. It was all as charmingly mad and chaotic as ever, yet you could sense that the hectic effort was leading somewhere. India was having its turn in the limelight and some of her citizens were enjoying a slice of the prosperity that we in the West often take for granted. There was a downside to this rapid development: Delhi sat in a cloud of dust and smog that the sun barely penetrated. It was easy to understand why increasing numbers of Indians were seeking sanctuary in the mountains of Nepal. At least now they had the money to do so.

I returned to Nepal the following spring, after a few months at home, and this time I brought my mobile phone. I even fitted a local SIM card as Pasang had suggested. I had become used to calling with my satellite phone, but because calls were expensive and drained battery power quickly I used it sparingly. However, this was something different and I was able to ping-pong texts with Jane and speak to the children almost daily. I lost the signal above the last village – Thame – but was pretty sure that by the next time I came back more masts would have extended coverage deeper into the mountains.

One night, in a high and remote valley I sat in our base camp kitchen with the Sherpas drinking cups of tea. Nima, as he often does, asked about our children. He nodded approvingly on hearing they were both in school, then he disclosed that over the years he had used the money made from working with me to send the youngest two of his five children to university in Kathmandu. I thought of my own charmed life and how it had led to this point, of my opportunities, experiences and achievements. Then I thought of my contributions: a little entertainment and inspiration through talks and writing, some new climbs for others to enjoy, perhaps a sense of wonder and scraps of knowledge passed to clients over the years... And I knew that these were minor and fleeting. I could see clearly that my only real legacy lay with our own children and those two students in Kathmandu. It was a contribution that spanned generations, time and place. The fact that Nima had never mentioned it before, and that I had been an unknowing benefactor made the feeling all the more special.

Later, I walked to my tent under a starlit Himalayan sky, grateful for just being there and spending time with such wonderful people. I was keenly aware that I had been one of the last generation to experience these mountains as something of a wilderness. The phone masts spreading up the valleys were merely the latest in a series of incursions. Perhaps that realisation had already occurred in my subconscious, and explained my own more recent explorations.

All mountaineers develop differently. Some go higher, some try ever-steeper faces and others specialise in a particular range or region. I am increasingly drawn to places where few others have trodden. However, communication by the touch of a button or the click of a mouse is now truly global and can penetrate even the remotest ranges. All progress comes at a price – and for me that has been the loss of my notion of real mountain wilderness. You might be physically isolated, but you no longer feel it. Even so, the mountains still retain a magical, almost sacred charm for me, acting as havens of sanity and calm in a life that otherwise can seem just a succession of consumer choices. Perhaps, more than ever, the mountains are what you make of them, or want them to be.

Now, the wild is within.

Acknowledgements

The narrative of this book follows my life over some 10 years. During this time I have travelled the world, meeting, climbing and working with many wonderful and kind people far too numerous to mention here. Old friends have also provided help, support and guidance along the way. To all of you, I would like to say a big thank you for contributing in your own special way to this work.

On a more specific level, my biggest debt of gratitude goes to my climbing partners, not only for their care, strength and judgement while in the mountains, but also for a lot of fun. I ended up climbing with Andy Parkin by chance and it has developed into an enduring partnership. His commitment to the cause over the years, in the face of great adversity, is inspirational. Paul Schweizer stepped up at the last minute for the first of our Wrangell climbs, and even after nearly 20 years of living in Britain he remains the coolest of Californians under pressure. Rob Gearing has paid to come on a number of trips with me, but I like to think of him more as a loyal friend. I am deeply privileged to have shared a rope with you all.

Although kit has all got lighter, mountaineering still remains an equipment intensive pastime. I am very grateful to Bradshaw Taylor for supplying me with Mountain Hardwear clothing, sleeping bags, rucksacks and tents over the last 10 years. Thanks also to First Ascent and Lyon Equipment for providing the vital hardware – the nuts and bolts, if you like, of climbing. Wallets have also got lighter over time, and mountaineering expeditions are good at accelerating this process. Some of the expeditions described in this book received funding from the British Mountaineering Council, the Mount Everest Foundation, the Mountaineering Council of Scotland and the Alpine Club Climbing Fund. Without this vital support the trips may never have happened.

Skippers are important people, and I would like to pay tribute to them. Celia Bull started the Fuegian ball rolling with the life-changing outing on *Ada II*. Many thanks to the subsequent torch bearers – Mono on *Mago del Sur*, Marcel on *Iorana* and Wolf on *Santa Maria Australis*. In Ushuaia, Luis and Carolina have provided base camp, friendship and assistance through their business La Compañía de Guías de Patagonia, Denis Chevallay has been similarly helpful in Puerto Williams. In Pakistan, Nazir Sabir Expeditions have done an exceptional support job and in Nepal, it is Iswari Paudel and Himalayan Guides Nepal that I have to salute. Paul Walker at Tangent Expeditions provided the vital logistics in Greenland.

I would like to thank my editor Stephen Goodwin for his hard work. Stephen is the third book editor I have had, but the first living just down the road. While most of our work has been done electronically, it was always reassuring to know I could pop over to the neighbouring village to sort things out if the need arose.

This is my first book for Vertebrate, and they have been a pleasure to do business with. In particular, John Coefield has been patient waiting for my manuscript and invaluable with help and advice.

Lastly, I would like to thank Jane – my wife – for her love, support and help over the years and for having Maisy and Lewis – who might just possibly grow into another generation of adventurers.